WINE JOURNEYS
Myth & History

First Edition

for Kim,
a true enthusiast

Patrick Hunt
Stanford University

cognella®
academic publishing

Bassim Hamadeh, CEO and Publisher
Michael Simpson, Vice President of Acquisitions
Jamie Giganti, Managing Editor
Jess Busch, Graphic Design Supervisor
Marissa Applegate, Acquisitions Editor
Jessica Knott, Project Editor
Luiz Ferreira, Licensing Associate

First published in the United States of America in 2013 by Cognella, Inc.

Printed in the United States of America

ISBN: 978-1-62661-064-4

www.cognella.com   800-200-3908

CONTENTS

PREFACE

"Never did a great man hate good wine." *Rabelais*

"… Summer when the woods were green and Old Silenus on his fat donkey would come to visit them, and sometimes Bacchus himself, then the streams would run with wine instead of water and the whole forest would give itself up to jollification for weeks on end." Mr. Tumnus the Faun, from *C. S. Lewis, The Chronicles of Narnia: The Lion, the Witch and the Wardrobe.*

Somewhere in my bloodlines vintners and winemakers must lurk, maybe a little *Vitis vinifera* poured between the alleles of my DNA. I find this imagined genealogy palatable because whenever and wherever I see rows of vineyards rolling across a valley or over hills, I have a spontaneous excitement, joylike and thrilling. It has been a lifelong experience and I don't have any other explanation. When I was a boy we had a few rows of vines on a little farm we rented and I loved watching them change during the year. I enjoyed touching the vines' shedding trunks in our mild winter. I derived so much satisfaction from watching the first greening and how the leaves popped. How lovely the light was when it was in either the east or west behind the leaves, causing them to glow vividly. I remember how the tiny flowers changed into small fruit and then how long I waited for them to grow pendulous and change color—from green to mixed with faint lavender to purple—and then ultimately swell and ripen. In fact, I couldn't wait for the ripening and usually tasted them on a daily basis through summer, especially when the grapes were warm with sunshine and finally sweet. We didn't make any wine, not the least because the clusters of grapes were picked clean one by one before the end of August and the fruit was long eaten, usually on the spot. A single harvest was nonexistent between my four brothers and me, equally lean and hungry and browned like raisins ourselves by the sun, long before we ever tasted wine.

Musing now, although I love cool spring water, wine is what water dreams of becoming. At this point in life I appreciate what philosophers have said for ages. Some forms of beauty may belong to the young but old wine does not. We may speak in metaphor of our growing years as vintage, best appreciated in reflection. This small book is best understood as a trifle, not intended in any way as globally comprehensive but rather highly selective, like Proustian memory. This is a personal *vinodyssey*—only covering places I've been where wine developed, and both its strength and weakness is that it is intimate, not encyclopedic in the least, with occasional literary notes interwoven where I found them apropos. If anything, this book's author sees it as a small cellarful of essays, part memoir and an extended opportunity for *belles-lettres* musings between wine notes.

Literary and philosophical notes on wine have been around for ages. One of my favorites is from Plato, ever the wise guide:

> When a man is entering his fortieth year … he may call on the other gods and especially invoke Dionysus to join the holy rites of the elders and also join their mirth, which the god gave to men to lighten their burden—wine, the cure for the pinch of old age, so we may renew our youth and enjoy the forgetting of despair.[1]

This comes from a philosopher who eschewed excess in every form and even fears the power of poetry in his *Republic*, so his wine encomium is all the more restrained.

As an historian, archaeologist, and archeoethnobotanist, I enjoy both the long journey in place and time that wine has taken through the millennia, as well as my own journeys through wine domains across multiple continents. Although I have also tasted wine in Africa and South America, with the exception of Egypt, these experiences will not be covered here. Instead, my little *vinodyssey* only selectively looks at some European, Western Asia, and the Levant contexts and wine history where I've spent sufficient time to make a few possibly useful observations interspersed with the wisdom of others. If I were Kermit Lynch, whose own passionate stories are inspirations, and like him a visionary wine buyer who steered others' palates and helped change tastes for decades to come, I might be more inclusive about topics. But this book is not intended to be comprehensive even about one wine region—for example, most of the best domains in Bordeaux are not covered and this is also indicative of other chapters—precisely because that is the purview of many other books, whereas this book is as much personal reflection as a summary of some specific stories, mythological or historical. Any one of these wine topics could produce a book in itself. If it is a fault of this book to have such a small focus, it is because I have not yet been able to discover other wonderful wine contexts beyond these few I know at this point of life. I hope to live long enough to remedy that lacuna. How lucky I have been to discover some great wines, how foolish not to search out more.

The last few decades have afforded me incredible privileges of sharing wine with many mentors, friends, and acquaintances who have taught me much about wine. Many are perhaps even greater than the world knows because they are humble. I hardly know where to begin thanking them and to them this little tome is dedicated, some now drinking wine in better places, like Robert Mondavi. This thank list includes Fritz Maytag, Paul Draper, Michael Marston, Fred Concklin, John York, Jenny March, Cordell Hull, David Stronach, Peter Herdrich, Dafydd Griffiths, Nina Wymess, Stanley and Helen Cheng, Michael Keller, Marie-Thérèse Noellat, Rob Cook, Dikran Karagueuzian, Michael Goldfield, Richard Reed, Dick Davis, Ed White, François Wiblé, Véronique Perrin, Léonard Gianadda, Arno Penzias,

Alex Greene, Charlotte Horton, Blake Edgar, Carolyn Lougee, Hiram Simon, Alex Bernardo, and many others unnamed. In admiration of her many skills and patience, I thank my editor, Jessica Knott. To these kind souls—with whom I have quaffed more than a glass more than one time and often in different countries—I am profoundly indebted. Much of this book also owes an enormous debt to pioneering oenoarchaeologist Patrick McGovern and encyclopedist Karen MacNeil, with both of whom my limited conversations have not been long enough. As the Psalmist says in gratitude, although not about a wordy encomia but a likely wine metaphor, "My cup runs over."

CHAPTER 1

Wine in Prehistory and Anatolia

"Noah, a man of the soil, proceeded to plant a vineyard." *Genesis* 9:20

What if wine grapes were the first plant humans cultivated and domesticated after tasting the juice of naturally fermenting wild grapes? Wine connoisseurs will certainly smile in appreciation of this possibility, which may have some truth to it, and scholars of the oldest religions will nod in understanding, not surprised at human ingenuity in finding "divine beverages" that may have given elevated meaning to an otherwise tough existence. Vintage stories about human appreciation of the earliest wine encounters take on many layers of legend. Nearly every culture seems to have lively narratives of ancestral experiments with wine and related beverages, often with humorous overtones on the one hand or moralistic subtexts on the other. One central idea is certain in human society: wine has been strongly tied to civilizing forces from the outset, connecting to social ritual, religion, and conviviality, also directly stimulating the arts of dance, music and poetry wherever humans have gathered for around 10,000 years and probably much longer.

Logical reflection on plant domestication suggests that grain should not be the first human cultivar but rather a fairly late comer to the process of human discovery. Fruits are—pardon the pun—much more lower-hanging food sources than grains, which generally require more sedentary practices. It is much easier to first obtain food from wild fruits without much work except to identify, observe, and harvest when ripe than to actually plant grain seeds, although harvesting wild seeds is not much different from picking fruit if identifying, observing, and harvesting was also an early step. Obtaining enough food value from wild grain seeds would probably not yield as much volume as from wild fruit, except in grasslands. Of course human ancestors no doubt did both, but the steps in the process seem much earlier for fruit, as our related primates have deduced for a long time. Fermented fruit, however, add a bonus that other species may not have fully appreciated.

Some oenologists and beverage historians theorize the grape (now known as *Vitis vinifera*) was the perfect fruit package for fermentation—with sugar content as high as 20–23%—and was thus the first cultivar, not grain, as the vanguard of agriculture. After airborne yeasts like the *Saccharomyces* genus penetrated the grape skin and altered it, humans were not far behind to discover its virtues, possibly while still on the vine. It is certain that animals beat us to this discovery, since birds have been lining up for old fermenting berries long before us, but even insects and other living things have been at it for possibly up to 100 million years. Given the hundreds of wild world grapevines and varietals on nearly every landmass, birds were the logical disperser of grapes to new lands. By eating the fruit and flying over bodies of water, they dropped the seeds, replete with fertilizer and dispersed grapevines flourished. Expanding the idea that grapes were the first cultivar, theorists who suggest wine came before bread include pioneering "oenoarchaeologist" Dr. Patrick McGovern, paleochemist and ethnobotanist extraordinaire of the University Museum, University of Pennsylvania, among others.[2] McGovern has coined this idea of the beginning human love affair with grapes and their effects the "Paleolithic hypothesis."[3]

The potent but then mysterious combination of psychotropic and elevating effects of grape fermentation were seemingly not lost on Neolithic humans. It is probably too easy and therefore a cautionary exercise of speculation to extrapolate how the fermentation products of the grape won something close to religious esteem among our Paleolithic and Neolithic ancestors. Archaeologists like McGovern have also been suggesting for decades that deliberate fermentation of alcohol is an evidence for the transition from late Paleolithic to early Neolithic cultures.[4] Archaeological technologists like Karen Vitelli had asked if early pottery was first even made for food, based on research from Franchthi Cave on the peninsular edge of the Aegean Sea, a dramatic collapsed massive cave place I visited when a graduate student at the American School of Classical Studies in Athens.[5] If early ceramic technology and pottery are also somehow connected to viticulture, one wonders what other pioneering human technologies that underlie civilization can be traced to viticulture. However, as difficult to answer such questions like why, how, and when, perhaps an easier question to answer is where more formal viticulture began.

Where Wine Originated

The full history of the cultivated grape and its exciting juice is not easy to deduce, lost in the dim forgotten memory of earliest agriculture that archaeology and ethnobotany are attempting to reconstruct. But Anatolia is also the locus where the oldest temples (ca. 11,000 BCE) yet known are found in places like Göbekli Tepe near Urfa in southern Turkey. It is unknown to date whether incipient agriculture may have been connected to Göbekli Tepe, but prehistorians like Rainer Vollkommer suspect the relationship was not casual or accidental.[6] This monolithic site is only partly excavated since the 1980's by the German Archaeological Institute (DAI) but its seminal history is being explored; perhaps it will yield evidence of the earliest agriculture yet known.[7]

Anatolia, the probable home of viticulture—covering modern Turkey and more—is no exception to this narrative where the names of both Noah and Dionysus exert enormous influence in the oldest tales about wine in Western culture, equally edgy and slightly numinous at the dawn of viticulture, suggesting wine is perhaps more a divine gift and first quaffed by gods before humans were ready to imbibe. Some of these may be sobering stories while not at all about sobriety, but many are also hugely entertaining and should make us smile at our own human foibles while seeking inspiration and elevation. Any history of wine should be enjoyed like wine itself but not just vicariously.

Even if biblical stories about ancient patriarchal Noah are mythologically suspect, nonetheless the expanse of Anatolia can claim several strands of a tangled story. Most historical ethnobotanists agree that *Vitis vinifera* originated as a cultivar between the Black Sea and Iran, roughly in eastern Anatolia,[8] where the families of grapes considered the oldest group (*Proles pontica*) originated.[9] The Anatolian traces range from the literary example of Noah on one hand—topographically consistent even if only a late literary echo—to archaeology with the world's oldest winery to date excavated in the land of Ararat (mostly contiguous with ancient Urartu) not far from the literary context of Noah's story and also somewhat related to Mt. Nisir in the Zagros Mountains where Utnapishtim's boat landed after the flood in the *Epic of Gilgamesh*. It may not be just the archaeological vestiges of ancestors of wild wheat in *Triticum monococcum* (*einkorn* wheat) found at Karaca Dağ in Anatolia from around 9000 BP (7000 BCE), but could be more provocative.

The Story of Noah from Genesis 9:20-24

In what may be the first Western literary account—or at least purporting to be—since Noah and family had just decamped from the cramped ark after the Flood, the patriarch Noah sets a new agricultural benchmark:

> Noah, a man of the soil, proceeded to plant a vineyard. When he drank some of its wine, he became drunk and lay uncovered inside his tent. Ham, the father of Canaan, saw his father naked and told his two brothers outside. But Shem and Japheth took a garment and laid it across their shoulders; then they walked in backward and covered their father's naked body. Their faces were turned the other way so that they would not see their father naked. When Noah awoke from his wine and found out what his youngest son had done to him, he said, "Cursed be Canaan!"

Reinforcing this Anatolian connection in myth history and biblical literature to early viticulture, this *Genesis* 9 account mentions Noah as planting and cultivating a vineyard then subsequently falling prey to the effects of overindulgence, including sleep. This is a subtle allusion to the idea of fallen humanity after being ejected from the Garden of Eden that God had planted, since the verb "to plant" only occurs before in *Genesis* 2-4 framed by the Edenic example of what had before been easy is now fraught with snares, including not being able to handle the results. The text quoted above notes that while he was sleeping off the effects, his sons encountered their own embarrassment at their father's loss of dignity in being found naked or at least uncovered in his vital parts (the anatomical area taboo to their gaze).

Talmudic commentary on this Noah story is often amusing in a macabre way. For example, the *Mishnah Tanhuma Noah* 13 relates that the devil was at play. As soon as

Fig 1.1 Noah, Ghiberti Door Florence 15th c.

Noah planted his vines, the devil buried several dead animals in the vineyard, squeezing drops of their blood into the soil. This included a lamb, a lion, a monkey, and a defiling pig. All these dead animals were somehow absorbed into the vine roots, which idea oenologists will not find all that strange. Now when someone drinks just one cup of wine, he or she feels lamblike. But with two cups, strong and lionly. After three cups, one behaves a bit silly like a monkey. Four cups makes one behave like a pig, out of control; wallowing will soon follow with more wine.[10] Of course, blame the devil! It couldn't be the wine, could it?

The biblical account of Noah makes it seem this was an unprecedented event and it is the first occasion of the state of "becoming drunk," as would be expected from someone without prior example of limits and behavioral expectations. Western art has depicted this story many times, from Ghiberti's 1452 door on the Baptistry of Florence to Michelangelo's 1509 fresco on the Sistine Chapel ceiling, among others. Both of these art historical images show a nearly naked Noah on display, almost supine or asleep near a huge wine cask or barrel.

Noah's experience is the earliest biblical wine venture and the *Genesis* account does not moralize against wine, rather only loss of control on the part of Noah and the inappropriate response of at least one of his offspring. But this is still a gloss on early viticultural practice, where one should expect a certain amount of uncertainty when probing behind the actual but vague historical kernel of a literary myth about the first winemaking in Anatolia.

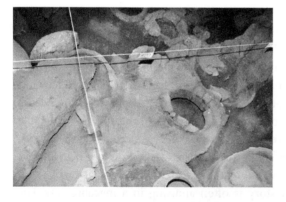

Fig 1.2 Areni Winepress, ca. 4100 BCE from Areni Cave, Armenia

Armenia, Home of The World's Oldest Winery to Date

Further reinforcing Anatolian primacy in viticulture, a starting discovery was made in 2007 in Armenia, again close to the presumed literary topography of Noah's vineyard. In deep cliff caves just outside Areni, Armenia, and a stone's throw from the Turkish border, a joint archaeological team from Armenia and international universities found a winepress and winery (or wine storage area). This winery cave excavation was led by Dr. Gregory Areshian of UCLA and the results are now well published.[11] The cave yielded multiple evidences of viticulture, including multiple large ceramic winemaking vats holding up to 14–15 gallons of wine each, as well as carbonized grape pips and stems of *Vitis vinifera* and tartaric acid with calcium salts. In addition, stronger corroboration comes from pigment *malvidin* found on three of the ceramic potsherds most likely from red wine from grapeskins. Radiocarbon dating of the organic artifacts confirms the date of this winery as soundly Chalcolithic: repeated results show the winery to date from around 6,100 years ago (4100 BCE). Anatolian origins for pioneering viticulture is, for now, agreed on by ethnobotanists until possibly earlier evidence is found elsewhere, which seems unlikely given that DNA evidence to date also sources all known *Vitis vinifera* back to the Ancient Near East through *Proles pontica*.[12]

Modern Turkish Viticulture

Far west from Armenia, along the Mediterranean seacoast are the mountains of Izmir, ancient Smyrna. The coastal steep slopes are intermittently decorated with the dark spires of vertical cypress trees. Here we bounced westward on the peninsula along a dusty Turkish road with the Aegean Sea shining on our right in the late afternoon, and as the topography became more gentle there were olive groves on our left, their leaves silver in the oblique light. On the horizon was the peninsular coastal town of Urla, whose ancient harbor was Klazomenai in Greek times, where wine may have been exported westward for centuries; nearby is Liman Tepe, another port where shipments like olive oil and wine may have originated as early as five millennia ago, long before the Urla region was known by these names.[13]

Fig 1.3 Urla Vineyard, Turkey

Inland, in the warm fall when it would cool quickly after sunset, we could finally see the revived vineyards of Urla Winery—in the same valleys where the Roman vineyards were—in their autumn colors. Being a white wine grape with translucent pale yellow-green hue, the indigenous *Sultaniye*[14] leaves were not as spectacular as other vines, which were splendidly hued in red and even purple, with yellow chlorophyll having long given way to xanthophyll and anthocyanin pigments. Recently I was very pleased to see that in Germany, the famous *Marzipanstollen*, especially enjoyed around Christmas, uses sultanas (*Sultaniye*, in fact) raisin grapes from Turkey, one of Turkey's best exports. I had some of this *Marzipanstollen* in the Rheintal of Switzerland and brought one home to enjoy after the 2012 holidays with family. *Sultaniye* grapes from Urla and its environs in Aegean Turkey are prolific as table grapes across Europe. *Sultaniye* is one of the 26 indigenous grape varietals originating from Turkey.[15]

These Urla (Şarapçılık) vineyards I visited have been revived on terraces at least a millennium old and next to the stone winery, the ordered rows of manicured palm trees in a grove with reflecting pool immediately struck me as being aesthetically derived from the palace gardens of Cyrus at Pasargadae in Persia. I was proudly told that many tulips bloomed here in spring; a sure sign of Ottoman Turkish heritage since sultans like Suleiman the Magnificent had state-organized tulip cultivation on a large scale in the 16th century. Even our word "tulip" derives from the Turkish word *tülbend*, originally from a word for a turban, and the resemblance is easily conjured up since one of the visual icons of Istanbul is a tulip. Ogier Ghiselin Busbecq, Hapsburg Ambassador from Vienna's Ferdinand I to the Ottoman court of Suleiman, was given tulips by the sultan and he shared them with Carolus Clusius, Prefect of the imperial medical garden of Maximilian II. When Clusius left Vienna he began the Leiden Academic Gardens (*Hortus Academicus Leydenensis*) in 1594–95 and wrote about, studied, and hybridized tulips, thus beginning the love affair of the Dutch with the tulip. But the tulip is a newcomer in Turkey since wine in Turkey harks back to the dawn of history, as already noted.

Fig 1.4 Urla Vourla, 2009

Not surprisingly, Urla Winery's vintages have done well in recent competitions in Europe and the U.K., including a Silver for its *Urla 2009 Boğazkere* in the Decanter World Wine Awards in 2011; a Silver for its *Urla 2010 Tempus* in the Decanter World Wine Awards in 2011; a Silver (Vinalies d'Argent) from Vins du Monde—Oenologues du France for its *Urla 2011 Sauvignon Blanc*; a Silver for its *Urla 2009 Vourla* from the International Wine and Spirit Competition 2012; a Silver for its *Urla 2010 Tempus* from the International Wine and Spirit Competition 2012; and a Silver for its *Urla 2010 Chardonnay* from the 2011 Concours Mondial du Bruxelles, among others. London's Decanter World Wine Awards judges are usually chaired by Steven Spurrier of 1976 Judgment of Paris fame. The *Vourla* cuvée revives the name *Vourla*, the old Greek word for Urla. Using steel tanks and French oak barrels (including Seguin Moreau from Chagny, Burgundy, and Radoux Tonnelerie SA from Jonzac, Bordeaux) for fermentation and storage before bottling, the state-of-the-art temperature-controlled facility is only a few years old and the whole operation, begun by Can Ortabaş, is just over a decade old (after 2001) despite the fact the Urla region has grown wine for millennia. At a small Istanbul dinner ceremony after a lecture I gave at the Sait Halim Pasa Mansion, I was given a bottle of Turkish wine from the Turkish Ministry of Culture, one of several to bring home. One of these bottles was a delightful golden-pink *Urla 2010 Serendias Roze Sek*, which we also tasted at the Urla Winery. It was a rosé made from Syrah, Merlot, and *Boğazkere* and has also been a 2011 gold-medal winner for Urla Winery.

For me, the most exotic Turkish varietal is the *Boğazkere*, whose long history reaches back to the Tigris River watershed of the edges of Mesopotamia. A very dark grape, it is harvested in October and because it has primarily been grown in hot, almost arid microclimates, it is fairly drought resistant. The Elazig province of southeastern Turkey has been its primary home, but it has spread over the centuries across Turkey. Because of its spice and high tannin density, its name has usually been interpreted as "throat burner" in Turkish, and its strong taste has lent it well to blends with softer varietals. I find it robust and when it can age for up to a decade, it is particularly satisfying with spicy dishes like *Tandir* lamb and strong cheeses that cannot overpower it.

Anatolian Viticulture from the Chalcolithic to the Bronze Age

Wine historians and oenoarchaeologists like Dr. Patrick McGovern have found wild *Vitis vinifera sylvestris* in the steep headwaters of the Tigris River in eastern Turkey's Taurus Mountains, near the site of Nemrut Dagh with its first century BCE colossal head sculptures and the Neolithic site of Çayönü.[16]

Some of the other early viticultural production or early wine consumption sites from the late Neolithic and early Chalcolithic periods onward into the Bronze Age in the eastern and southeastern regions of Anatolia include Shomutepe, Shulaveri in northeastern highlands, Aslan Tepe—especially its Hittite phases—as well as Korucutepe in Central Anatolia, and Hasek Höyük and Kurban Höyük in the southeast.[17] Vines "were extensively cultivated in Hittite times" where at one point in the time period somewhere around the Late Bronze Age (ca. 1500 BCE), an acre of vineyard was worth a Hittite silver *mina* of weight as the Hittite Law Code stipulates.[18] Wine was both popularly consumed in Hittite urban wine bars and taverns as well as ritually poured in libations on royal funerary pyres as a sendoff from this world, as archival tablets from Boğazköy (ancient Hattusa) require for the latter.[19] Showing an official wine hierarchy, there was a royal officer whose Hittite title was "Chief of the Wine Stewards" (*Gal Gestin* in Hittite).[20] Although other ancient Anatolian words for wine are also attested, one Luvian word (Western Anatolian ancient language of Lycia, somewhat Hittite-related) for one alcoholic beverage is *maddu* and another directly Hittite word is *wiyana*,[21] very much a direct parent word to the later Indo-European "wine" word now used in English. Thus it appears that the Hittites were very wine-conscious in Anatolia in the second millennium BCE.

Ottoman Fancies

More in keeping with modern Anatolian wine, I was a guest of the Ministry of Culture of Turkey at a posh private dinner in Istanbul. My host had asked where I wanted to spend an enjoyable evening meal and I chose the magical Çırağan Palace Kempinski on the Bosporus. At the opulent palace restaurant overlooking the water, in this incredible setting with the old Ottoman imperial palace gardens surrounding us and the amber evening lights twinkling across the water against the purple dusk, my Turkish dinner companion, poet Çağla Demircioğlu, and I had an exquisite meal, including an aubergine salad with lemon juice, garlic, and olive oil and another eggplant dish with cheeses, *Hünkar Beğendi*, which translates as "Sultan's Delight." I looked at the wine list and there to my delight was listed the same *Urla 2009 Vourla* vintage I had tasted at the Urla winery, with its spicy Boğazkere, Merlot, Syrah, and Cabernet Sauvignon combination. The only difference one might expect to find was the elevated cost: instead of its more modest price, it was around 150 Turkish *lira* at this dizzyingly expensive palace restaurant. The added value must have been that it was sufficiently appreciated by Turkish connoisseur wine lovers to be on the wine list (given its European awards), but I could add in my mind how beautiful the natural Urla landscape was on the Aegean coast not far to the south, especially with the autumnal colors of the Turkish vines and the reflecting pool at sunset reminding me of what we imagine the Garden of Cyrus to have been like at Pasargadae.

It is well known that despite the Islamic ban on alcohol, Turkish sultans and the court had a deep appreciation of fine wine, and not only European, since vast wine estates could be found in Turkey, although managed by infidel Greeks, Armenians, and other Christians. The religious restrictions were not strictly enforced, so wine cultivation continued, either under the radar or not, and the vines were rarely ripped out of their vineyards even if allowed to go wild a while every few generations. By 1904 Turkish vineyards were producing 340 million liters of export wine, although both 20th century world wars severely dented this production, and it wasn't until near the end of the millennium that wine production again melded quantity and quality.

If during my Istanbul evening dinner I felt like an indulged pasha myself, noting the huge hookahs in the Çırağan garden gazebos with their perfumed smoke, I was also reminded of one of my favorite passages in odalisque literature, faintly redolent of the beauty of an Ingres fantasia or a Pierre Loti prose poem. This circa-1785 passage is in the rococo collection of tall tales, that incredible medley *The Adventures of Baron Munchausen* collated by polymath Rudolph Eric Raspe and embellished by Gottfried August Bürger. Its imaginary mendacities have amused and engaged such caricaturists as Thomas Rowlandson and engravers like Gustave Doré.[22] The whimsical part in question is set in the Turkish Sultan's palace, not far from the harem or seraglio. The inimitable baron wagers with the Sultan that in the Vienna Hapsburg imperial palace wine cellar are bottles surpassing that of the sultan's single bottle of Tokay. Starting with the Sultan's boast and Munchausen's wager:

> "Munchausen ... Here is a bottle of Tokay, the only one I possess, and I am sure that never in your life you have tasted better." So saying, His Highness filled his own glass and mine. We touched glasses and we drank. "Well, what do you think

Fig 1.5 Sultan's Palace, Topkapi, Istanbul

of that? That is something out of the common, is it not?" "The wine is not bad," I answered, "but if Your Highness will allow me to make the remark, I must say that I have drunk a better bottle of Tokay from the cellar of the Empress of Austria, of quite another brand than that sour stuff ..."

The Sultan is slightly peeved at Munchausen but the baron swears he can procure such a bottle from Vienna before an hour passes.

"Well let your Highness deign to accept my challenge. If I do not fulfill my engagement—and you know that I am a sworn foe to bragging—your Highness shall have full leave to cut my head off, and my head is no pumpkin. There are my stakes, what are yours?" "Agreed, I accept the challenge," says the Sultan. "If when the clock strikes four, the bottle is not here, I will have your head cut off without mercy. ... On the other hand, if you make good your promise, you are at liberty to take out of my treasury, as much gold and silver, with as many pearls and precious stones, as the strongest man can carry. ..."

The imperial Tokay in Vienna must be summarily fetched from the cellar of the Empress-Queen Maria Theresa by the baron's fleet manservant who, once his weight belts are let go, runs so fast he can ostensibly cover the impossible return distance in a matter of a quarter hour. Instead, after almost an hour has passed, the bottle of imperial Tokay still has not arrived—the speedy manservant indeed has the bottle from Vienna and was returning but has instead fallen asleep under an oak near Belgrade—and the Sultan is about to summon his executioner to summarily dispatch Baron Munchausen. Outside the seraglio, Munchausen quickly has his marksman wake up the distant snoring runner with an unbelievably long musket shot, and the manservant:

"set off to run again with such swiftness, that he arrived at the Sultan's cabinet with the bottle of Tokay …"[23]

Just in the nick of time, after tasting it, the Sultan agrees this Tokay surpasses anything he has tasted before and Munchausen empties the Sultan's treasury because he indeed has the strongest man in the world as another of his servants. If history is even slightly pass-able here in such a literary stretch, such a rare imperial bottle might be a legendary *Tokay Eszencia* (above 6 *puttonyos* of highest sweetness) from the old Hapsburg imperial vineyards of Hungary, a delectable and syrupy topaz-hued botrytized late-harvest wine produced and consumed then as well as today by connoisseurs—note Mozart's flamboyant librettist Lorenzo da Ponte (1749–1838) claimed in his memoirs that he could write continuously for 12 hours with "a little bottle of Tokay to the right."[24] That *Tokay Eszencia* can theoretically last 200 years is not disputed, although not in a sultan's sarai. But the Munchausen yarn does somewhat justify the exquisite tastes of sultans.

Recalling this literary fancy about Ottoman indulgence while dining in Istanbul's Çırağan Palace brought a reflective smile. Even though the last of the Ottomans did not survive this, their final palace, built by Sultan Abdülâziz only in the mid-19th century, its archaized architecture is reminiscent of the ornate Baroque style of bygone Ottoman splendors in such a magical Istanbul landscape.

Phrygia, Home of Dionysus

Phrygia is on the Aegean Coast of Turkey and is the region where ancient Greeks thought the wine god Dionysus originated. This myth source is plausible because the Phrygians grew vines extensively, made a fairly high volume of wine, and exported what surplus they didn't consume locally across the Aegean Sea to Greece. Ancient sites from where wine was shipped westward include *Tabae* (Tavas, near modern Pamukkale) and as mentioned, Klazomenai (adjacent to Urla). The Phrygians also hybridized one varietal grape, *Misket*, which then became known as *Muscat* to the Mediterranean world. Phrygia also produced the famous *Pramnios* wine, which Homer sang about in the *Iliad* 11.639 in the company of Nestor and especially in *Odyssey* 10:235 when the sorceress Circe mixed it with honey to drug Odysseus' men, so it already had a potent reputation to be so allied with the bewitching Circe.

The wine god Dionysus himself, before he left Turkey, spent at least a great deal, perhaps all of his mythical youth in Phrygia, such that his name sometimes is thought to mean "God of Nysa" (*Dio* + *Nysa*),[25] after a Phrygian peak said to be haunted by satyrs and lush with wild vines. The Greek tradition of Dionysus is least as early as Mycenaean tradition by around 1200 BCE as Linear B clay tablets attest. Because he was a god who could not be controlled, like his sacred drink, this divine connection underscores how wine was deeply embedded in religion and ritual through prehistory.

While modern Turkey is often ranked no lower than fifth in global volume of grape production, less than 5% of this harvest is made into wine; instead it is the world's largest source of table grapes.[26] Although understandable in Islamic tradition, this dichotomy is ironic given that ancient Anatolia was the likely source of vine cultivation for millennia and, as mentioned, that the wine god of the Western world seems to derive in name from Anatolia's Mt. Nysa in Phrygia, like his rich but foolish devotee the legendary King Midas from Phrygian Gordion in ancient Turkey.[27] Midas' Phrygian capital Gordion is not far from the modern capital of Ankara where modern wine Turkish production is regulated, possibly much to the consternation of the spirit of Dionysus himself.

Dionysus and viticulture migrated across the Aegean from Anatolia to Greece, sometimes depicted in the mythologizing Greek art as in the famous fifth century BCE Exekias black figure vase, discussed in more detail in the chapter on Greek wine. The later myths have him landing first in Attica although the island of Crete has the proven archaeological evidence for earliest Aegean island viticulture in proto-Greek contexts. Regardless of where Dionysus went first, Crete or the mainland, nearly all the myths accurately have the journey of Dionysus beginning in Anatolia before he ventured across the wine-dark sea.

CHAPTER 2

Wine in the Ancient Near East: Between Mesopotamia and Egypt

"He makes ... wine that gladdens human hearts." *Psalm* 104:15b

Wine More Powerful Than Gods

Mesopotamian and Ancient Near Eastern literature have many tales about the enormous power of wine and how even the gods can be overcome by it. Sumerian texts attest to some kind of wine legacy by at least 2650 BCE but it is likely already known from the Uruk Period more than a millennium earlier. In the Sumerian creation the gods, especially Enki and Ninma, made humans after a drunken banquet. Other drunken Sumerian gods include Ashnan and Lahar in related stories, mainly gods who argue and fight as wine inebriation brings chaos and dissolution of order. In another Sumerian text, Ninkasi is the goddess of winemaking, brewing, and alcohol, the "Lady Who Fills the Mouth."[28] Also an intoxicated and merry Enki, "having consumed wine and gulping down beer ... in goblets deep as boats" over-generously gives the goddess Inanna his gifts of civilization for her city Uruk.[29] Utnapishtim also tells Gilgamesh in the *Epic of Gilgamesh* Tablet 11 that he plied the men who built his boat to escape the flood with both beer and wine as plentiful as water.[30] In Ancient Egypt, the goddess Hathor was the primary patron deity of merrymaking, intoxication, and wine in general; she had an annual festival at Bubastis where excess in wine drinking was not discouraged. In Ugaritic myth, the drunken god El and his three sons, Thukamuna, Shunama, and Haby, wreak havoc after a *marzeah* or wine banquet.[31] The power of wine over gods is a human caveat that wine and its effects are very hard to control. If even gods can lose sobriety, what might happen to humans?

Overall, early wine in Mesopotamia was often imported due to the hot climate that made it difficult to sustain vines unless somewhat shaded from the wilting aridity. The climate made brewing of beer more prevalent than vine production, especially in southern Mesopotamia, but in the more mountainous northern Tigris-Euphrates and in the Zagros Mountains to the east, winemaking still had a fairly early start, of which the Sumerian myths retain an echo. Viticulture in Upper Egypt was also difficult at first given the ambient desert heat, since it is generally accepted that *Vitis vinifera* is best grown where the average annual temperature is between 10 and 20°C with a winter minimum of 3°C, where long warm summers are balanced by cool winters.[32] The heat of Egypt would be a long-term obstacle to viticulture except in enclosed fields and gardens, where shade was provided, made it easier in Upper Egypt, whereas viticulture in the Nile Delta began much earlier due to lower temperatures.

Egyptian Wine History and Deities

The oldest wine traces found in Ancient Egypt were dated to Predynastic history from Abydos tombs during the Naqada III period (ca. 3150 BCE) and into the First Dynasty, including several hundred imported wine jars from the former period.[33] The evidence was from ceramic vessels that yielded grape seeds, yeasts, and residues of both tartrates (calcium salts) and terebinth resin as a wine preservative. These earliest ceramic vessels were not necessarily indigenous since their decoration was mostly consistent with Levantine or Syro-Palestinian style, found elsewhere in Palestine to the east.[34] On the other hand, some debate the late date of indigenous Egyptian viticulture, since grape seeds have also been found at Predynastic el-Omari before the third millennium BCE.[35] By the Old Kingdom, at least five kinds of wine were known to Egypt, as shown in the funerary offerings to King Unas (ca. 2494–2345 BCE) of the 5th Dynasty.[36] Even the most representative Egyptian hieroglyph for "grapevine" also doubles at times for "garden."[37] In the Old Kingdom, during the 4th Dynasty around 250 BCE, Metjen was one official who had significant estates in the Nile Delta, including vineyards, "… plentifully planted and a great deal of wine was made there."[38]

Wine (known as *irep* in Egyptian), both red and white, was produced in Egypt in the Old Kingdom onward, especially in the Delta but also in oases like Kharga and Dakhla as well as in Kynopolis[39] and the walled fields of temple precincts in both the Nile Delta and Luxor, the latter by Amenhotep III (ca. 1417–1379 BCE).[40] While beer may have been the most available beverage of Egypt, it was more associated with the common people, whereas wine was more rare and was the drink of gods, royalty, and wealthy.[41] Private home gardens often had grape vines in pergolas where the fruit could either be eaten or used

Fig 2.1 Egyptian Grape Harvest, ca. 1450 BCE

for homemade wine.[42] Other Egyptian means of supporting the vines included forked props or stakes or merely training them to grow on other trees or even columns.[43]

Wine was also used extensively in Egyptian medicine as both a carrier (or a vehicle)[44] for other medicine as well as an analgesic[45] for alleviating general pain and internal medicine,[46] and as an aid in childbirth.[47] Often taken with honey, the antibacterial properties in the combination of wine and honey were seemingly unknown in Egypt. Offering tables shown in tomb paintings or other media often had wine vessels depicted underneath for funerary or afterlife consumption.[48] In the famous tomb of King Tutankhamen in the Valley of the Kings (known as KV62), 26 wine jars were found for his afterlife enjoyment, although this volume of vessels was by no means large compared to earlier dynasties.[49]

Other Egyptian deities connected with wine and viticulture include Osiris, who presided over the *Wag* Festival (also known as *Ouag* or *Wagy*) when libations of wine were poured to Osiris on days 17 and 18 in the first month of the year.[50] His epithet *Wennefer* can mean "eternally good" as well as "eternally incorruptible" and it is likely at Abydos that his main rites or mysteries were commemorated with wine. For these and other related reasons, Herodotus (*Hist.* 2.42.2) links Osiris with Dionysus.[51] The cobra goddess Renenutet, "Lady of the Fertile Fields," was also a deity presiding over and protecting harvests, including that of the grapes, where a small shrine would often be placed near the wine press. She was also connected to Osiris in his divine protection through the royal *uraeus*, the flared cobra on the headgear guarding Egyptian kings.[52]

Wine-making scenes are known from many New Kingdom Egyptian tomb paintings, for example, well represented in the Tomb of Nakht (ca. 1390 BCE) at Thebes and even more extensively in the tomb of Khaemwaset (ca. 1425) at Thebes. The systematic process is depicted in Egypt in various media, from picking the ripe harvest hanging from overhead trellises, to treading the grapes underfoot, to squeezing the juices by twisting the presses, to filling and storing the contents in ceramic vessels.[53]

By the Late Roman period, several wines from Egypt had received sufficient recognition to be noted by Athenaeus (ca. 172–220 CE) of Naucratis, the Greek city in Egypt. In his famous *Deipnosophistae I.33de*, Athenaeus praises white *Mareotic* wine from the region of the northwest delta near Alexandria, described as "abundant, pleasant, fragrant" as well as a "pleasant and aromatic *Taeniotic* wine…even better than Mareotic" from Tanis in the eastern Nile Delta, and then the Coptic *Thebaid* wine "thin but easily digested and suitable for fever patients."[54]

Much like modern vintage recording, Egyptian wine-vessel stamps recorded a substantial amount of information, including the reigning king's year, the wine varietal, the vineyard, the owner of the vineyard, and even the winemaker.[55] If the winemakers changed, their clients who appreciated their wine could follow them to new

Fig 2.2 Egyptian Wine Amphora, 18th Dynasty

vineyards, much like today. Thanks to Egyptian scribes who stamped such details for the wealthy or noble wine connoisseurs of antiquity, this carefully recorded information allows modern scholars to locate vineyards otherwise lost from the ancient records.

Egyptian love poetry also speaks about the intoxication of love like wine, for example:

"New wine it is, to hear your voice; I live for hearing it"[56]

Other Egyptian poetry texts add to this treasury, where the lovers are endearingly referenced as "sister" and "brother":

"… wonderful are the seasons that the sister spends with her brother. They sit in my spreading shade while drunk with wine …"

"… the breezes blow as I say in my heart, 'Let's get drunk with sweet wine', for I am consecrated to you through the powers of love …"

"… with wine for her to set aside that you may intoxicate her and fulfill her desires in the night …"[57]

Wisdom literature also attributes wine as a divine gift: "He [the god] created remedies to end illness, wine to end affliction." Elsewhere the royal scribe Nebmare-nakht praises the art of writing and its satisfaction to his pupils: "Befriend the scroll and the writing palette… Writing is better than all other professions. It pleases more than wine…."[58] Of course, Nebmare-Nakht is biased and uses the wine metaphor to motivate his scribal students.

Neolithic and Early Bronze Age Viticulture in the Ancient Near East

In the Neolithic sixth millennium BCE—more than 7,000 years ago—at Firuz Hajji Tepe at the south end of Lake Urmia in the Zagros Mountains of what is now Iran, six 1.5-gallon pottery jars bear evidence of wine in chemical residues of calcium salts from concentrated tartaric acid, traces that can be found in such high concentration only in wine, along with a shellac of red malvidin pigment, also a wine residue, and terebinth tree resin was also used as a wine preservative. These vessels were excavated under the direction of Mary Voigt and analyzed by Patrick McGovern using infrared spectrometry and liquid chromatography.[59]

Additionally, elsewhere in the Ancient Near East, viticulture can be seen as early as the sixth millennium BCE (based on the differences between wild grape seed of *Vitis vinifera sylvestris* and cultivated grape pips of *Vitis vinifera sativa*). Again in the Zagros Mountains of current Iran, another ancient place, Godin Tepe, a Chalcolithic archaeological site from about 3500 BCE, yielded storage of flattened ceramic vessels laid on their sides like modern bottles to reduce oxidation.[60] In the Chalcolithic Levant of what is now Palestine and Israel, viticultural evidence can be found in the fourth millennium BCE at Tell esh-Shuna in the Jordan Valley.[61]

King Gudea of Lagash in Neo-Sumeria is one of the first to impose state control of irrigation and canalization of the Tigris-Euphrates,[62] including "irrigated terraces protected by trees to be used for planting grapevines,"[63] although viticulture was not entirely successful here until later. This illustrates how the heat of Mesopotamia needed mitigation with other taller vegetation, possibly also reducing damage from shredding sandstorms that swept eastward from the Nefud desert.

Wine Imports at Middle Bronze Age Mari in Mesopotamia

History often preserves for us small but significant personal details. Mari, a city along the middle Euphrates now in Syria, also had extensive wine imports in the Middle Bronze Age recorded in its annals. Much of the wine was brought down the Euphrates from Carchemish in the hillier and cooler region of what is now Turkey's border with Syria above Mesopotamia's river plains, a distance of about 500 miles. Cuneiform clay correspondence from around 1800 BCE found in Mari's archives from elsewhere tell that Shamsi-Adad, an early Assyrian king, heavily criticized his son Yasmah-Addu, the predecessor of King Zimri-Lim at Mari, for poor governance. Yasmah-Addu apparently loved good wine more than governing, and the rise of wine imports apparently increased dramatically under his otherwise lax administration, aided by Aplahanda, the king of Carchemish. Mari's state archive clay tablets record that Aplahanda supplied Yasmah-Addu despite the considerable distance, and some of Aplahanda's royal shipments to Mari from Carchemish are known to have been at least 50 jars of wine from his own royal Carchemish stores ("…I'm sending you the kind of wine I drink…"). Most of the Carchemish imports at Mari were then protected and allocated by Mari's royal family over generations.[64] Prices were also accordingly much higher in Mari—at least triple at the equivalent of $10 per liter higher than in Carchemish—so the king of Carchemish could make a nice profit if transport was easy and unencumbered downriver going with the water flow.[65]

Mari's next king, Zimri-Lim—not an Assyrian but actually from this city, unlike Yasmah-Addu—did not curtail the Carchemish wine imports, and continued to store the imported Carchemish wine in sealed rooms in his 300-room palace at Mari, the largest palace of the era and fairly well preserved archaeologically. Zimri-Lim also sealed his wine collection inside rooms, sealed by clay stamps with his own royal seal ring, and his wife in his absence had to borrow the seal as needed to send wine to Babylon but had to reseal the room and return the king's seal ring.[66] Qualities of wine at Mari—also from Aleppo and elsewhere—were differently described as "red," "of good quality," "second-rate," and "old."[67] There was also an old Sumerian goddess originally worshipped in the region of Mari and Karana, *Geshtin-anna*, whose name appears to mean "grapevine of heaven, with a variant of *Geshtin* appearing as *Karana* or *Karanum* in Akkadian, and wine was also drunk in her religious rituals as a divine beverage. Plus court musicians at Mari were allotted a modicum of wine, possibly for before or after performing[68]

Assyrian Wine

Eventually, viticulture flourished in Mesopotamia to make such imports less necessary. The Assyrian king Assurnasirpal (883–859 BCE) had his scribes inscribe the celebratory inauguration of his new capital Nimrud (Kalhu) where 10,000 skins of wine were consumed, and Assyrian palace reliefs commemorates literary accounts with visual imagery of grape clusters hanging from the vines to prove they were grown in Assyrian kings' own "fecund" gardens.[69] The original Boğazkere varietal of Anatolia may also have been cultivated in

Fig 2.3 Assurbanipal drinking in his Vineyard

Assyria along the upper Tigris River. Elsewhere, among other wine bowl-wielding Assyrian kings like Tiglath-Pileser III and Shalmaneser III, a famous 6th c. BCE Assyrian relief of the king Assurbanipal (668–627 BCE) depicts him reclining on a couch, his wine bowl held almost to his mouth, under vines whose luscious clusters of prolific grapes hang just above his head. This British Museum relief was originally in the royal palace at Nineveh, just at the junction of the Khosr River with the greater Tigris River in the Assyrian heartland.[70] Assyrian wine use is well documented by David Stronach, where using only golden wine bowls would do justice to royal wines.[71]

Canaanite Wine

In the Canaanite Levant, both the Judean Shephelah and the upper Jordan Valley of Palestine have long supported vineyards in places like Gibeon and Gilead, "renowned for its fine wines."[72] The distinctive "Abydos-Canaanite jug" was found in Egypt as early as First Dynasty Abydos (3100–2890 BCE), already mentioned in this chapter on Egyptian wine imports. Tell es-Sa'adiyeh, important from the Chalcolithic onward, lies just east of the Jordan River on the Wadi Kufrinjeh just south of Gilead, and its region was a site of importance for viticulture in the Early Bronze Age from around 2900–2650 BCE, as the tell's palace evidences with several industrial wine production complexes that exported wine to Abydos, among other contexts.[73] Bronze artifacts at several sites also demonstrate wine-drinking sets of bronze bowls, strainers, and juglets at Megiddo, Tell es-Sa'adiyeh and Beth-Shan in the Late Bronze Age. Additional bronze wine-drinking sets are found in the Persian Period at Tell Mazar.[74]

Persian Wine

Perhaps the most famous Near Eastern wine yarn comes from Herodotus and is about the Achaemenid Persians' legendary love of wine. Whether the following is true or not, Herodotus recounted the controversial anecdote that when the Persians met at council, they drank lots of wine and then made a state decision, possibly in their cups. If when they met again in the next council on the following day and came to the same conclusion in concord while sober, the Persians knew it was a good decision.[75] Strabo and Athenaeus tells us that the Persians introduced wine to Syria, especially Damascus, that subsequently the Persian kings loved Chalybonian wine,[76] which may have been cultivated on the slopes of Mt. Hermon above Damascus.

Wine appears again in the medieval poetry of Persian epics like Ferdowsi's *Shahnameh* written between circa 977 and 1010. Not only is musk-scented ruby wine savored in festivals under teak and ivory canopies but the great Persian national hero Rostam is bathed in rosewater, musk, and wine at his death like other epic heroes in Hittite lore and the *Iliad*. In this epic is the amusing story of the cobbler's son who drinks eight glasses of wine and then rides a lion, after which

Fig 2.4 Achaemenid Persian Wine Rhyton, 5th-4th c. BCE

wine becomes permissible to drink again with reasonable limits when the astonished king and his court find out. Also in this epic is the harp-playing jeweler's daughter Azezu who plays silken harp strings and serves red wine to Bahram Gur with great grace, her house filled with jasmine scent. Another harp girl, Azadeh, who was also a servant of Bahram Gur, was said to have cheeks red as wine.[77] Later Persian poets like Rumi (1207–73) and Hafez (ca. 1315–90) also mutually celebrate love and wine, so often inspiringly paired together.

Wine in Lebanon and Baalbek

The Canaanites of Ugarit and the adjoining area were involved in the wine trade, whether it was their own or others' wine they shipped. As mentioned earlier, the Canaanite jars found at Abydos even in Predynastic and First Dynasty Egypt were Levantine, and this trade continued through the Bronze Age, as seafaring ships that plied the Eastern Mediterranean continued the wine trade. In Phoenician, *cherem* was a Semitic cognate word for wine fermentation related to the Hebrew word *kerem* for vineyard. Later in Arabic the same word or a cognate is apparently metathesized, reversing the *r* and *m* to *khamr* or *chamr*. Regardless of the linguistic connections, it was the Phoenicians who were responsible for spreading much of the viticulture across the Mediterranean. Some think the name of Lebanon may be derived from the trade in frankincense, one of the early Phoenician monopolies, since the Semitic word cognates include *libanon*, the Hebrew word for frankincense, the sap of the *Boswellia* shrub from Red Sea where the Phoenicians traded; another etymology for Lebanon may be from Semitic words like *l-b-n* for "white" that may be descriptive of the coastal limestone and related geology or the snow-covered Amanus Mountains visible from the sea.

Poetry from Late Bronze Age Ugarit, circa 15–12th c. BCE, the Canaanite precursor kingdom to Phoenician culture, also rhapsodizes about wine, especially in the *Rap'iuma* where the shades of departed are feted at banquets where the chief god El favors wine: "Poured wine flows all day, sweet and ample choice wine, nurtured by El and fit for a king ... to the banquet house on the summit ... in the heart of Lebanon."[78] Wine from ancient Lebanon or Phoenicia was also renowned elsewhere, as the eighth century BCE biblical prophet Hosea exhorted the Israelites "to return to God, and they would then blossom like the vine with the fragrance of the wine of Lebanon." (*Hosea* 14:7b). Later traditions associate Canaanite wine ritual with the upper Beqaa Valley, possibly even related to the above *Rapi'uma* text in that a Phoenician banquet house on the summit may predate the Roman Classical site of Baalbek if toponyms can be connected.[79] Baalbek is 50 miles northeast of Beirut and is formerly known as Heliopolis. It has one of the largest surviving temples in the world: at 66 meters long it is almost as large as the Parthenon in Athens (69.5 meters long). This temple was dedicated to Dionysus about 150 CE. The Baalbek (Heliopolis) site had been visited by Marc Antony in homage to Bacchus in the first century BCE before the current temple of Bacchus was erected. The Temple of Bacchus has many relief scenes of grapevines and wine drinking as expected for a wine god.[80] One famous wine from the Roman period praised by Athenaeus was the *Bybline* wine from Byblos.[81]

Most historians suggest during the Roman destruction of Carthage in 146 BCE, extant Punic agricultural treatises on viticulture—partly deriving from earlier Phoenician texts—were saved by the Romans, especially the work of Mago of Carthage (third–second c. BCE). Some of Mago's 28 books were translated into Greek by Cassius Dionysus (second century BCE) of Utica, adjacent to Carthage, also into Latin by Decimus Silanus (second century BCE) by decree of the Senate; successive Romans like Varro and Columella, among others, read some of these Punic texts and partly incorporated them into their own work.[82]

Beirut, ever the Paris of the East, demanded more sophistication and tolerance by the mid-nineteenth century. Thus Lebanese viticulture was revived during the late Ottoman period around 1857 when Jesuit monks planted hardy and heat-tolerant Cinsault vines from North Africa in the lower Beqaa Valley at Chateau Ksara. Within a few generations, others had followed suit with Domaine des Tourelles in 1868 and Chateau Musar in 1930 so that the Beqaa Valley, especially Chateau Ksara—no longer in Jesuit hands—today produces almost 70% of Lebanese wine.

Biblical Evidences for Viticulture

Long after the Noah episode from *Genesis* 9, reportedly far to the north in Anatolia as already discussed, biblical viticulture recounts several famous vignettes. One is the literary tale of *Numbers* 13:23-24 about the Israelite spies sent in to explore and canvass the Promised Land. In amazement they return, reporting in hyperbole that one gigantic harvest grape cluster ('eshkol) typical of Canaan—the land of Nephilim giants in *Num.*

13:33—cannot be carried by one person but must be supported by several men carried on poles across their shoulders:

> When they reached the Valley of Eshkol they cut off a branch bearing a single cluster of grapes. Two of them carried it on a pole between them, along with some pomegranates and figs. That place was called the Valley of Eshkol because of the cluster of grapes the Israelites cut off there.

Elsewhere, wine is mentioned about 200 times in biblical texts, most often in a positive context. In I Kings 21:1–16, Naboth the Jezreelite loses his life when he refuses to relinquish his family vineyard to King Ahab and his wicked wife Jezebel, both of whom act above the law and pervert justice.83 Not the least of positive wine references is the first gospel-attested miracle of Jesus turning water into wine at the wedding feast of Cana in the Gospel of John 2:1–11 and beautifully rendered by Venetian artist Paolo Veronese (1528–88) with his huge canvas (6.66 x 9.90 meters) at the Louvre, painted circa 1562. Some say putative wine lovers like the Turkish Sultan Suleiman the Magnificent appears on the left among other famous contemporaries in Veronese's biblical subject. But an earlier vital biblical literary metaphor on wine is found in Isaiah 5 where Israel is the "Vineyard of God": kerem-El as the "Vineyard of God" becoming Carmel in English. x

In far more iconic references during Roman occupation, in *John* 15:1, Jesus refers to himself as the "True Vine and My Father is the husbandman" of the ecclesiastic vineyard of his followers. Furthermore, Jesus commanded the celebration of the Eucharist in all subsequent

Fig 2.5 Veronese, Marriage at Cana, 1571

Christianity to be commemorated with his blood represented in wine in *Matthew* 26:27–29 where he tells his disciples to drink the cup of the grapevine ('*ampelos* in Greek). Paul even recommends a modicum of wine for stomach health in *I Timothy* 5:23. The effect of wine is also a reverse metaphor for spiritual elevation in *Ephesians* 5:18. Naturally, responsible self-control and understanding limits are always called for in this biblical literature as well, as seen in the much earlier Davidic encounter with Nabal, who loses his life not over wine but because he lacks overall self-control.[84] Given the contemporary biblical encomia for wine, it is very difficult to comprehend or swallow ultra-conservative religious bans on wine when even Jesus' enemies called him a "wine-bibber" in *Luke* 7:34 and *Matthew* 11:19.[85] But such restrictions usually derive from hierarchical fear of losing control over people to something possibly more powerful than mere human authority. In the next chapter on Greek wine, some of the same fear is seen literarily in Euripides' *Bacchae* with the fatal reactions of King Pentheus of Thebes against the worship of Dionysus. How could any who claim to know and love the Bible dismiss this already-mentioned verse from *Psalm* 104:15b, "He makes … wine that gladdens human hearts."

Religion and wine have such long-standing connections beyond the perception that wine was a divine beverage and wine in ritual libations as well as conferring mutual elevated spirit. Paul in *Ephesians* 5:18 cautions not to be drunk with wine but to be filled with the Holy Spirit, since both appeared to have some common behavioral aspects. Voltaire tells the humorous story in his *Philosophical Dictionary*[86] that Lord Cromwell was putatively once dining with Lord Bolinbroke and the company had brought out a bottle of wine and a corkscrew when the corkscrew fell under the table. Just then a deputation of church elders arrived unannounced when everyone was under the table on their knees searching for the corkscrew. Putting off the churchmen with this explanation, the divines left, Cromwell tells the others, "They think we are seeking the Lord when we are only searching for a corkscrew."

CHAPTER 3

Greek Wine Tradition and Dionysus

"What is better adapted than the festive use of wine, in the first place to test, and in the second place to train the character of a man, if care be taken in the use of it?" Plato, *Laws* I[87]

A Cretan Visit

I walked that early summer morning along the sunny vineyard hill south of Archanes, Crete, passing seemingly endless trellised vines on both sides of the valley interspersed with olive groves and a magnificent view of the cloud-dappled slopes of Mt. Juktas, its peak in shadow. The destination I could already see was a Late Minoan villa and shrine at Vathypetro with an ancient winepress, where long ago the grapes were probably crushed by dancing feet in cadence to music, a feature of Minoan culture. The limestone-channeled winepress was around 3,500 years old, covered with old lichen and employed huge ancient ceramic pithoi storage jars set in the stone. Nearby is another Minoan winepress at Phourni just outside Archanes. At the time in 1984, I was a graduate student attached to the American School of Classical Studies at Athens and studying archaeological sites around Greece and its islands. An ancient Minoan roadway, now a scenic path, led along woodsy vales from Archanes to Vathypetro and up Mt. Juktas as well as south down to the Messara Plain. Archanes has been a viticultural region for about 4,000 years and remains so today.

While the ancient Minoan stamping of grapes accompanied by music is only a reconstructed idea, we know that music accompanied Minoan harvests from the famous singing vase, The Harvester Vase of Hagia Triada, where men bringing in wheat have their mouths open singing and are led by a man in ritual dress also singing and shaking a rhythmic sistrum.[88] Although we also have ample evidence for Minoan dancing on various media from ancient paintings to sculpture to jewelry, we can only imagine how Minoans celebrated when the harvest was grapes for wine. In many ways these Minoan traditions are precursors to Greek culture, often absorbed or incorporated in various stages from earliest moments onward, as in this passage from Homer's *Iliad* 18 561–72 as a description of a scene on the mythical Shield of Achilles:

> Therein he set also a vineyard heavily laden with clusters, a vineyard fair and wrought of gold; black were the grapes, and the vines were set up throughout on silver poles. And around it he drove a trench of cyanus, and about that a fence of tin; and one single path led thereto, whereby the vintagers went and came, whenever they gathered the vintage. And maidens and youths in childish glee were bearing the honey-sweet fruit in wicker baskets. And in their midst a boy made pleasant music with a clear-toned lyre, and thereto sang sweetly the Linos-song with his delicate voice; and his fellows beating the earth in unison therewith followed on with bounding feet mid dance and shoutings.

Whether or not this relates to a Bronze Age wine ritual connecting to Minoan tradition remains to be seen, but there are definite Mycenaean fragments to be found in the Homeric epics, much more than just epithets attached to names.

Back in the shaded town of Archanes, surrounded by traditional hill vineyards filled with Kotsifali and Mandilaria vines—also known as Amorgiano—and famous for "rozaki" table grapes as well, I had my first lyrical experience with Greek wine of these Cretan varietals. In the town I smelled wine in the air and followed my nose to the huge open winery door. Walking in, I was immediately faced with a huge wine vat. A welcoming bearded winery worker with typical friendly *xenophilia*, "hospitality to strangers," greeted me with a "Yassou," handed me a glass, pulled me by the arm, and brought me right to the wine tap of the large vat. He opened it up and laughed as amber wine splashed right over the top of my quickly filling glass and spilled onto the floor. The man smiled as I tasted the wine, nodding at my appreciation and refilled my glass. That Cretan morning was splendid and the birdsong from the trees outside was amplified in the winery doorway. I almost felt ready to dance.

Dionysus, God of Wine, and Transformation

According to myth, the wine god Dionysus came to Greece from Phrygia in Anatolia,[89] and according to archaeological evidence, viticulture came to Proto-Greek culture via Crete and the Aegean islands. Archilochos was an Archaic Greek poet (ca. 680–645 BCE)[90] from the island of Paros. Legend says even the Delphic oracle commanded certain Greeks to honor in order to appease the anger of Dionysus.[91] Archilochos describes a Dionysian experience thus:

> For I know how to take the lead in the dithyramb,
> the lovely song of lord Dionysus,
> my wits thunderstruck with wine.[92]

Among many other references in his poetry, Archilochos makes several known early references here to the mythical god of wine, drama, and transformations. For the Greeks, Dionysus also mediated profound philosophical implications of transformation. As Seaford has noted, "It is the joyful transformation of identity that underlies the importance of Dionysos in several spheres" and he mentions wine first and theater as well, among others.[93] Being half-mortal, half-divine, Dionysus had a special relationship between gods and humans through

Fig 3.1 Greek Wine Amphora with Dionysus

drama, especially the performance or reading of tragedy. According to Burkert, "Classical tragedy portrays the suffering and destruction of the individual caught in the mysteries of the divine."[94] Wine had another mediatorial element because it could temporarily confer an illusory divine state on mortals. The dithyramb is the "type of song especially associated with Dionysus."[95] As Archilochos may join the dance of satyrs and maenads (other translations exchange "song" for "dance" since *chorós* is "dance" and *choreía* is "choral dance with music" in Greek[96]) the wild attendants of Dionysus, his steps will be less stately than the gods' but less abandoned than the satyrs' and maenads'. Because Dionysus was also *Bromios*, "thunderer," and wine could strike humans with loss of control, Archilochos implies his mind is empowered and possessed by the god rather than led only by his own nature. The cadenced dithyramb was the precursor of choral dance, eventually incorporated into ritualized drama. As a lyric poet who often praises Dionysus, Archilochos was highly familiar

with Dionysian tradition, so his allusions and statements about his wine-god-altered state are perfectly apropos.

Dionysus can always be recognized in Greek art on wine vessels carrying his drinking cup and wearing a wreath of ivy, the plant that, like him, cannot be controlled. His imagery in art can include a panther leopard (*panthera* means "all wild" in Greek) with maybe a bearded snake as his harbinger of virile earth power. One of the most expressive red figure Greek wine amphora vases by the Kleophrades

Fig 3.2 Dionysus by Kleophrades Painter, 5th c. BCE

Fig 3.3 François Vase, volute krater, Florence

Painter (ca. 510–470 BCE)[97] has the god dancing with ecstatic Maenads, some of whom dangle bearded snakes and carry thyrsoi, the wand of the god that can touch dead wood and make it sprout again. A dancing bearded Dionysus wears his ivy crown and a spotty leopard skin tied around his shoulders, and carries his high-handled kantharos drinking cup in one hand and a purple grapevine in the other ready to be planted somewhere.[98]

As the god of wine, the ancient Greeks believed Dionysus brought divine elevation and relief from sorrow. As the god of freedom, Greeks linked *Dionysus Liber* to lowered inhibitions from wine's behavioral modification. As the god of changing boundary lines, dissolving constraints, and even chaos, most Greeks thought *Dionysus Lusios*, "the Liberator," was "the god who enables you for a short time to stop being yourself and thereby sets you free."[99] This was the god, "the Loosener"[100] who at certain times relaxed social strictures, with wine often the agency or the medium. On the other hand, Dionysus was also a god of both freedom and communality simultaneously, an idea that "derives in part from his association with wine," which relaxed constraints but also bound people together in conviviality since wine aided social integration.[101] As the god of tragedy, Greeks thought Dionysus helped humans to find purpose and meaning in dramatic enactment. The judges of tragedy in the festival cycles were generally priests who awarded prizes to the best dramatic trilogies.

Dionysus and Drama

I will never forget my first foray in Greece to the Theater of Dionysus at Athens. On scholarship I had arrived a week ahead of the start of my graduate program at the American School of Classical Studies. At a June's summer dawn I was probably the first to arrive at the Acropolis before the heat rolled across the city and much of the city was still in shadow, including the west colonnade of the Parthenon. Walking around the great temple, I finally peered over the south parapet to glimpse the shadowed ruined theater staring up like an eye fixed below me. I was soon wandering below the Acropolis around the old theater, most of its encircling rows of seats long gone from the hillside. I studied the Hellenistic frieze on the marble *skene* as I ambled between the cypresses and was especially struck by the first row of formal seats—the only ones with backs. Here the judges of drama sat, with every seat in that bottom row bearing an inscription about the seat holder, in each case the office of a priest cut into the marble. The high priest of Dionysus in this his precinct held the best, highest seat in the middle with its carved legs and adjacent pavement holes. This experience told me more than anything I had previously read elsewhere that Greek drama had an indelibly strong connection to religion. Greek dramatic tragedy enacted here, profound and often disturbingly paradoxical, was never intended as entertainment.

Aeschylus was the first tragedian of Athens to win greatest acclaim in the Dionysus festivals of the fifth century BCE, winning 14 times, and according to tradition, had a calling from Dionysus himself:

> Aeschylus himself said that when he was a youth he fell asleep one night while watching grapes in a field. Dionysus appeared in a dream and asked him to write tragedy. When day came, he tried to write tragedy in obedience to the vision, after that Aeschylus found this task easy. Pausanias, *Description of Greece* 1.21

The connection of Dionysus to tragedy as well as wine should not be overlooked. The great surviving altar or *thymele* from the Athenian theater is sculpted with satyrs and grapevines with clusters of fruit. What happened at this theater altar, set in the middle of the originally circular orchestra, is terribly important. Before dramatic performances like the Great Dionysia festivals, the cult statue of Dionysus would be brought into the theater. To invoke the real god's presence, a live goat would be tied to this marble *thymele* altar. Perhaps to solemn music, the priest would raise the knife over the wide-eyed goat, possibly struggling, and slit its throat. Now the theater crowd, already on the edge of their seats, would be hushed. The goat's death cry would echo across the theater and with the magnified acoustics, a shiver would ripple through the crowd, because while humans heard the scream, it was said the god Dionysus only heard a song. That explains the etymology of the word *tragōidía*, from *trágos* for "goat" and *'ōdé* for "song."[102] Such is the profound wildness of this god who is also the god of wine.

Fig 3.4 Greek Theater Segesta, Sicily

Both Dionysian theater—less directly wine-influenced—and Dionysiac wine ritual—more directly wine-influenced—were cathartic, meant to release some of the cognitive dissonance when dramatic resolution came to the riveted, motionless audiences, although Euripides challenged even that tradition. As Dodds noted, "[in] early Dionysiac ritual ... its social function was essentially cathartic in the psychological sense."[103] Wine was also a vital part of the Bacchic Mysteries, where worshippers partook of the god through his drink.[104] Other Dionysiac cult rituals emblematized the raw grape juice, itself altered naturally to transformative wine, as the god's blood, and certain Dionysian festivals like the three-day *Anthesteria*, celebrating the flowering or bloom of the vine, had its days even named after iconic wine vessels.[105] Theater and Dionysian festivals as cathartic are followed by the transformative symposium where wine was again an agent of catharsis.

Wine, Philosophy, and Politics

Wine was also the celebrated drink of the Greek symposium, where Athenian aristocratic citizens and their philosophers—often one and the same, especially in this context—gathered on reclining couches for social occasions to be entertained by flute girls and bards, to engage in sexual dalliance, to rhapsodize or recite music and poetry, or to engage in dialogue with freedom, sometimes witty and often profound, just as Socrates reigned in Plato's work named *Symposion*, expounded to understand the true nature and purpose of *eros* and its higher mysteries.[106] Plus, in his *Laws*, Plato advances the idea through his Athenian interlocutor that the ethos of wine symposia had great value to safeguard education.[107] If the musicians were quieted a bit, the wine sipped could, by releasing a certain amount of social tension and even intellectual inhibition, inspire novel pathways of thought if possibly no more than a second cup was imbibed, generally well diluted with water. Continuing on to further cups could likely bring back the atmosphere of flute girls and result in further loss of inhibition. Some of the deepest thought surviving from antiquity was generated in such symposium contexts, even if artificially recreated in Plato's *Symposium*, and this Greek moment was foundational not only to philosophy but also to civilization itself. Even in modern parlance, a symposium is hypothetically a place where scholars of academe present, hone, and debate new ideas, ever an echo of Athenian Socratic tradition. Two Greek writers, Theognis and Pindar, equate the wine *krater* as a metonymy, a substitutable literary figure representing the *symposion*.[108] Not only is wine kathartic like Greek drama but Belfiore reads Plato in her seminal commentary on his *Laws* 2.666 & ff. as saying that wine rejuvenates the old and that Dionysus gives his initiation rites to the human race as a *pharmakon*—a healing medicine—to remedy the dryness of old age and make the old young again.[109]

The role of wine in Greek social, ceremonial, and even political life has been explored by many, including eloquently by Joanna Luke, who stated the importance of the Greek wine *krater* transcended far beyond mere symbolic value. Owning a wine-mixing *krater*, especially the artistically rendered ones by master artists like Exekias or Euphronios, demonstrated that the owner was not a barbarian who drank potent wine unmixed, and also showed that one was aristocratic, able to supply enough wine surplus to fill a *krater*, not a small vessel, and that this wine could be distributed widely among others to convey leadership over a social hierarchy and a community, since hosting a symposium was not only an aristocratic perk but an obligation to the *polis*.[110] While there is no immediate philological connection between *kratēr*, "wine mixing bowl" (from *krasis*, "mixing"); *kratēsis*, "might power, dominion"; *krateo*, "rule or hold sway"; and *kratos* ("might," "power," and "rule")[111] there must have been an appreciation of the potential word play, even if by antithesis.[112] Political exile, *ostracism*, in the Greek world was also communicated through the agency of a ceramic potsherd, an *ostrakon*. If communality was a shared sacred identity represented in a wine vessel like the *krater*, then this idea could be potentially much larger in ancient Greek society as democracy began to change civic focus from the elite aristocrat as the focus of power to the common citizen in solidarity with other citizens. In the same way, symbolic power as transferred from the wealthy *krater* owner to the far more popular *demosion* pottery that was the state property of the Prytaneion that governed Athens, again mediated through communal feasting with wine drinking that bonded the *prytaneis*, those who circulated in ruling as civic foremen.

Wine's Power

Greek wine cups—especially the kylix and kantharos—frequently had images painted at the bottom with a defined purpose and many can still be seen in museum collections or elsewhere. When you drained a cup, you would often see the painted *gorgoneion* of Medusa or a satyr or other hybrid monster, a bestialized, humorous or even scary visual device. This was not merely decorative. One general purpose of the image inside was *apotropaic*,[113] a protecting idea to remind you of what wild thing you could become if you continued to imbibe the god in his wine. For certain you could lose yourself for a time, especially your own self-mastery, and who knew what you might do in such a state. The god was believed to certainly enter your person, possessive and larger than could be contained, so a certain caution was encouraged. Some ancient Greek words have very pointed original meanings exactly along these lines: our modern word "enthusiasm" has its roots in '*enthousiasmós*

Fig 3.5 Greek Bronze Satyr Handled Wine Vessel

from 'énthous ('éntheos), suggesting the god (theos) comes in (en) and "inspires or possesses"[114] via drinking his wine. Of course, we don't usually catch this ancient Dionysian connection when we think of the excitement of enthusiasm today, but I enjoy remembering Robert Mondavi's whoop of enjoyment when I shared this with him in 1996.

Attic Ikaria

My first visit to the Attic site of Ikarios was also an inspired event. During the summer of 1984 I was living outside Athens to the northeast of the city in the village of Kifisia near Mt. Penteli and spending my days hiking over and around the mountain range, whose west-facing slopes were covered in scrub and wild thyme and whose east-facing slopes were cooler and more wooded. I had a rudimentary map from 1888 and I knew the myth of Ikarios,[115] the man who had welcomed the incognito Dionysus from the east to Attica. The god soon showed Ikarios how to plant vines. This famous myth story purportedly took place in the deme of Ikaria, named after Ikarios.[116] One version of the story says his daughter Akme became the first maenad and ran off with the god. Other versions give his daughter's name as Erigone[117] or Aletis.[118] But at harvest Ikarios and some local shepherds became drunk because Greeks had never experienced the effects of wine. In fright at their loss of control, the shepherds killed Ikarios and his daughter Erigone found his body. This sad end to Ikarios and the visit of Dionysus are commemorated on mosaics, marble reliefs, and other ancient media at the site of Ikaria. But the ancient site purportedly had contained a small temple and shrine to Apollo as well, excavated in 1888 by the American School of Classical Studies at Athens where I was about to study. In my weeks of exploring the Attic countryside, I was shirtless with a deep tan and my shoes smelled strongly of wild thyme from hiking over goat paths through all the Greek hills.

I was determined to find this site of Ikaria, the legendary birthplace of Greek viticulture based on my 1888 map where annotations marked that late-nineteenth-century discovery of Ikaria's site. I hiked over Mt. Penteli to the village of Dionysos, figuring it was aptly named, which it was. After some exploration off the road and hidden behind a century of overgrowth were the small ruins, some stones with inscriptions and one stone's inscription even

Fig 3.6 Ikaria site, Attica Greece, (note vineyard right rear)

read *IKAPIΩN* in confirmation. But more remarkable to me were the old vineyards just beyond the oaks and ruins. The gnarled but well-tended rows had trunks thicker than any I had ever seen, some wider than my waist. I sat next to the Ikaria ruins and was playing my flute for about a quarter of an hour. I was suddenly surprised to hear a girl's voice calling out to me from the vineyard, beckoning me to the fence. I stopped playing and walked over. The girl was about eighteen and very animated as I approached.

In our quick creole conversation, halfway between Greek and English, her curiosity demanded what I was doing there in this remote place.

"*Apó poú eísai*? Where are you from?" she asked boldly. "*Yiatí eísai edó*? Why are you here?"

I told her I was from California. I could have asked her what she was doing there, but I didn't have to. She proudly told me this was her family's vineyard for many generations, and when I simply remarked, "It looks so old, *Phaínetai tóso paliá*," she answered matter-of-factly without a flicker of disbelief.

"Our vineyard is old because it was planted by Dionysus himself."

Loving mythology as I do, I laughed genuinely without a trace of skepticism, which pleased her. "Come with me, please, *'Ela mazí mou, parakaló*," she said. She immediately took me to her villa about a kilometer north of Ikaria in rural Dionysos to meet her parents, who graciously housed and feasted me for the next few days in wonderful country *xeno-philia* generosity because they wanted to honor this stranger from half the world away who had found Ikaria on his own when much of the modern world had forgotten it. A month or so later when I was at the American School of Classical Studies in Athens, after talking with archaeologist John Camp from the school, we revisited the site with a few fellow grad students and this time I found Ikaria easily. I didn't dare play my flute in front of my staid peers and this august professor, and no girl appeared at the fence separating the site and the old vineyard, although I was half hoping she would and I could prove I'd been there with local Greeks from Dionysos. That year I came to understand how much even modern Greeks still love their civilizing mythology. I kept those old hiking shoes for a decade because for several years they were still faintly perfumed with wild thyme.

Mt. Kithairon

That same July, filled with thunderstorms, when I was in the region of ancient Thebes, the chief city of Boeotian Greece, I spent a bit of time climbing around Mt. Kithairon, the mountain on the border and identified with Dionysus from antiquity. Near Thebes is the sanctuary site of Kabirion we visited where the Kabeiroi were mysterious minor deities, often believed to be guardians of vines.[119] They often seem physically related to the Egyptian dwarf god Bes, bestower of blessing in childbirth. Here too on Mt. Kithairon in myth was the Sophoklean peak where the infant Oedipus was chained to the mountain crest to be eaten by wild beasts in order to avert the oracles, a useless attempt. Perhaps more important, Kithairon's wild and thickly sylvan precipices towering overhead were darkening in the stormy dusk, as the former haunts of Dionysian ritual where I could almost imagine the wild ecstatic screams of Bacchantes (from Dionysus' Romanized name of *Bacchus*) coming from its mossy shadows. Bacchantes invoked Dionysus here in dances with their thyrsoi,[120] and on this mountain nature obeys the god.

Here on Kithairon is where Euripides' *Bacchae* 724–7 places the wildest encounters, where "the whole mountain and the wild animals join in the bacchanale and nothing remained unmoved in running."[121] Kithairon is where unbelieving Theban king Pentheus was torn apart by his own sister and mother, both Dionysiacs overcome by the god who thus punishes the king for trying to impede and stamp out his holy rites. This mountain became for me a haunted place even when I knew much of its reputation was imaginary, although on the top of the peak one can see remnants of recorded ancient activity around the rocks, fragments of broken pottery even after millennia. I half expected to catch a satyr in my peripheral vision, reminding me of a few months earlier when a few goats on Mt. Penteli's wild thyme hillsides butted me repeatedly until I turned back and found another pathway. When the wind rustles the leaves of Mt. Kithairon, perhaps one might think of distant echoes of something Greek like Euripides' strophe line "*Bákchai 'íte, Bákchai 'íte*" in his chorus cry of the god's worshippers in *Baccchae* 84.

Remembering this numinous time spent on Mt. Kithairon and the tragic Pentheus story from Euripides, as the *Bacchae* 1177 line of the chorus repeats, "Why Kithairon?" to Agaue, the mother of Pentheus, I wrote the poem below, much later published by Jenny March in her *Penguin Book of Classical Myths* (2008).[122]

Kithairon

Pruning wild limbs on Mt. Kithairon
is no impediment to a vine god,
dismemberment to him is temporary
like the faith of mortals.
Here on this ivy mountain
some see his beard in the clouds
or his thigh knotted in a root.
But in the eyes of Pentheus
pruning was in troubled wood,
powerless to take root again
since his sad mother has both
knit and unknit the cloth of him.
Is it wind we hear howling on Kithairon?

Because of my unforgettable time almost living within the mythology of Greece, during that summer in 1984 I wrote a book of poetry *Wings Over Hellas*—a fair bit of it published later piecemeal by Jenny March in London, some of which I even read publicly at her encouragement between 1989 and 1990 at combined Classical Association and Institute of Classical Studies events when living in London, and Jenny became a dear friend. I also composed a fair bit of music that summer in Greece and quite a bit later, distilled by that time and subsequent visits to Greece, a magical place where the myths seemed far more real than in any books, especially those of Dionysus.

Naxos, the Sacred Island

I visited Naxos, the sacred island of Dionysus in 1999 by invitation from Greek archaeologist Vassilis Lambrinoudakis to explore the sites, as I had hosted him at a winetasting in California during his Stanford sojourn. Naxos—also known as Dia—was far more lushly forested in antiquity, and its woods were long celebrated as his myth haunts, and his temple at Iria, about 5 kms from the main island town of Chora was one of his holiest cult sites. This temple was later converted to a Christian church, and some associations between Dionysus and Christ encouraged this synthesis about wine and miracles.

Marc Antony (83–30 BCE), the ill-fated Roman triumvir notorious for his wine escapades, lack of self-control, and affair with Cleopatra, once made his entry into Ephesus dressed as Dionysus, wearing ivy, flanked by fluteplayers and men and boys in satyr costume, and was even often hailed as the "New Dionysus."[123] According to legend, as Plutarch describes him as having a "graceful length of beard,"[124] Antony had also commissioned a bearded statue of himself as Dionysus for the Temple at Naxos about 39 BCE and even some of his tetradrachma coins bore on the reverse an image of Dionysus. As the legend goes, after Christianity had triumphed over Greco-Roman religion, some Naxian Christians had nonetheless believed this statue of Marc Antony-Dionysus in the old temple, now converted to a church, to be a statue of Jesus because visual associations between Jesus and Dionysus were believed by many credulous Christians. Accordingly this statue was re-erected in the church for some time despite the dissolute name of Marc Antony whose likeness had been forgotten.[125]

Naxos was also famous for its many wines blessed by Dionysus. At a simple but perfect restaurant right on the beach lit by lanterns, we tasted some modern Naxian wine (a crisp Prompona white, if I remember right) over dinner—with local fresh fish, *choriatiki* salad and Naxian Graviera cheese—as guests of Lambrinoudakis. Some Dionysus myths have the god born here in a cave on the island instead of coming by sea from Phrygia in modern western Turkey, while other myths instead say he was nurtured on Naxos by Iphimedeia and Pankratis[126] along with the semidivine Lenai nymphs, and some Greek myths also maintain the Lenai become nymphs of the wine press. A fragment of Sophokles from one of his lost satyr plays, *Dionysiskos* (*Infant Dionysus*), has an episode where in the infancy of the god, satyrs assist in the god's wonderful discovery of wine.[127]

Naxos as the sacred island of Dionysus has long been rendered in art. After the Ancient Greeks, artists have celebrated fragments of the Dionysus/Bacchus myth, often based on ekphrases of poets like the Greek bard Hesiod or the Roman poet Ovid, especially his *Ars Amatoria* 1.535–64 and Catullus' *Carmen* 64. Some artists even attempt to depict Naxos in its thick vegetation. Titian's 1523 *Bacchus and Ariadne* in the National Gallery of London is one such masterpiece, depicting the meeting of Bacchus and Ariadne on the edge of Naxos Island, where Ariadne still looks out to sea after Theseus had abandoned her, his ship barely visible on the marine horizon.[128]

Titian's majestic painting shows Bacchus leaping from his chariot just as Ovid describes, and among the many ironies, rather than panthers, which would be his normal large cat or tigers from India from where he arrives, his steeds are cheetahs, the fastest land animals, but fully at rest while it is the god who is hyperactive and more wild.[129] Empty in the foreground beside Ariadne is an upturned wine amphora (with Titian's name "engraved"), now facing the god, showing she has consumed enough, possibly in grief at her abandonment, to be ready for the god of wine. Jenny March made the interesting observation that underneath the amphora is a discarded yellow garment, possibly evocative of the life of the courtesan since this was the *krokotos* garb of the Greek *hetaira*; she has now given up this unmarried life with Theseus to enjoy the sacred marriage with Bacchus.[130] Their eyes locking, Bacchus promptly weds Ariadne and gives her the crown of stars above in the rich Venetian blue sky above burgeoning cumulus clouds. The frenetic retinue or *thiasos*[131] of the wine god off to the right includes dancing maenads, satyrs shaking haunches of dismembered deer, and a drunken Silenus on his donkey followed by satyrs lugging wine barrels, among others. Perhaps the most intriguing part of the painting is Ariadne's small domestic dog wearing a collar but both attracted to and repelled by the strangeness of the faun, half human and half animal, dragging on a string the severed deer head trailing blood. Titian makes clear the wine god is mediated through the agency of his drink by several visual references: the empty wine amphora, the drunken Silenus followed by the huge wine barrel, and possibly the purple robe he wears below his vine-covered head, all normal attributes of the god.[132]

Another *Bacchus and Ariadne* painting, far less allegorical than Titian's, is from 1754 by Rococo artist Jean-Baptiste-Marie-Pierre (1714–89). It has Ariadne deeply asleep on the lap of Bacchus secreted in a forest of Naxos, similar to woodsy landscapes of his contemporaries like Boucher and Fragonard.[133] With the light falling fully on her, Ariadne is ambiguously flushed with wine and love while the tawny god, clothed only in a leopard skin, reaches over her for grapes; the both of them also wreathed in grapevines. Empty wine vessels are strewn on their sides about the forest around them on the right with shiny grapes interspersed at different places on the canvas. Much larger than his half-naked sleeping female companion, the god's capacity for his wine seems logically greater than Ariadne's capacity. But if love is also part of the equation—as the ancient Greeks could expect *eros* to be mediated by wine—Bacchus should be sleeping too except that he is a god after all. Speaking of love and wine, Athenaeus philosophizes, quoting another poet (Antiphanes) that "There are only two secrets a man's face cannot keep, one when he is flushed in love, the other when in wine drunk deep."[134]

Ancient Greek Wine

How early the Greeks developed winemaking and grew vines is established at least by the Neolithic, where carbonized grape seeds have been excavated in the region of Thessalonica and in Toumba, Macedonia.[135] Also evidenced viticulture in the Early Bronze Age has already been mentioned from Minoan Crete at the outset of this chapter at least as early as 2000 BCE but likely much earlier. Mycenaeans also made, drank, and exported wine as literarily mentioned from myth figures like Nestor, furthermore contexted grape seeds have been found in more than a few Mycenaean sites like Pylos, Mycenae, Tiryns, and Sparta. Mycenaean wine amphora fragments have also been found in the Levant and Egypt.[136]

Homer tells in the *Odyssey* that old King Laertes of Ithaka grew over 50 different types of grape varietals on the island, which may not be mere literary hyperbole in terms of existing ancient Greek varietals.[137] Other Archaic Greeks like the lyric poet Alkman (seventh century BCE) mention Denthis wine from Messenia, a wine that "smelled of flowers" (*anthosmias*). The great encyclopedist Theophrastus (ca. 371–287 BCE), pupil and successor of Aristotle, gave ample descriptions of differences in regional Greek viticultural practice—like vine planting and the timing of pruning, and in his *De*

Fig 3.7 Greek Wine Transport Amphorae, Stoa of Attalus, Athens

Causis Plantarum, also stating that grape varietals should be matched with their optimum territories and soils.[138] Greek wines praised in antiquity include the wine of Attic Ikaria, Naxos, Mende, Nemea, Peparethos (Skopelas)—mythically founded by Staphylos, another Greek word for grape) a son of Dionysus but more likely from Crete—and *Pramnian* wine from Smyrna across the Aegean, already mentioned in a previous chapter, to name only a few. Some coins from Mende (Macedon) even had images of Dionysus holding a kantharos wine cup and riding a donkey,[139] others from this ancient city had both donkey and vine with full grape clusters. Wines were also produced and shipped from Aegean islands like Chios (*Chian*), Thasos (*Thasian*), Chalkidike (*Chalkidikian*), Lemnos (*Lemnian*), Kos (*Koan* or *Choan*), and Lesbos (*Lesbian*), often said to be the best, like ambrosia, and sometimes also said to be specifically *Pramnian* from Lesbos.[140]

Given its oenological longevity even during Ottoman times, Greece is home to over 300 indigenous grape varietals,[141] including some in Italy today that bear names like Aglianico—from Helleniko—in Campania and Grechetto in Umbria as well as Greco in Campania and Calabria.

Fig 3.8 Mende Tetradrachma 5th c. BCE

Many of these South Italian varietals were likely brought by early Greek colonists to Magna Graecia and Campanian cities like Neapolis (Naples) from the ninth and eighth centuries BCE onward. Both Nemea and Nauplion in the Peloponnesus also have old wine traditions, and an ancient text of the second century CE Roman doctor Pausanias' (*Travels in Greece* 2.38) noted a donkey carved on a rock at Nauplion; the carving was said to have celebrated a local donkey that severely consumed a grapevine but it flourished so well the following year it was accidentally thought to have discovered the virtue of pruning.[142]

Fig 3.9 "Greek Wine Vessels, 6th c. BCE, Agrigento Museum Sicily

Signifying how extensive the Greek wine trade was in antiquity, the vast distribution of Greek wine amphorae is well known, ranging from the Black Sea all across the Mediterranean and even outside Gibraltar—the ancient Pillars of Herakles—along the Atlantic coasts, vital sources of wealth for Greek city-states.[143] The remains of Greek shipwrecks, including one just outside Marseilles—the ancient Greek colony of Massilia—have produced many wine transport amphorae. One shipwreck alone yielded up to 300 wine amphorae from Greek colonies in South Italy from about 100 BCE.[144]

Modern Greek Wine

Modern Greek wines, many continuing the tradition even if in new hybridized varietals, include the already mentioned Archanes red Kotsifali and Mandilaria (Amorgiano) wines of Crete, along with Naoussa (red), Mantinea (white and rosé), Goumenissa (red), Rapsani (red), Assyrtiko (white), Patras Mavrodaphne (sweet red), with many of these red wines coming from Greece's near-ubiquitous great red xynomavro grape.[145] Most of Greece's grape varietals are not well known outside Greece, like the red Agiorgitiko ("St. George") and rosy Moschofilero (used in Mantinea wine), both popular around Nauplion and Nemea. From Monemvasia one local grape of the eastern Peloponnesus was brought to Sicily presumably in the early medieval period, where the name Monemvasia became shortened to Malvasia (for a group of grape varietals, especially Malvasia Bianca) and taken by the British from there to Madeira where the name was again altered to Malmsey for producing sweet white wines.[146] Savatiano is the white grape used for Greek retsina.[147]

Some of the Greek wine producers and cooperatives that have flourished since the 1980's with higher standards include Boutari, Achaia-Clauss, Tsantali, Kourtakis, and Karonis, among many others.[148] The *Boutari Moscophilero 2007* from the Peloponnese has been widely praised (*Wine Advocate* among others), as has the *Domaine Sigalas Assyrtiko Athiri 2007* from Santorini. Gaia Wines received the accolade of Winery of the Year in 2007, 2009, 2010 from *Wine and Spirits Magazine*, especially noting their Assyrtiko and Agiorigitiko; *Decanter* World Wine Awards also confirming the same prize-winning winery and wines with gold medals from 2009–12.

Greek Love of Wine

The full richness of Greek culture and especially Greek art and poetry on wine can hardly be summarized here. Athenaeus and his fellow Greeks understood vintage when he said in *Deipnosophistae* 13.46, "Old wood best to burn, old wine to drink, old friends to trust, and old authors to read." Leave it to elegaist Theognis to pour into a poetic verse some of this Greek literary wine treasure:

"Drink wine which under the peaks of Taygetus
has been produced by vines which the old man planted
in the mountain glens—old Theotimus dear to the gods -
channeling cool water to them from Platanistous.
Drink some of this and you will scatter dire cares,
And well fortified you will be much lighter in heart."[149]

Thus the ancient Greeks had one of the most balanced perceptions of wine's divine blessings: they loved its paradoxical dissolving of cultural inhibitions and at the same time offering communality and social integration through both public ritual for the many as well as the clubby closeness of symposium for the few; they were profoundly appreciative of the elevated state and philosophical openness equated with divine enthusiasm; they noted and needed the wine god's transforming power in mediating civilizing arts like music, dance, and tragedy and drama; while they were also well aware of the dangers of excess. Yet

Fig 3.10 Rhodian Greek Bronze Krater
6th c. BCE

in all this the ancient Greeks also knew well that wine brought a slight modicum of happiness, not a false hilarity but a given ability to lighten, even if temporarily, some of the weight of the heavy mantle of mortality and take the mind away for a brief blessed respite from the stressful cares of the human struggle against fate, destiny, and one's own inability to always succeed at everything attempted or dreamed. For these gifts the Greeks were grateful.

CHAPTER 4

Etruscan Wine and Banquets

"Death to the Etruscan was a pleasant continuance of life with jewels and wine and flutes playing for the dance." D. H. Lawrence, *Etruscan Places*[150]

Tarquinia

In the old Palazzo of the Tarquinia Museum its astonishing size immediately seizes your attention, the largest two-handled wine cup I've ever seen—a Classical red figure kylix "wine cup" with convivial wine scenes like Ganymede serving Zeus—easily two feet in diameter. It seems unlikely one person could lift it when full of heavy wine, so it was likely intended for a communal quaff as a deeply social experience. Of course, the Etruscans loved wine and dance-filled banquets in death as much as in life, just like their underground painted tombs show across ancient Etruria in Central Italy, to-day's Tuscany and Umbria.

More than a few times now I've visited the sea-ward side of Tarquinia, seemingly always toward

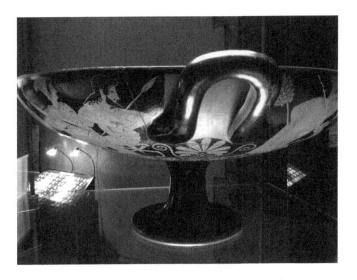

Fig 4.1 Giant Kylix, Tarquinia Museum, side view
(main subject is Ganymede Serving Zeus)

Fig 4.2 Tarquinia, Tomb of the Lionesses

Fig 4.3 Detail of two dancers from the Tomb of the Triclinium, Tarquinia

late afternoon, with the western sun slanted dramatically on the slopes of Monterozzi. Its sparse trees are angled along the hilltop of the Etruscan necropolis where hundreds if not thousands of Etruscan tombs rest. Etruscan tombs often have banqueting scenes, and Tarquinia's are no exception, some with high-kicking dancers circling around enormous wine kraters. The Tomb of the Leopards has young males bringing *oenochoe* vessels; the Tomb of the Lioness depicts both male and female dancers carrying the same vessels, with large black bucchero wine vessels adjacent to the dance. Many of Tarquinia's tombs date from the early 5th century BCE and their narrow descending staircases dot the hill.

After D. H. Lawrence's journey to Tarquinia in 1927, he was one of the first to describe some of the banquet and drinking painted tomb scenes, published posthumously in his *Etruscan Places*. Excerpted here is his Tomb of the Hunters and Fishers visit:

> Behind the man stands a naked slave-boy, perhaps with music, while another naked slave is just filling a wine-jug from a handsome amphora or wine-jar at the side. On the woman's side stands a maiden, apparently playing the flute: for a woman was supposed to play the flute at classic funerals; and beyond sit two maidens with garlands, one turning round to watch the banqueting pair, the other with her back to it all…[151]

Lawrence entered and wrote about at least five of the Tarquinian tombs with their painted banqueting scenes where wine plays a large role in afterlife joy. Quite often the wine vessels drew his attention, as well they should. The late esteemed J.K. Anderson, emeritus Classics professor at Berkeley, spoke and wrote about the wine god as salvific, a god who brought afterlife joy in his purple wine.[152] Lawrence writes more about his Etruscan experience:

> The *Tomba dei Vasi Dipinti*, Tomb of the Painted Vases, has great amphorae painted on the side wall, and springing towards them is a weird dancer, the ends of his waist-cloth flying. The amphorae, two of them, have scenes painted on them, which can still be made out. On the end wall is a gentle little banquet scene, the bearded man softly touching the woman with him under the chin, a slave-boy standing childishly behind, and an alert dog under the couch. The *kylix*, or wine-bowl, that the man holds is surely the biggest on record; exaggerated, no doubt, to show the very special importance of the feast.[153]

One of these painted kylix images in Lawrence's second description may be the same as or very similar to what I'm still astonished by after multiple visits to the Tarquinia museum. If it was thought in antiquity that a little wine elevated the spirit, "the more the merrier" seems an apt conclusion because in the afterlife, one could drink as much as one wanted without any ill effect once the limits of mortality were gone. Tarquinia's *Orcus Tomb* paintings even show multiple rows of huge wine amphorae and related vessels.[154]

Even a famous ceramic sarcophagus in Rome in the Villa Giulia National Etruscan Museum, *Sarcofago degli Sposi* ("Sarcophagus of the Spouses"), almost 2 meters in length,

Fig 4.4 Etruscan Sarcophagus with Banqueting, Chiusi

from the Banditaccia Necropolis of Cerveteri, depicts a smiling couple reclining together at an afterlife banquet, as many other Etruscan sarcophagus motifs also expressed the same wishful thinking.[155]

Early Etruscan Wine History

It was quite possibly the richly trading Phoenicians who introduced wine to the Etruscans at least by the late eighth or early seventh century BCE, given the mid-seventh century Regolini-Galassi Tomb at Caere has Orientalizing motifs and other Phoenician-style objects in Etruscan tombs, including ostrich eggs and jewelry and the famous Populonia Lamp.[156] Possibly more telling, the first wine ceramic amphorae in seventh century BCE Etrurian sites have Levantine shapes that are either Phoenician in origin or merely brought by Phoenician ships,[157] since the Phoenicians were some of the best sources for wine elsewhere in their trans-Mediterranean network of emporia, and bringing not only luxury items but important commodities and ideas, including the alphabet that the Etruscan also borrowed and made their own. There remains scant history about early indigenous Etruscan wine-making and Etruscologists offer few confirmations.[158] Livy mentions a wine party given by the Etruscan Tarquins and involving Romans around 509 BCE in the context of the Lucretia narrative.[159] Other evidences may include a wine jug with grape must from an Etruscan farm in the Albegna Valley near Grosseto and several small Etruscan bronzes from Ghiacco Forte near Saturnia with men holding the *roncola*, a special grape-harvesting scythe-like tool.[160] In any case once the Etruscans were involved in their own winemaking, they became very proficient in making local wine even when they must have still imported Greek wine, all of which they enjoyed immensely judging by the prolific tomb banqueting scenes.

Beyond ancient texts—many purged by the Romans—the archaeological evidence for Etruscan wine is scant but growing. Much of the prior scholarly emphasis on wine in Etruria has justifiably centered on funerary ritual due to the primarily tomb contexts, but this is changing.[161] In 2011 around 150 intact grape seeds from were found by Nancy de Grummond's excavations in the Etruscan site of Cetamura del Chianti in a waterlogged well. Datable to the first century CE, they appear to date from earliest Roman vineyards in Chianti, but whether or not they are precursors to Sangiovese varietal remains to be seen.[162]

Other ancient vineyards in Etruria are known from Cosa, Statonia, Graviscae, and Caere[163] but these are mostly from Roman records and it is unknown how early viticulture can be proven for Etruscan sites. Even if the Etruscans consumed more wine from Greece and produced outside their homeland than wine they produced regionally, it does little to diminish their love of banqueting and the role of wine therein. One of the most intriguing archaeological evidences of wine ceremonies is the recent discovery at Populonia (Poggio del Telegrafo) of a cache of over 100 buried wine cups and *kyathoi* ladles in a posthole of the "King's House," already buried by the seventh century BCE.[164] Since Etruscan records were likely diminished by Roman conquest, their tomb artifacts and tomb paintings are a better record of their love of wine. It is no surprise that nearly every Etruscan museum in Italy has more bucchero wine vessels displayed than can be easily counted, most of them from Etruscan tombs.

At the Tarquinian Necropolis

Although I've seen them over and over since, I will never forget my first viewing of the painted Etruscan banqueting scenes in Tarquinia's tombs. Living in London, we had rented a small Fiat wagon in Verona as a family—my wife Pamela and three young daughters, Hilary (Hilaria), Allegra, and Beatrice—and drove all over Italy in 1988. Of course, thinking we could fit anywhere in this diminutive Fiat, we drove up to the very top of the old hill town in Montepulciano and were temporarily wedged between the stone walls of a medieval alley, with hardly any room to back up, until townsfolk helped us extricate ourselves from the alley, naturally more by animated hand signs than words. With daughters named in recognizably Italianate fashion, and because the Italians love children, our girls always seemed to receive free gelati everywhere. At first we were worried that the Fiat had no seatbelts in the second row of passenger seats, but after a week covered in accumulated layers of gelati, the girls stuck to the seats.

While our children accreted strata of gelati, we adults sampled the local classic *Vino Nobile di Montepulciano*, for which the red wine Montepulciano has been famous for eons, praised in Italy as early as 789 by the medieval cleric Arnipert. The vestiges of the Etruscan hill town underneath the medieval town of Montepulciano may have been founded by Etruscan king Lars Porcena around the end of the 6th c. BCE about the same time Rome threw out the Tarquins. Much later, Renaissance Florentine poet Angelo Poliziano (14545–94) was born here in Montepulciano and his poems probably helped inspire Botticelli's 1482 *Primavera* and 1486 *Birth of Venus*,[165] among other works, and he was ostensibly Michelangelo's teacher of humanities as well. Driving over the hills to the coast and Tarquinia has always been magical, as was the honey-colored Vernaccia wine we bought in villages and tiny roadside vendors at various times along the way in the Etruscan hill country coming from Siena.

At the Tarquinian necropolis, it was midsummer and we could hear bees buzzing slowly in the heat even as we descended the cool stairs into the painted tombs, the only visitors at that moment. Our eyes adjusted to the dim light and we only wanted to whisper as we saw the 2,500-year-old paintings of dancers and reclining banqueters sipping celebratory wine. In the silence we imagined the music of the dancers—maybe some had even echoed within this very tomb in the last party of the resting occupants.

In the *Tomb of the Hunters and Fishers*, banqueters in the tympanum wait for the serving boy to fill up a

Fig 4.5 Enoteca Pinchiorri, Florence

small drinking jug from a huge wine krater on the right. Underneath the banqueters, birds scatter. Etruscan augurs had determined the future from many things including bird flight, which we could vicariously glean from the obvious seasonal migrations of birds north to south and vice versa. After we had seen quite a few banquets and were returning to the sun outside, we had just climbed the stairs when a lovely butterfly floated by and landed on our eight-year-old daughter Hilary's sunny forehead, slowly resting its wings about a minute as she didn't dare move, only smiling at the serendipity. I was astonished, knowing butterflies were the ancient symbols of a soul (*psyche*) en route to the underworld and we had just stepped out of an Etruscan tomb and that asphodels still bloomed on the necropolis hillside. We took a photo of the butterfly on Hilary's brow and although now faded, it's still in a photo album somewhere at home. I soon wrote a poem about the event as well. Down in Tarquinia Lido by the beach below the Etruscan town, we regaled ourselves with this story over a few glasses of local wine. Thus fortified I explained to our young children how propitious it was to see this necropolis butterfly and how meaningful that it rested on a child's forehead. At the time they probably lapped up the *tartufo* creamed pasta and *basilico* salad more than my retelling of old myths, but we often remind each other of this Tarquinian event when together; they are all adults in their own right who appreciate this special part of Italy on their own.

Castello di Potentino's Origins and Connections

This early childhood Italian magic proved irresistible to our daughter Hilary who, after several years of elementary school in London, later spent undergraduate time in Rome at the Centro, followed by a graduate fellowship in Fiesole and master's and doctoral dissertations on Italian artists. In graduate school in London she was the wine buyer for a restaurant. But when she moved to Kensington (London), the family of her friend Alex Greene in London provided deeper, more venerable Etruscan authenticity. The old Castello di Potentino in the Maremma of Italy now belongs to the family of Alex Greene and his sister Charlotte Horton, heirs of novelist Graham Greene. Castello di Potentino is within the commune of the hill village of Seggiano in the hills high above Grosseto. The castello can be triangulated between Orvieto, Montepulciano, and Grosseto, approximately 30 kilometers from each of these cities and thus in

Fig 4.6 Castello di Potentino

the heart of Etruscan hill country. Local legend has it situated on an old Etruscan hill site here in the Orcia River Valley watershed. Approaching the castle from almost any direction requires visitors to circle some of the slopes of the Etruscan sacred mountain, Mt. Amiata, a peak that dominates the Italian landscape for many miles. From the slopes of Mt. Amiata en route to the castle it is also possible to view the Tyrrhenian Sea around some twists in the narrow road.

It was in Kensington that we first tasted the Greene family's wine *Sacromonte* 2006, a Sangiovese from the castello estates. Soon thereafter this was the featured red wine at Hilary and Bradley's 2009 wedding reception in Kensington at the Royal Geographical Society where I've been a Fellow since 1989. It was the perfect elegant wine for a posh wedding. Wine connoisseurs have justifiably raved about different vintages of the *Sacromonte* and good wines have apparently been made in this valley since the Etruscans. We also had a wonderful winery lunch at the castle where we had the Sacromonte wine again. Nearby Monte Amiata was a sacred site known even then for its hot springs, and some of its two-thousand-year-old olive trees are almost as old as the Etruscans themselves who also grew olive trees in this area. But the more recent history of the Castello di Potentino is somewhat connected to some of the most illustrious Renaissance notables.

Duke Ferdinand I de' Medici (1549–1609), one of the more enlightened Medici rulers, gave the Castello di Potentino estate to Marchese Giovanni Battista Bourbon del Monte (1541–1614), who also had a nearby palazzo in Piancastagnaio on Monte Amiata. Much of this Medici activity happened when Tuscany became a Grand Duchy around 1601. Giovanni was a first cousin of the famous brothers Francesco (1549–1627) and Guidobaldo Bourbon del Monte (1545–1607). Their father was the soldier and military strategist Ranieri Bourbon del Monte, brother of Giovanni's father, the Marchese del Monte. Ranieri was also elevated to the rank of marchese by the Duke of Urbino. Guidobaldo was also a famous mathematician and close friend of poet Torquato Tasso. His brother Francesco Bourbon del Monte became a cardinal in 1588.

These two brothers assisted the early career of the even more famous Galileo, helping him obtain his first professorships in Pisa then Padua, so both of them can be named as noted patrons of Galileo, the pre-eminent scientist of his era. It is apropos that Galileo is purported to have said, "Wine is sunlight, held together by water." Cardinal Francesco Maria Bourbon del Monte is most famous for being revolutionary artist Caravaggio's main patron and a connoisseur collector of great art, and Titian

Fig 4.7 Tuscan vines and olives

was Francesco's godfather at his christening.[166] We know from records that Galileo even visited both Bourbon del Monte brothers' houses. Over the castle doorway is the old carved limestone Bourbon del Monte scudo bearing the family heraldry.

These are lasting Castello di Potentino connections to the Bourbon del Montes, one of the most intellectually prominent families in Tuscany. Whether Caravaggio also ever spent time here at Castello di Potentino may remain a mystery, but local historians have suggested Caravaggio hid out here when he disappeared from Rome as a fugitive in 1605–6;[167] not implausible because of the Del Monte family connections and because this quietly remote estate was just outside the papal states in Medici Tuscany, out of reach of Rome. The 11th century castello perches high on a rocky outcrop, easily defensible and with great views over the surrounding countryside with its rich vineyards and old olive trees, about a mile west of Seggiano's hill town and the national road SS323.

This venerable viticultural area around Seggiano and Monte Amiata is also rich in Etruscan wine stones—*pestarole*—where the local grapes were trampled. Generally out of regional volcanic rock—Monte Amiata is volcanic—the grape juices were drained through rock channels in the *pestarole* and collected below in waiting pithoi to ferment before being transferred to amphorae after six months. Local articles about these local wine stones also suggest they are most likely Etruscan:

> These *pestarole* artifacts … most likely to be considered as Etruscan … are composed of an upper tank dug into the *peperino* stone of Monte Amiata, material particularly suitable for carving. Part of it consists of a bath that has a spout of stone beneath which opens another collection tank. They are real stone monuments that tell of a civilization dedicated in particular to grape growing and wine production … the [grape] bunches were piled in the upper tank largest and pressed so as to remove the liquid that flowed through the hole, in the lower container.[168]

Additional wine pressing vats with pressing basins—referenced by another name as *pigiatoi*—are also known in the vicinity of Monte Amiata from the Abbadia San Salvatore.[169] Yet another Italian name for related wine stones like these may be *palmenti*.[170] The process of using stone vats was practical in several senses because the volcanic *peperino* stone is fairly soft, but it doesn't decompose like wood. The stone vats or "baths" had low enough rims and were sufficiently large for several people to easily step inside and trample the grapes side by side.

The winemakers at Castello di Potentino and the commune of Seggiano have experimented with grape crushing in these pestarole vats below the castle, especially with the Sangiovese grape that is the main local varietal. One early indigenous grape most often thought to have been cultivated by the Etruscans was *Vitis silvestris* as an ancestor of the modern Sangiovese:

> Cultivars of wild *Vitis silvestris* are attributed to the Etruscans, the indigenous ancestors of Trebbiano, Sangiovese, Falanghina … Sangiovese, in the opinion

of many ampellographers, was born in Tuscany Etruscan and, indeed, precisely in the Chianti territory....[171]

Since Sangiovese is also Italy's "most famous grape, responsible for the three great wines of Tuscany: Chianti, Vino Nobile di Montepulciano and the magnificent and expensive Brunello di Montalcino," history may have been made here in Etruria by the Etruscans even though now the "Sangiovese vine has many genetic variations or clones."[172]

Castello di Potentino's organic vineyards are also completely hand-harvested. Among the 20,000-bottle annual yield, beside the *Sacromonte* Sangiovese from the Montecucco Rosso DOC (*Denominazione di Origine Controllata*), the vineyards also produce a crisp tinted white *Lyncurio* that Potentino winemaker Charlotte describes as "the pale cold pink of a winter sunset" made of 100%

Fig 4.8 Brunello di Montalcino Casanova di Neri, 2007

Pinot Nero, as well as a red *Piropo* from Pinot Nero, Sangiovese, and Alicante and a solo *Alicante*. Having now tasted all the Potentino wines at the castle, I'm not surprised that their wines have also been praised by discerning wine writers like David Way who notes "there are very few producers in Montecucco of that quality" and others.[173] Castello di Potentino also produces highly esteemed extra virgin olive oil from their vintage olive groves, some of which have been rooted here for around a millennium. Famous novelist Graham Greene, one of my favorite writers, began the family's British transplant here by owning another prior local castle in this same Maremma region of old Etruscan Italy in the mid-20th century, and Alex and Charlotte follow this expatriate family tradition of their great-uncle, although they have dug roots deeper by re-introducing winemaking in restored vineyards that recall the Etruscan tradition.

Fig 4.9 Etruscan Corinthian style wine vessel

Tomb Wine Vessels and History

Etruscan love of wine is not only manifest in the tomb paintings of banquets. The tombs themselves were packed with wine vessels, originally brimming with Etruscan wine, especially amphorae, kraters, oinochoe, kylikes, kantharoi, kyathoi, psykters, and skyphoi, among others. In fact, there are more Greek vases found in Italy thanks to the Etruscans than in Greece itself, partly because they were better preserved in Etruscan tombs carved out in Italy's tufas. Many of the indigenous wine vessels are black bucchero ware. Famous wine vessels, many ceremonial black or red figure, are now in world museums and made by Greek artists like Exekias and Euphronios from Etruscan sites like Vulci, Cerveteri, Tarquinia, and Fiesole; many other Etruscan wine vessels or cosmetic ceramics like alabastron and pyxis vessels are Corinthian or East Greek in design. Conversely, in contrast to Greek wine vessels in Etruria, by 575 BCE Etruscan wine vessels have been found in shipwrecks from Ampurias Emporion (near Barcelona) to Cap d'Antibes as well as in Marseilles and in the interior of Midi in Gaul ("masses of bucchero kantharoi, oinochoe and cups") and even at Motya, more than a few of these due to Punic trade.[174]

Other Etruscan sites across Etruria, including the Mugello Valley north of Florence, have also yielded bucchero pottery with numerous wine vessels like kantharoi, especially Poggio Colla.[175] Back south in the Maremma, only about 15 kms north—as the bird flies—from Castello di Potentino is the famous town of Montalcino, whose environs are so esteemed for its Brunello di Montalcino wine. Only 3 kms away from Montalcino is the Etruscan site of Poggio alla Civitella. Although not fully excavated, Poggio alla Civitella's Etruscan history with surviving ceramic wine vessels may yet be connected to Montalcino's long wine legacy. These dual traditions of Etruscan and Montalcino winemaking have been tentatively explored and will no doubt become more secure in Etruscan wine history.[176]

Although not enough evidence exists from scanty Etruscan text to know a lot, techniques of making Etruscan wine also may have included an additive sweetening, possibly with honey, not unlike Roman mulled wine (*mulsum*), as we have Etruscan language words like *math-* for "sweet" as an adjective for their wine.[177]

Fig 4.10 Etruscan Bucchero wine vessels

Chianti Country

The Chianti wine region is rich in Etruscan remains, including Montecalvario tumulus, Poggino necropolis, Poggio di Salivolpe, Piano Tondo, Radda in Chianti, Bosco le Pici, Castellina, Castelnuovo Berardenga, and Cetamura del Chianti, already mentioned. Some Chianti place names like

Starda, Vercenni, and Nusenna have Etruscan origins and it is not unlikely that the very word "chianti" is Etruscan. Like ancient Etruscan *Clusium*, which later becomes Chiusi, "Etruscan" words like *Clante*—the name for an Etruscan family—with the possibly related old *Clanis* river name later changed to Masellone, where the *cl* sound often becomes *ch* so that the ancient local wine name *clante* can become *chiante* and chianti. Cetamura and other Chianti sites are also rich in Etruscan black bucchero pottery, with extensive wine vessel fragments such as kantharoi drinking cups.[178] As the bird flies, Cetamura itself is very close to Gaiole, around 5 kms directly north of this famous chianti town, not far from the heart of the Chianti Classico DOCG (*Denominazione di Origine Controllata e Garantita*) region. Even the town of Gaiole has yielded Etruscan bucchero pottery.

Fig 4.11 Tignanello 2007

At least 47 Etruscan bucchero pottery vessels have been excavated or reported from the Chianti region, 22 alone from Cetamura.[179]

Not in Gaiole but instead also the Maremma near Poggi del Sasso is another notable organic Sangiovese, the high quality *Salustri Grotte Rosse Sangiovese Montecucco* 2007 with high scores across different rankings, including international competitions in Germany and Britain. The Salustri family has been involved in viticulture between Montalcino and Scansano since the 13th century and the Italian wine magazine *Civiltà della Bere* ranked the *Salustri Grotte Rosse Sangiovese Montecucco 2007* as one of the best 100 wines of the world.[180] Montecucco has recently (2011) been made a DOCG region.

Up to 1996 my favorite Tuscan wines have usually been Antinori's *Tignanello* or *Tenute Marchese Antinori Chianti Classico Riserva* (also much enjoyed at Villa San Michele in Fiesole), but in 1997 while in Gaiole I had visited the former 1,000-year-old abbey Badia a Coltibuono, built by Vallombrossa monks and now noted for its Chianti Classico DOCG of the same name produced by Conte Roberto Stucchi Prinetti and the cooking school (Villa Table) of his wife Lorenza de' Medici. After visiting the old abbey, the cooking school, and even walking around some of the estate, including vineyards, I also ate heartily at Coltibuono Restaurant managed by their son Paolo on the estate and brought back home a 6-liter bottle of *Riserva Badia a Coltibuono* 1995 in simpler days when airlines still let one hand carry wine. I cellared the bottle half a decade and we consumed it at a

Stanford archaeology party in 2003 where its vintage was appreciated. I had brought a bottle of excellent *Robert Mondavi Cabernet Sauvignon* 1995 for Lorenza and Roberto and presented it to Lorenza during the visit. Emanuela Stucchi Prinetti now manages the *Badia a Coltibuono* viticulture.

Savoring and mulling on these 1995 Tuscan memories from Badia a Colitbuono and Gaiole, a year later I composed parts of an unaccompanied "Medici Suite" for any one of several stringed instruments in honor of the Medici legacy in being such huge art patrons for centuries, and not the least because several of Lorenza and Roberto's family members, including Roberto's father Piero, play the cello. A dance from this *Medici Suite* was premiered in early 2011 on a live radio KZSU broadcast at Stanford, performed by violinist Joseph Gold on a 1692 Stradivarius. Although I performed it on the piano rather than on cello, the Italian premiere of this musical piece was held at Castello di Potentino because Duke Ferdinand I de' Medici gave this same castle to the Bourbon del Montes. The musical inspiration was the lively, colorful dancing banquet scenes of Tarquinia's Etruscan painted tombs, where D. H. Lawrence's observations of Etruscan love of wine are just as valid after almost a century of added archaeological and historical validation, a tradition living on in modern Tuscan and Umbrian Italy as Castello di Potentino amply justifies.

CHAPTER 5

Wines of the Roman World

"Thus Bacchus conquered India With Wine."

Rabelais, *Gargantua and Pantagruel* Chapter 5

Wine Amphorae in the Alps

B rushing dirt off the old Roman wine amphora handle that had clung to it for 2,000 years was exciting for me as an archaeologist. In the high Grand-St-Bernard Pass between Italy and Switzerland, an old Roman road was preceded by the Gaulish tribal pathway. Long buried in shallow, rocky soil at the top of this alpine pass around 8,000 feet in elevation, the old ceramic shard in my hand now saw intermittent sunlight and shadow as racing clouds sifted through the high peaks all around me. I turned the old amphora piece over, placing my fingers through the handle as a natural fit. I'll never forget pondering how the amphora had arrived long ago at such a remote place. I hoped its wine was consumed there before it was broken in the rocks. The Gauls loved wine and this pass was a major trading route between Gauls and Romans (and earlier Greeks) where wine was such a prized commodity, exactly as amphora studies have shown their impact on the diverse Roman economy.[181] Such fragments of Roman ceramic wine cups and ceramic amphorae excavated from such high and remote ruins—this was only the first of quite a few excavated here[182]—clearly show Roman wine traveled far and was appreciated everywhere as one of the hallmarks of civilization.

Amphorae and Economics of the Roman Wine Trade

Roman oil and wine were so voluminously traded across the Roman Empire that we have whole indices of Roman amphorae classifications and the system set up by the exacting German scholar Heinrich Dressel (1845–1920) for identifying amphora stamp types for

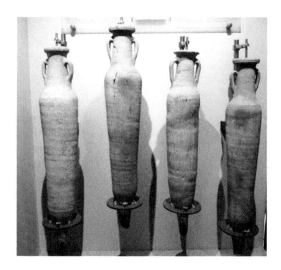

Fig 5.1 Roman Wine Amphorae, Museum of the Roman House, Caelian Hill, Rome

origins has been long acknowledged in archaeology.[183] Important for Roman wine, the earlier Coan wine amphorae, the "Dressel 2–4" wine amphora types at Rome's zenith and the following flat-based wine amphorae, have been carefully tracked all over the Mediterranean, from Spain and Gaul to Asia Minor as well as to London and in the interior of the empire along the great rivers like the Rhine, Rhone, and Po, Ebro and Nile, among others, although each of these river regions also produced their own wine during Roman times and had their own local transport vessels.[184] About 110 cm in height with an average wall thickness of 1–2 cm, the Italian Dressel 2–4 wine amphora had advantages of being not as awkwardly heavy as others and with sufficiently strong walls to guard against breakage in transport.[185] Some Roman provincial areas were bulk wine producers even during the late Roman Republic, including Laietania in Catalonia (Spain)[186] and Gallia Narbonensis (Provence).

Conison's new study documents the volume of the Roman wine consumption as being in the hundreds of millions of liters per year and Roman consumption ranged across all levels of society.[187] Roman amphora studies established a foundation as "the single most important material for studying Roman commodity trade."[188] Although coinage and monetary transactions are amply represented in the wine trade, whereas the unskilled labor may be paid in coin, in Roman Egypt payments of kind in fruit may be made for the labor contractors who supplied the vineyard workers for harvest; they could receive a third of the fresh juice, presumably for sale.[189] The estate accounts from Egyptian papyri from Oxyrhynchus in the late Roman period also show how much responsibility the wine steward (*oenocheiristes*) of such an estate assumes as a key figure in the agricultural life of Roman Egypt.[190]

Our best ancient sources for Roman viticulture are the Roman themselves, writers whose agricultural manuals have survived, although only parts of these manuals deal with viticulture. Marcus Porcius Cato—Cato the Elder—(234–149 BCE) wrote *De Agri Cultura*, Marcus Terentius Varro (116–27 BCE) wrote *Res Rusticarum* (or *De Re Rustica*), Lucius Junius Columella (4–70 CE) wrote *De Re Rustica*, and of course the encyclopedist Pliny the Elder's (23–79 CE) *Natural History* also provides viticulture details and vintages spread across several books. In addition, the epic poet Virgil also gave advice in his *Georgics* and the poet Horace also praised wine in many of his poems. As mentioned in an earlier chapter on Phoenician details, during the destruction of Carthage in 146 BCE, Punic agricultural treatises on viticulture written by Mago of Carthage (third to second c BCE)—likely partly deriving from prior collected and edited Phoenician texts—were translated into Latin by

Senatorial decree; Varro, Columella, and Pliny read some of these Punic texts and incorporated them into their own agricultural texts.

Roman Wine of Pompeii

That wines had daily importance and easy accessibility in Pompeii is confirmed by the presence of at least 59 different commercial *thermopolium* vendors selling food and wine at many street corner stalls in Pompeii. In the newest estimates of Pompeian food (*popinae*) and wine (*tabernae*) establishments, 94 are listed; Pompeii had "roughly one drinking establishment for every 100 people."[191] Other local places like Herculaneum even had the prices listed on painted walls in coinage for different qualities of a cup of wine (1 *as*, 2 *asses*, etc.). But how were Roman wines qualitatively scaled and evaluated?

Fig 5.2 Roman Bacchus Wall Painting, Pompeii

Take, for example, one of the Roman "first growth" *Aminaean* vines producing wines that improve greatly with age, according to Pliny.[192] There was a local *Aminaean* grape varietal grown on Mt. Vesuvius whose wine was sometimes called *Pompeiana*, coming from the rich volcanic slopes of Vesuvius.[193] This wine grown even on the fateful mountain just above Pompeii was a great source of local income until AD 79 when all the liquid assets went up in smoke like everything else in the vicinity. Prior to the cataclysmic eruption of Mt. Vesuvius, vintners of *Pompeiana*, like their modern counterparts, could obtain bank loans on the future strength of an upcoming vintage if Roman banking practices are any indication.

The Roman fresco [55 by 40 inches] shown here is from the House of the Centenary, Pompeii, and now in the Museo Archeologico Nazionale, Naples. It is almost a Roman-style late "Impressionist" wall painting, finished not long before Vesuvius made *Pompeiana* an, alas, extinct treasure. The Roman wine god Bacchus stands at the left in an amusing but perfectly logical designer garb: his body is a *racemus*,[194] a cluster of ruby grapes that are shining and glabrous, translucent with juice. While the best Roman wines were mostly white, this must have been a red-skinned grape if the painting is

Fig 5.3 Detail of Roman Bacchus, Pompeii

not overly imaginary here. Wreathed with grape leaves and ivy, Bacchus holds his *thyrsus* wand, symbol of his divine vegetative prowess, in his left hand. From the *thyrsus* he unfurls his protective ribbon-like banner circling the mountain and its vineyards. The right hand of Bacchus holds a wine jug from which a stream of *Pompeiana* pours into the throat of a thirsty golden *panthera*, his animal totem. The panther's dyspeptic leap for the cascade of wine is understandable given the Romans' high regard for wine. This pouring of wine down a panther's throat is an image appearing in several surviving Roman paintings if this and a counterpart painting in the British Museum are representative. It may also be important to remind again from the original Greek [*pan* + *thera*] that the word panther means "all wild." This wild cat is appropriate as a totem for Bacchus who is the dissolver of inhibitions.

Below the main grouping on this Roman painting, a great bearded snake sacred to Bacchus rears up before an altar to the wine god. Birds also flit about the garland festoon at the top of the painting, but our attention is drawn to the mountain itself in one of its few pre-AD 79 images.

This is no cameo appearance because the mountain is center stage, not yet having blown its cork in the huge volcanic event in CE 79 that buried Pompeii and neighboring towns under tons of ash, in places more than 30 feet deep. In the Roman painting between the grape cluster of Bacchus (who could even be a living advertisement for the wine) and the peaceful-for-the-moment peak, there are multiple rows of trained trellis vineyards. In a vinous excerpt of his country gentleman treatise,[195] the Roman writer Columella describes such trained vines as either "staked" [*characatus*] or "horsed" [*canteriatus*] with trellises framing vines much like our own vineyards today. Pliny, however, maintained (*Nat. Hist.* 17.199) the best Roman wines were not made from vines raised on trellises but those growing on trees, especially elms or poplars.

Highly Praised Roman Wines

What would be a dream vintage for an archaeologist? The very idea of "vintage" is an old one referring to a particular year's crop, and has come to generally mean a distinguished year. I find the idea of vintage appealing since "ancient" and "vintage" seem to pair well, especially as I age, and now I often refer to my elders as having greater vintage. The very ideas of vintage and select growths are at least as ancient as Roman viticulture. The praise of Cato, Varro, Columella, and Pliny for select Classical wines like *Falernian, Caecuban*, and *Massic* sounds amusingly like our modern purple prose enthusing and celebrating premium 20th century vintages. Where we often think appellations are relatively modern, Pliny devotes many pages of his *Natural History*, especially Books 14, 17 & 23, to Roman wine cultivation and regional classifications. Varro and Pliny both praise Falernian wine profusely in comparison to other Roman wine that often lasted only a year in contrast to Pliny's assertion that Falernian wine's taste improves annually up to its twentieth year.[196]

While *Pompeiana* may not have been at the absolute top tier of Roman wines even though it was an *Aminaean* growth, what was the value of one of the more fabled Roman wines? Some were very expensive like those of the year 121 BCE, which was the so-called *Opimian* vintage named after a 2nd c BCE Roman consul, Lucius Opimius. It had the ancient equivalent value of a venerable modern Petrus, Batard-Montrachet, or Romanée-Conti discussed in a later chapter. By Pliny's time this Opimian vintage could easily occasion a valuation of 1,000 sesterces a cask and, according to Pliny, it was somewhat bitter but still drinkable after almost 200 years, although said to be reduced to the viscosity of very thin honey.[197] While it had an initial price tag of 100 silver sesterces per amphorae, interest accumulated up to 6 percent per annum—calculate that after a century or so!—nearly the equivalent of $16,000–20,000 today for a few bottles or $50,000 or more for what volume might be in a case, although some doubt the wine could have lasted this long and retain any drinkability.[198] From Campania, and thus not too far from Pompeii, *Falernian* was often the most highly regarded Roman wine. It could continue improving after several decades, which suggests a late-harvest grape to some. Varro[199] writes in 37 BCE that *Falernian* becomes more valuable the longer it is cellared. While *Pompeiana* shone best at under 10

Fig 5.4 Petrarch's *Virgil* (title page) by Simone Martini (c. 1336)

years vintage,[200] *Falernian* would turn amber as it increased in drinkable vintage.

While finding extant ancient Roman wine names in France may be difficult, the best Roman wines in antiquity from Italy were *Falernian* and its compatriots, the marvelous *Caecuban* or *Massic* that have also long been the toast of Roman poets. In his odes, often written in praise of wine, Horace nostalgically remembers such classics two thousand years ago:

Aulon, now cherished by fertile Bacchus, envies less the clusters of Falernum. [*Carmen* II.6]

A worthier heir will drink your Caecuban now guarded by a hundred keys … glorious wine more choice than that drunk at pontiffs' feasts. [*Carmen* II.14]

Since Corvinus orders a far mellower wine, fetch the Massicum that you guard, fit to be brought out on some auspicious day! [*Carmen* III.21]

The geographer Strabo (ca. 63 BCE–ca. 24 CE) also praises the most excellent Roman wines from south of the city of Rome, many along the famed Appian Way:

The Caecuban Plain borders on the Gulf of Caietas; and next to the plain comes
Fundi, situated on the Appian Way. All these places produce exceedingly good
wine; indeed, the Caecuban and the Fundanian and the Setinian belong to the
class of wines that are widely famed, as is the case with the Falernian …[201]

Strabo is not exactly following a map for these famed Roman vineyards. When driving
south along this ancient route, the flat blue sea is on your right and the foothills of the
dramatic Apennine Mountains on your left. One can still choose the more tranquil coastal,
nearly arrow-straight Via Appia than the ultra-fast modern A1 autostrada clipping through
interior valleys. Still an agricultural cornucopia, even the coastal Italian landscape is rarely
flat, and in the Apennini Meridionale range of Central Italy the mountains veer west, loom-
ing much closer to the coast than near Rome where they disappear east to the horizon.

The locations of these celebrated Italian viticultural areas can be easily found by track-
ing from north to south and starting at the southernmost part of Lazio (ancient *Latium*).
Setinian Wine was made in the foothills east of the Appian Way at Sezze (ancient *Setia*) and
northeast of the ancient *Forum Appii* on the northeastern edge of the Pontine plain just
where the rising slopes of the Apennines begin. Further south, *Caecuban* wine was from the
small plain of the same name surrounded by the arc of the Monte Ausoni and Monte Lepini
hills above Campania where the straight Appian Way coming down from Lazio (*Latium)* ran
into the edge of the Gulf of Caietas and had to turn inland at Terracina around the narrowest
of coasts until opening up by the Lago di Fondi (*Lacus Fundanus*). *Fundanian* wine was here
from Fondi (ancient *Fundi*) where the Appian Way turned south again. *Massic* wine was
from Mt. Massico (*Massicus Monte*), a little further south of the *Caecuban* and *Fundanian*,
east of Simuessa (*Sinuessa Sinope*) and north of Mondragone and just west of the edge of
Campania. *Falernian* wine was from the Falerno plain (*Falernus Ager*), immediately east
over the hill of Mt. Massico, west of Capua and north of Castel Volturno (ancient *Volturnum*)
where the Volturnus River flows west into the sea on the edge of traditional Campania. Thus,
the most famous Roman wines were from the region south of the city of Rome itself and
clustered around Campania and closer to Naples, ancient Neapolis.

Although Strabo doesn't mention the long-lasting *Surrentine* here, it could also be located
in the hills around modern Sorrento (ancient *Surrentum*) and its 25-year longevity is also
mentioned by Athenaeus.[202] Perched on the Sorrentine peninsula south of ancient Pompeii
just before the beginning of the Amalfi coast before it swings southward, Surrentum has
some of the best views of Campania looking north and west. But looking south, one of the
most dramatic, indeed vertiginous, views of the Sorrentine peninsula is from the island of
Capri where the Emperor Tiberius had his Villa Jovis perched on the dizzying cliffs looking
south across the strait to the Amalfi Coast or southeast toward Surrentum. The poet Statius
also describes the context for Surrentine wine in his *Silvae* II.2 in his praise of the Villa of
Pollius Felix at Surrentum:

> There's a villa on high that gazes down on the deep,
> where the countryside's dear to Bacchus,
> where the grapes ripen on the slopes of the hills,
> without envying Falernian vines …

Here cliffs are awash with grape-juice,
the nectar of Bacchus, often in autumn
when Lyaeus' crop is ripening on the vine ...

Many Roman poets and other writers praise some special wines with extra attention. *Setinian* wine, sometimes called the very best of all Roman wine, had ancient fans including Martial, Juvenal, and Cicero. But while individual Romans likely had favorite wines, each wine had its own geographical and climatological niche in the Italian landscape. In addition to these premium wines above, Athenaeus also discusses and compares the various Roman wines from other regions of Italy, including Rhegium (far south in Calabria across from Messina, Sicily), Alban (just south of Rome), Praenestine and Tiburtine (both just east of Rome), Spoletine (central Italy in Umbria), and Tarentine (in the foot of Italy), to name only a few.[203]

Terra, the Origin of Terroir

The Romans were probably also the first—or have the earliest surviving works—to classify *terra* or context based not just on soil but also on local conditions—including directional exposure (e.g., southerly toward sun or not), wind, slope, and elevation, etc.—for wine production, although the word *terra* suggests that soil was at least as important as grape type or even more so, anticipating the sagacious French by at least a thousand years with the concept of *terroir* (and maybe even the textual source of the later idea). Pliny says of *Campania felix*, "Happy Campania," the province around Naples:

These instances, if I am not mistaken, show it is the country and the soil, not the grape, that matter ... since the same vine has a different value in different locations.[204]

Clearly the idea of *terroir* derives from *terra* as Pliny describes it here, with the variables of soil, sun, wind, and cardinal direction, elevation, gradient, rainfall, water drainage, and every other microcontext influence making a difference in the ultimate wine product.

Of some interest related to implicit Roman understanding of *terra*, earlier than Pliny by almost a century, Varro notes that some locations are better than others for vines, especially that not all crops are as successful on the same land (*Res Rusticarum* I.7.5), and while forests are better suited for mountains and grain better suited for plains, vines are best suited for hillsides (I.6.5). Plus, he notes that some areas like Smyrna in Asia Minor can produce two grape harvests per year (I.7.6) [in contrast to Italy's one] and that the leaves of the grape are not deciduous in Egypt [in contrast to Italy] (I.7.6).

Wine Recipes

The Romans often spiced their wine, sometimes with ingredients that might radically alter the taste. A book attributed to a noted gourmand of the Tiberian epoch, Marcus Gavius Apicius (1st century CE)—although it is unlikely to be his authorship—has several recipes in this compilation, *De Re Coquiniaria* ("On the Subject of Cooking"), that instruct how to prepare spiced wines. Several of these Apician recipes for spiced wine (*conditum*) call for ingredients like honey as a sweetener but also ingredients for flavor, including floral notes from rose petals, violets, soaked date pits, or leaves from laurel or perfumes like nard as well as saffron and ground pepper. Many of these ingredients are soaked and strained and are to be served heated as mulled wine. The Apician text is also astute to suggest fining "muddy" wine with egg whites or pulverized bean meal.[205] Mentioned briefly in the chapter on the Etruscans, Roman *mulsum* was a honey-sweetened wine, but mixed in just before drinking rather than fermented with the honey throughout like mead.

Some Roman wine was heated for winter consumption. For the wealthy, a bronze or silver vessel for heating wine was called a *miliarum*, looking much a samovar with tripod legs and appearing in a third century CE mosaic of a Roman banquet at Sepphoris in Galilee.[206] A *miliarum* is often double walled with interior middle space to heat water, and there was usually a separate container for glowing coals. Wine strainers for removing lees or sediments were also fairly common, occurring in several parts either in metal or ceramic as a set and including a perforated intermediary colander. Whether or not Horace is referring to wine in winter, he mused regarding Cato the Elder, whose viticultural knowledge was voluminous as mentioned, "They say that even old Cato, for all his virtue, warmed (*caluisse* in Latin) his heart many times with good wine."[207]

The Villa of the Mysteries and Bacchic Rites

The Villa of the Mysteries just outside and north of Pompeii's Porta Ercolano in the old vineyard environs has one of the most complete yet enigmatic Roman wall paintings in the world along two preserved walls of one room, thematically related around the wine god Bacchus who had his own mysteries.[208] Discovered in 1909, these divided scenes in dramatic red are skillfully framed by green floors and lines and with meanders and *faux marbre* upper decoration, all rendered with consummate skill and incredibly costly even when painted. After more than a century they still defy full understanding, not the least because ancient mysteries were never intended to be divulged to the uninitiated. Some have even claimed the villa belonged to Livia, wife of Augustus.

One basic thread of interpretation of the Villa of the Mysteries scenes—still highly debated—suggests a Bacchic initiation sequence,

Fig 5.5 Roman Mosaic Dramatic Mask, Naples Museum

beginning with a noblewoman receiving an invitation to become a *mystes* or initiate of the god. A hooded mystagogue or teacher then instructs the deeper meaning of the familiar myth of Bacchus. Along the way, an increasingly wild transformation takes place. Each vignette is more attended by satyrs, fauns, and goats. Empty wine amphorae are prophetically read by silens and bestial characters peering into the depths. It looks like an all-night vigil unfolding as the dancing performant's eyes become increasingly underlined by dark sleep-deprived bruises. Even while her garment billows around her in the sacred dance, her eyes are finally dilated and hollow as if

Fig 5.6 Roman Dramatic Mask Wall painting, Pompeii, Naples Museum

the god himself gradually possesses her. Each paradoxically silent scene screams out to the overloaded senses. Even Bacchus the god is overcome by the experience and finally draped in exhaustion across the lap of Ariadne while the eye-popping psychotropic experience of the woman initiate yields to a sweaty flagellation by a semidivine winged creature. Did a weary sleep finally follow the event or was it met by dawn? How can we know what happened in this room? Many such questions remain unanswered.

We can only imagine the dizzying surges of accompanying music, the divine meal, and the heady fragrances spinning around the room in the swaying light of flickering lanterns or candelabra in this private place far from the Roman public eye. These depicted rites most likely appear to mirror an event that would ostensibly take place in this same room, ultimately leading to a sacred marriage (*hieros gameos* union) with the god where the initiate takes on the transformative role of Ariadne as outlined in the prior chapter on Greek wine and Dionysus. If all this is as interpreted, these hauntingly evocative Roman wall paintings in the Villa of the Mysteries may form our most complete—yet frustratingly hermetic—images of Bacchic rites in the Roman world. It seems foolish and almost impossible to take the transforming agency of wine out of the equation. Some say the excesses of such bacchanals led to imperial censure and the brief closing down of Bacchic rites during the reign of Tiberius in the first century CE, where the enjoyment of the many who were mostly well behaved was limited because of the behavior of the few who were out of control. Mostly quiet complaints in the patrician circles were made at times by shocked Roman parents whose adolescent children may have been sexually victimized—both girls and boys—by Bacchic revelers in full abandonment. But Roman viticulture, the vast wine trade and the overwhelming popularity of wine were mostly unaffected by the peripheral minor eccentricities of those generally few uncontrolled Bacchanalia. After all, wine was a time-honored staple of a healthy life in the Roman world for rich and poor alike.

The Wine Edict of Domitian

In 92 CE there was a famine in the Roman Empire and the emperor Domitian responded with his famous vine edict banning new vineyards and cutting back others. The immediate expectation was that new grain would be planted for food in place of the vineyards. In effect Domitian ordered half of Asia Minor's vineyards and other non-Italian vineyards to be ripped out, uprooting local economies as well. Although Roman legions were employed in places because of stiff resistance from farmers and general recalcitrance from the Roman wine trade, the vine edict was mostly ignored, especially in *Burdigala* (Bordeaux). Some suggested he was merely protecting Italian viticulture from outside competition, but this is difficult to prove even though it was the first recorded Roman wine law. Domitian's name was hardly an honored one due to his seizure of private property and profligacy along with the public suspicion that he had murdered his predecessor, his emperor brother Titus, and four years later Domitian was assassinated by his attendants and his memory damned,[209] although Domitian's brutal reputation may have slightly improved in modern scholarship.[210] Outside of Italy the Roman wine trade was not the only entity to have likely rejoiced at his death. While largely ineffective, Domitian's Vine Edict was on the boards until the Emperor Probus repealed it in 280 CE. How much his repeal had to do with the fact of his being from Sirmio in Lower Pannonia (Serbia) where viticulture had been going on for a millennium—albeit not as successfully until after his repeal—remains to be seen, since Pannonian wine took off with his removing the constraints of the old Domitian edict. Viticulture in Carnuntum in what is now lower Austria and in Dalmatia, now Croatia, subsequently also flourished as a result.

Virgil's Georgics on Wine

Ever appreciated even from the outset for his lofty beauty of thought and mastery epic in the *Aeneid*, Virgil also wrote tracts for gentleman farmers; urban patricians tried to emulate his Acadian principles in their rural getaways. In his *Georgics*, Virgil made honored pastimes like beekeeping and viticulture appear simple, which it rarely was unless one had slaves to do the hard work. But his imbibed ideas were certainly sound for making good wine assuming the capricious timing of a long sunny harvest season in *Georgics* 2.408–10: "Be the first to dig the ground, first to carry away and burn the prunings ... but be the last to harvest." This admonition for late harvest hints to many that the best Roman vintages were sweet white wines[211] like *Opimian, Falernian,* and *Surrentine* (from Sorrento)—the wine good for 25 years—precursors to Sauterne and other dessert wines.

Virgil's lyricism on viticulture mentions (*Georgics* 2.333–4) the hardiness of the young vine: the "vine tendril does not fear the south wind's rising or showers launched from the skies by the blustering north wind." The poet also encourages good seasonal timing:

Already whenever the vineyard has shed her autumn foliage, and the north wind has shaken their glory from the trunks, the keen farmer extends his care to the coming year and pursues the vine he had left, lopping it with Saturn's crooked knife and pruning it into shape.[212]

A lasting link from Virgil is that modern viticulture around the world still often uses a similar curved knife or billhook—the sickle used by Saturn to castrate his father Uranus in Greek myth as Virgil alludes—in both harvesting grapes and pruning. While often serrated, it may go by various names in Europe, including *serpe* and *serpette* (French), *roncola* (Italian), and *Hippe* (German). This *Georgics* passage is also illustrated by Simone Martini in the frontispiece of the famous Virgil manuscript that belonged to Francesco Petrarch (1304–77) the seminal Humanist, with an obvious *roncola* billhook in the vinedresser's hand, much like the one a Roman farmer would use and Virgil would also recognize.

Roman Wine Cultivation

Roman cultivation of vines ranged from small individual vineyard farms to vast patrician estates, with some intended for private consumption and worked by family members, while other wine estates were for investment income and export with intense slave labor, although for more than a few many wealthy or patrician Romans, vineyards were playthings.[213]

Columella's *De Re Rustica* 3.3 tells that the Roman economics of viticulture could return a 10% surplus profit even at 3 tons of grapes per acre; other Romans maintain a possible yield of up to 23 tons of grapes per acre, but Roman vintners looking for the highest quality would prefer a considerably lower yield. Varro in his own *Rerum Rusticarum* I.2.7 makes an extravagant yield claim:

> What wine is compared with that of Falernum? Is Phrygia, which Homer calls *ampeloessa*, more teeming with vines? In what land does one half acre (*jugerum*) produce 10, no even 15 *cullei* of wine, as in some regions of Italy? Has not Marcus Cato written in his book of *Origines*, "That region lying this side of Ariminium and beyond Picenum, which was allotted to colonists, is called Roman Gaul. There in several places a single half acre of land produces 10 *cullei* of wine." Is it not the same in the

Fig 5.7 Ancient Roncola (wine bull-hook pruner), Fiesole Museum

region of Faventia where the vines are called *tre centaria* because a half acre yields 300 amphorae of wine, … indeed L. Martius … said that the vines on his Faventine farm yielded that much.

To make the comparable complicated calculations, 1 Roman *culleus* = 20 amphorae = 120 gallons = 600 bottles; 10 *cullei* = 200 amphorae = 1,200 gallons = 6,000 bottles; 15 *cullei* = 300 amphorae = 1,800 gallons = 9,000 bottles. If there were 2.5 lbs of grapes per bottle of wine; 9,000 bottles = 22,500 lbs = 11.5 tons x 2 = 18,000 bottles = 23 tons per acre. This does not, however, compare favorably to deliberately lower-yield acreage producing high-quality wine nor to Columella's suggested yield under a range of natural circumstances that could vary widely depending on a given year. In comparison, Columella's figures for highest-quality wine are not that different from Napa Valley's 2010 data where an average yield was around 4 tons per acre depending on location, whether valley floor or hillside, east or west side, north or south along the valley.[214] On the other hand, in regard to how plausible the Roman viticultural manuals were for Roman farming, the discovery of a large vineyard at Pompeii has "substantiated in remarkable detail the recommendations of Varro and Columella."[215]

As Conison has astutely summarized, the three primary Roman written sources for wine agronomy—Cato, Varro, Columella—wrote their manuals for both wealthy landowners and for those who managed the wine production, especially the wine foreman, the *vilicus* who might actually be a slave, and these Roman oenology manuals address a practical spectrum of wine estate management advice from which wine varietals to plant, how and when to prune, where to plant vineyards and in which wind and sun direction depending on which type of vine, how to best make the wine from each type of vine, and many other related viticultural topics.[216] One of Cato's most lasting maxims said it was better and more profitable to farm a small vineyard well than a large one badly.[217]

The Roman premium vines like Aminaean have been mostly hybridized out of the vineyards of Italy, but some names recall their origins and may be their descendants like Falerno del Massico, grown in roughly the same location. This 1989 DOC in Campania can be found from about four dozen producers. I've had this heady wine many times in Campania, and yet my first time is still the most memorable. I had ordered it for an early-dusk dinner at the Enrico Caruso Ristorante on the open pergola rooftop of Naples' best hotel, the Gran Vesuvio. Off to the south I could easily see across the Bay of Naples the brooding presence of Mt. Vesuvius towering over the region, purple-hued against the dusk. Musing on a hot day on that fateful week in 79 CE when its eruption destroyed much of the plain, I found my thirst slaked by the spicy coolness of the 1989 DOC. The old Roman vineyards may have gone but to the north of Rome now we also have Amarone, Vino Nobile di Montepulciano, Chianti, and Brunello di Montalcino as well as many other excellent wines across Italy— more about Campania south of Rome in the following chapter—so viticulture has hardly lost out on an ancient Italian legacy.

Although Roman wine will continue to be mentioned in following Italian chapters, to close a specifically Roman chapter with Virgil's *Georgics* is apropos, here from II.388–94:

We call on you Bacchus in joyous songs and to you hang amulets from the tall pine. Hence every vineyard ripens in generous increase; fullness comes to hollow valleys and deep glades, and every spot towards which the god has turned his comely face. Duly then in our country's songs we will chant for Bacchus the praise he claims.

This Roman invocation lyricized by a great poet into a wish for bounty seen in the Bacchic amulets is one every vintner has echoed—maybe not as articulately—for millennia in whatever dream, to whatever god or saint, because wine was understood as a divine gift.

CHAPTER 6

Campanian Wine and Vesuvius

"Bacchus the wine he poured for all about." Chaucer, "The Merchant's Tale"

Last year I was standing in the Campanian hills by Casagiove above Capua and seeing miles of green vineyards spread out to the horizon, including the old Falernian plain. Although these vineyards are not the same concentration of plantings as those of antiquity, nonetheless the continuity is still here and the vine roots often drink from the underground streams flowing west from the Apennines as they have for millennia. While many Italian vineyards also had trees like poplars where the vines were cultivated to climb, Varro says in *Res Rusticarum* 1.8.2 that at Falernum, the vines were yoked on poles. No doubt across Campania in his day the ancient Roman *Vinalia* festivals celebrated the bounty of the land, especially the grape harvests.

Vinalia prima was the spring festival on April 23 when the Romans tasted the wine from the previous harvest and prayed for a good season, and both Venus and Jupiter were invoked. Some of this spring festival was sacred to Venus and both girls and women (including prostitutes under the aegis of Venus) gathered to offer the goddess mint, myrtle, and roses. The other festival, especially celebrated in Campania with its

Fig 6.1 Cantina del Vesuvio Campania

concentration of quality vines, was the late summer *Vinalia rustica* on August 19 just before harvest and gratitude for what the almost-ripe coming harvest promised was joyfully heard in music and liturgies. Although Venus was also invoked in the *Vinalia rustica*, Jupiter's priest picked the first bunch of grapes at the late summer festival because Jupiter controlled the weather. The priest also blessed the harvest with a sacrifice of a young female lamb.[218] In the breeze coming from the sea shining in the west I imagined I could almost hear the ancient pipes and songs rising from the plain above old Capua.

Campania Felix

Roman Campania was renowned in antiquity for its wines; although its wines in modernity may not quite measure up to this legendary standard, this place of such natural beauty is nonetheless producing high-quality viticulture.[219] If young wines and wines with little longevity were for plebeian consumption, fine and costlier Campanian wines were usually better aged and more for patrician consumption.[220] In Campania, geological sources are at times mixed with volcanic ash, soil that the vine roots probed and from which they drew sustenance in the heat of the Italian sun.

Although Columella's *De Re Rustica* III.1.4 advised farmers to choose the land carefully for different vines, Campania seems perfect for so many varietals it might have been hard to take him seriously here about *terra* contexts:

> Nevertheless an important consideration is the variety and the habit of the vine which you propose to cultivate, in relation to the conditions of the region. For its cultivation is not the same in every climate and in every soil, nor is there only one variety of that plant; and which kind is best of all is not easy to say, since experience teaches that to every region its own variety is more or less suited.

Today the region of Campania has at least 20 different DOC (*Denominazione di Origine Controllata*) varietals and some listings count up to 38,000 small wineries across Campania, so winemaking here seems to not have lost much importance since the times it was special to the Romans. Perhaps the most abundant at slightly higher elevations, Aglianico is a black-skinned grape originally from Greece by way of the Greek colonists at Naples (old Neapolis) and now one of Campania's most widespread varietals.[221] In addition to its many DOC wines, Campania has even higher-ranked wines with DOCG (*Denominazione di Origine Controllata e Garantita*). One DOCG wine is Aglianico del Taburno using a different varietal of the Aglianico grape and produced in Campania around Benevento, about 30 miles east of Capua and the same distance northeast of Naples.

Benevento is the venerable Roman town where the old Appian Way turned east and went over the Apennines into the more arid Apulia. Benevento has Roman monuments such as the richly red-bricked Roman theater and the white marble Arch of Trajan, romantically depicted by Piranesi. The Aglianico del Taburno DOC or DOCG is from mostly north or northwest of Benevento or on the eastern foothill slopes of Monte Taburno about ten miles west of the town. The Aglianico grape is high in both acidity and tannin, adding muscle to any blend, but mostly on its own here in the Aglianico del Taburno DOC/DOCG, it makes a huge hit, especially wine from around Torrecuso 10 miles mostly north of Benevento or the highly rated winery *Fidelis Cantina del Taburno* whose grapes are from about 1,000 feet elevation. Antonio Galloni rated the *Fidelis 2006* with a 90-point Wine Advocate score. Back in the town of Benevento, I've followed the old Roman road Via Appia over the Apennines and you can still see the ruins of small old Roman bridge arches over valley streams en route toward Foggia.

Other Campanian DOCG high marks are found in the wine-rich area of Avellino south of Benevento. The Fiano di Avellino is made from the famous and possibly ancient white Fiano grape, the Greco di Tufo is from the white Greco grape, and the Taurasi Rosso Riserva is from the Aglianico grape.

The Fiano di Avellino and may be very similar to or the descendant of the grape in the ancient Roman wine *Apianum*, so named from *Vitis apiana* because it is a grape loved by bees (*Apis mellifera*), as Pliny said (*Nat. Hist.* XIV.4.24), "The *Apianis*—'bee vine' is called this because bees are especially fond of it." The Fiano di Avellino wine must be at least 85% Fiano grape. Some Fiano di Avellino producers even put the ancient classification "*Apianum*" on their labels honoring the Roman tradition mentioned by Pliny.

Taurasi is a part of Avellino also rich in volcanic soil and since the Aglianico grape typically thrives at elevations above 1,200 ft., it is well suited to the hills of Avellino. The Taurasi Rosso Riserva must age for 4 years before release and must be at least 85% Aglianico grape. The long-standing (130-year-old) Mastroberardino Winery in Atripalda (Avellino) produces highly rated Radici Taurasi Riserva from their vineyards in Montemarano at about 1,650 ft. elevation of 100% Aglianico and also an equally regarded Radice Fiano di Avellino, the latter from their Santo Stefano del Sole vineyard at about 1,800 ft. elevation and 100% Fiano grape.

Eight villages of Avellino are the only ones that can legally produce what is named as Greco di Tufo DOCG, all at a fairly high altitude, generally between 1,200 and 1,600 feet. These villages are Tufo, Torrione, Irpina, Petruro Irpina, Prato di Principato Ultra, Altavilla, Montefusco, and Chianche. The local volcanic tufo is high in sulfur and other minerals. Some of these towns are hill towns like Montefusco perched above the Sabato River Valley surrounded by its vineyards. Greco di Tufo must be at least 85% Greco grape. Some local Greco di Tufo juice is also used to produce a sparkling *spumante*.

Modern Avellino itself is named from the ancient Roman town of *Abellinum*, and remains of the ancient town are on the hill in the village of Atripalda, itself possibly over an earlier Samnite village. Atripalda has the remains of a beautiful Roman villa (*domus*) once belonging to Marcus Vipsania Primigenius, a freedman of the famous general Marcus Vipsania Agrippa. Agrippa was the closest friend of the Emperor Augustus, perhaps almost equal to the emperor in wealth and power, and married Augustus' daughter Julia the Elder, to whom almost all the Julio-Claudian emperors were related. Marcus Agrippa was also a brilliant strategist who not was only credited with the naval victory in the Battle of Actium in 31 BCE but also was responsible for overseeing the renovations of the urban aqueducts of Rome and many other public works. The Roman town of *Abellinum* was enclosed by well-preserved *opus reticulatum* walls. The 2,500-sq.-meter Abellinum villa of this freedman named after his sponsor has fresco fragments of the highest-quality artistry, very similar to Marcus Agrippa's own Villa at Boscotrecase on the lower slopes of Mt. Vesuvius about 20 miles away and possibly painted by the same artisans, notably in what is called "Pompeian Third Style" in the latter part of the first century BCE, so this former slave must have been extremely capable in service to be so highly regarded by the most important citizen of Rome in his day.

Vineyards of Vesuvius

At first we could see Mt. Vesuvius silhouetted in June morning light as we came from Naples, and as we came closer we could make out the intermittent stone pines on the lower slopes. As our car wound slowly up from the Bay of Naples, the mountain dominated the landscape. On the southern flanks of Mt. Vesuvius in Campania south of Naples above the farming village of Trecase, we began to pass vineyard after vineyard and it was much cooler higher up than below, just as Varro said in his *Res Rusticarum* I.6.3 several millennia ago, "in mountain regions as on Vesuvius, the air is lighter and therefore more wholesome." Like Columella's variety of classy *Aminaean* grape in the same work (III.2.10), "everywhere very well known, because it covers those most famous slopes of Vesuvius," the mountain continues its role of a select viticultural *terra*.

The top of Vesuvius is often capped in puffy white clouds and the light is dappled across the vineyards. Every once in a while, even in June, one can see a stream of water coming down from some mysterious spring on Vesuvius toward the vineyards. This is when I muse that wine is what water dreams of becoming.

On these southern slopes of Vesuvius at Trecase, winemakers like Maurizio Rosso continue traditions that are several thousand years old. No doubt the fertility of Campania is assured by the rich volcanic soil of Vesuvius, and everywhere on the ground one can see bits of volcanic rock scattered along the topsoil between the rows of vines. One of these famous wines noted in Campania for centuries is the Lacryma Christi ("Tears of Christ"). This just happens to be a literary wine mentioned in Christopher Marlowe's play *Tamburlaine the Great*, Voltaire's *Candide*,[222] Alexander Dumas' *The Count of Monte Cristo*,[223]and Nathaniel Hawthorne's short story "Rappacini's Daughter,"[224] so this is a distinctive bookish pedigree for a famous wine. For example, at the dramatic climax of an act, Christopher Marlowe's protagonist Tamburlaine exultantly wishes:

> Then will we triumph, banquet and carouse. Cooks shall have pensions to provide us cakes, and glut us with the dainties of the world, Lachryma Christi and Calabrian wine…[225]

Trecase's Cantina del Vesuvio

In June 2011, I visited Cantina del Vesuvio in Trecase for a *degustazione* and lunch. Among the wines tasted from this 11-hectare vineyard were reds Aglianico and Lacryma Christi (also spelled Lacrima Cristi), and the white Greco di Tufo. While, as mentioned at least 20 different varietals are grown in Campania, the Cantina's fabulous Lacryma Christi is 80%

Piedirosso and 20% Aglianico varietals. Maurizio Rosso's *Lacryma Christi Rosso* DOC delivers immediate full-bodied taste and shows long legs down the side of the glass, with a high viscosity. The deep ruby color of the Lacryma Christi makes it almost opaque.

The Cantina del Vesuvio is in the National Park of Vesuvius covering thousands of hectares surrounding the volcano. The Rosso family has been making wine for the last century in this rich Vesuvian soil, bringing a

Fig 6.2 Cantina del Vesuvio Lacryma Cristi 2009

considerable bulk of the wine to Naples for generations, including by horse cart, even up to 1948 when postwar petrol shortages were still common in rural Italy.

Our winery lunch was under the olive trees at the edge of the vines and included a zesty pasta *pomodoro* with *basilico* and local Campanian *salzichi*. Local breads were also liberally doused with their home-pressed cantina's extra virgin olive oil. If any food can taste better outside in the fresh breeze off the Bay of Naples and the sweet odor of an olive

orchard surrounded by vines, this delicious lunch at Cantina del Vesuvio would be hard to top given all the fresh quality ingredients and ambience of these vineyard slopes.

After lunch a walk through the vine rows under Vesuvius was highly recommended. They were trellised high overhead much like many of their Roman ancestors were—as seen in wall paintings from Pompeii—nearly two thousand years ago on that fateful day in late August 79 AD/CE when Vesuvius exploded. The Monte Somma cone of the original Roman period Vesuvius stratovolcano was apparently higher than the present double cone that reaches 4,200 ft elevation (1,281 meters).

Fig 6.3 Winery Lunch, Cantina del Vesuvio

Fig 6.4 Pietro Antoniani, Eruzione del Vesuvio vista da Torre del Greco

Subsequent eruptions have continued repeatedly in the last 500 years, with especially frequent episodes in the 18th century, as seen in paintings by the likes of Pietro Fabris from 1767 and Pietro Antoniani onward to Giovanni Lusieri in 1787 and 1794 and Xavier Gatta in 1794.[226] The Antoniani painting from around 1774 shows the direction of the lava flow southerly toward the commune of Trecase where Cantina del Vesuvio is now located high above the town. Although this list of recent historic eruptions is far from complete, Vesuvius blew again in 1834 and the last major eruptions of Vesuvius were in 1906 and again in 1944.

Sir William Hamilton, the British diplomat to the Bourbon Court as Minister Plenipotentiary of King George III, and immortalized in fact and fiction by Susan Sontag as "The Volcano Lover,"[227] also roamed these same Trecase slopes for volcanic lava and scoria samples for his geological collection, just as he also scoured Pompeii for antiquities while his infamous wife Lady Emma Hamilton did more than merely entertain Lord Nelson. When I gave an invited lecture for a Hamilton Colloquium at the British Museum in London in 1996, I remembered my own ambulations under Vesuvius.

Trecase is only a few miles northwest of Pompeii. Just east of Trecase was the already-mentioned famous Augustan period Roman villa now known as Boscotrecase, extremely rich in Roman paintings and artifacts—many now in the Metropolitan Museum in New York—after excavation from the Vesuvian destruction of 79 CE. This sumptuous villa was originally owned by Marcus Agrippa, general, friend, and son-in-law of the emperor Augustus. The emperor's daughter Julia herself oversaw much of the finest Roman wall painting in Boscotrecase that is among the best in the Roman world for Third Style from imperial artists.[228] Marcus Agrippa must have chosen this region for his villa due to its great vistas and its lush volcanic fertility. Although Trecase is not as forested now due to many

Vesuvian eruptions in the interim, the word *bosco* means woods and Boscotrecase, while a modern name, suggests a more forested landscape in the recent past.

Today the Trecase trellised vines climb the lower slopes of Vesuvius, their tendrils almost appearing to grow before one's eyes because of the rich volcanic mafic minerals that are refreshed with every eruption. The local Vesuvian soil around Trecase is made up of fragmented lavas, scoria, ash, and pumice. Its mineral content is low in silica but high in potassium and high in feldspathoids.[229] Cantina del Vesuvio is on the upper reaches of Trecase in the foothills of the volcano above 500 ft. elevation and some of the vines are even higher. Everywhere I walked in the vineyards here, pieces of lava rock were interspersed in the rich soil. Cool, dark, and heavy to the touch, it is hard to imagine these small stones were once glowing lava.

The clouds that often cover the heights of Vesuvius because of its elevation foster agricultural plenty by orographic precipitation where dew point in condensation is reached here first rather than in the much hotter Naples plain below, so it has the best of all possible worlds to satisfy that old Roman epithet that Pliny described as *Campania Felix*, or "Happy Campania," for its fertility. The undergrowth here would be overly lush if vine growers didn't constantly work to keep the soil bare except for the vines, preserving the nutrients for the vines instead of other vegetation, although the soil seems sufficient to share fertility with whatever plants might root here. Most of the vine rows I examined were up to 20 to 30 years in age, although the family still maintains older vines that continue to produce good fruit quality each year.

Maurizio Rosso culls most of the grapes produced, concentrating them on the lower vine branches in order to maximize fruit concentration. Thus his wines are opulent and deliver full taste even after two years in the bottle. The longevity of the wines is also likely for up to ten years because of concentrated tannins, assuming good storage in cool cellars. Rosso's vision for Vesuvian wines promises a long legacy, not only for his family but for the other Trecase growers as well. If other local *viticoltori* are as sensitive to the ecology and the land-use needs as Maurizio Rosso, the future of Vesuvian wine has still yet to reach its great promise as well as the past renown of its long Roman ancestry. Cantina del Vesuvio is high enough on the mountain to see the island of Capri across the shining bay in one direction southward and northward to the cloud-shaded cone of the modern summit of Vesuvius, itself less than a mile away. But like Nietzsche who ironically warned against the folly of building houses on Vesuvius (but stated satirically, "Go ahead, build your houses on Vesuvius"), Maurizio Rosso agrees that Vesuvius is even better for great wine than great views.

CHAPTER 7

Wines of Sicily

"O Father of the wine-press, come, and stripped of deerskin stain your bared limbs in the new must with me." Virgil, Georgics II.8–10

Homer and Mythology in Sicily

The best sunshine in winter is likely reflected off the Ionian Sea in Taormina. When sailing wine-dark seas is not an option, one reads Giuseppe Tomasi di Lampedusa's magical *Il Professore e la Sirena* to catch a glimmer of Sicily's place in myth, preferably with a mesmerizing glass of Nero d'Avola. Looking south from Taormina to the curving bay of Giardini Naxos and Mt. Etna along the Ionian Coast, this is where the haunting siren Lighea must still be heard in faraway conch soundings from the blue deep. Here is Lighea, Lampedusa's youthful but immortal Siren, drinking wine for the first time:

> Once I gave her some wine; she was incapable of drinking from a glass, and I had to pour some into her minute and slightly greenish palm, from which she drank by lapping it up with her tongue like a dog, while surprise spread in her eyes at that unknown flavor. She said it was good…"[1]

More than any other literary topography in the Mediterranean, Sicily has been traditionally tied to Homer's *Odyssey* and Greek myths of agricultural plenty, and especially regarded by ancient Greeks as Persephone's Island. According to Goethe in 1787 in his *Italianische Reise*, the most beautiful view, *la bella veduta* in Italy—or the world for that matter—may be from the top row of Taormina's Greco-Roman Theater cavea, looking through the ancient ruined arcade. But to enjoy the best view with a comparable bit of divine elixir, almost anywhere from the Grand Hotel Timeo ought to suffice. Taormina's glory after the fourth century BCE was due to Hellenistic Greek general Timoleon who reestablished *Tauromenion* (so named because its high double peaks were thought to resemble bull horns). Even the

Corso Umberto, this picturesque town's main pedestrian street with the lovely evening passagiato, has its restrained Baroque buildings along its east side entirely anchored by the arcade of an ancient Roman *naumachia* several thousand years old.

As a caveat for anyone doubting Homeric ken of Sicily, whoever this bardic not-so-blind Homer was, enough mention of Sicilian contexts in the epic of the Odyssey should convince otherwise. Scylla and Charybdis were the horrible dangers of rocky cliffs on one side and whirlpools on the other side of the Strait of Messina where two seas meet; Polyphemus the Cyclops, son of Poseidon blinded in his Mt. Etna cave by Odysseus and his men, threw out the Faraglione Rocks attempting to sink Greek ships (possibly the source of the myth phrase "blind rage"), to name but a few. Odysseus and his men overpowered the Cyclops by wine, and although it was a sweet and powerful wine like the wine of Sicily, it was unlikely to be so local. Homer describes the grapes of Cyclops' land:

> Wine grapes in clusters ripen in heaven's rain...all good land, fertile for every crop in season, lush well-watered meads along the shore, vines in profusion...[2]

Ancient Tauromonium, Mamertine, and Morgantina Wines

Under privileged Roman status Pliny notes that the region of *Tauromonium* (Latin spelling of Taormina) had excellent wines,[3] although he also says that while they grow well on the hills around Taormonium, these vines do not translate well from there to other contexts. Wine stock from Tauromonium was even exported to Pompeii to be grown on Mt. Vesuvius.[4]

In antiquity the fame of Sicilian wine was well known, sometimes for its sweetness, as in Messina's *Mamertino* wine—praised by Strabo as rivaling the best Italian wines of his era[5]—and also a favorite of Julius Caesar; it was served at the third annual celebration of his consulship according to Pliny *Nat. Hist.* XIV.8 where Mamertine wine "was given by the late Emperor Julius at the public banquets—he was the first, in fact, that brought them into favor, as we find stated in his Letters—to the Mamertine wines, the produce of the country in the vicinity of Messana, in Sicily." Roman poet Martial also said, "If a jar of Mamertine, as old as Nestor, be given you, you may call it by whatever name you please."[6]

Today's wine going by the name of Mamertine is very different from the ancient Mamertine, and the modern varietal of the name is not so connected to Messina. While the modern Sicilian Mamertine is named Mamertino di Milazzo, it is not so much a product of the Peloritani Mountains above ancient Messana (modern Messina). Here in antiquity the unique microclimate climate was due to a dual marine influence on the northeastern tip of Sicily, where the steep highlands of Messina on the eastern side of the Peloritani were surrounded west and east by water as Cape Peloro tapers and narrows to its point. The modern Mamertino di Milazzo is instead mostly grown to the west on the northern coast of Sicily and thus on the western side of the Peloritani peninsula above the town of Milazzo. Here the maritime influence is solely from one coast for the modern wine. In antiquity Mamertine viticulture was mostly on the eastern side of the Peloritani Peninsula—although at least one ancient Mamertine seems to have been on the westward slopes—therefore the ancient context just above *Messana* was more complicated, moderated by the Peloritani Mountains as an orographic microclimate between two different marine coasts. Even though the distance between the primary ancient and modern context is only about 25 miles, the terroirs are themselves are very different. Modern varietals that make up the reds and whites of Mamertino di Milazzo DOC are also likely very different, mostly being a blend of Nero d'Avola, Grillo, and Inzolia, sometimes Nocera, although we do not know the ancient

Fig 7.1 Sicilian landscape

makeup, which may have been a single varietal but might have entirely disappeared and replaced by the Greek Aminaean varietal if *Sikelikos aminaios* is meant in later texts.[7] Hybridization in the interim has certain changed viticulture comprehensively since Roman times. Nonetheless there are excellent modern Mamertino di Milazzo producers, including Mimmo Paone and La Cantina Vasari. This DOC spread around about 30 villages in the region requires its Mamertino di Milazzo Rosso to be least 60% Nero d'Avola and no more than 10% Nocera.

Another favorite of ancient Sicily was the wine of the region of Morgantina, also called *Morgantina* and praised by Pliny (*Nat. Hist.* XIV.4) as *Vitis murgantina*, the best wine to come out of Sicily, a varietal also transplanted earlier to mainland Italy. Cato (*De Agri Cultura* 6.4) and Columella (*De Re Rustica* III.2.27) also highly praised *Morgantina*. Perhaps it is significant that the site of Morgantina and the vineyards associated with it are in the region of Enna. Morgantina is specifically just east of the Monte Erei uplift and mostly in its watershed where streams drain eastward. Here the Bosco di Rossomanno lies between Piazza Armerina and Aidone and Morgantina itself is less than 3 miles east of Aidone on a once-forested plateau where the hills gradually diminish into the plain. Although more usually associated with the city of Enna slightly north, the Vale of Enna in myth was the locus of Demeter's palace and Persephone's haunts in Roman literature at least since Ovid (*Metamorphoses* V.385 & ff.), surrounded by lush fertility befitting these vegetation goddesses,[8] since the island of Sicily has also long been called Persephone's Island.

Following Ovid, Late Roman poet (ca. 390 CE) Claudian tells in *De Raptu Proserpinae* Books I–III his version of the story even in "epic hyperbole,"[9] where the lushness of nature is believable in his time due to the legendary fertility of Sicily and the Vale of Enna (called *Henna* by Claudian), "mother of blossoms" (II.72) and where "the vine clothes the elm" (II.111). Claudian describes oaks and holm oaks (II.108–10) near *Lacus Pergum* (II.112), which is modern Lago Pergusa—also mentioned in Ovid (*Met.* V.385)—about 4 miles south of the modern city of Enna, half way toward the top of the Monte Erei uplift another 4 miles distant. Modern Enna is about 14 miles from ancient Morgantina. The Bosco di Santo Pietro preserve on the south side of Monte Erei between Piazza Armerina and Caltagirone is still rich in flora of over 300 species with a dense oak and holm oak biosome within 5 miles of Aidone. In Claudian's epic poem grape vine growing up the tree—just as viticulture is described in Pliny—is called *pampinus,* a vine shoot or tendril.[10] The site and city of Aidone is also very close to Morgantina, and its name may bear more than superficial resemblance to one of the Greek names of the god of the underworld, *Aidoneus,* who abducted Persephone from the Vale of Enna in myth, retreating back east toward Mt. Etna, about 30 miles mostly east. Note Milton's *Paradise Lost* 4.269 refers to Persephone (Milton's *Proserpin*) in Enna. Claudian's topography then seems fairly knowledgeable about this part of Sicily. Wherever the Vale of Enna was thought to be, the central Monte Erei uplift is still one of most lush parts of Sicily, once rich in conifers, and the soil balance not far to the east is often a richly balanced mix of calcareous, argillaceous, and volcanic soils. Did Morgantina wine—near all this literary topos—profit from logical natural resources for winegrowing?

The Lure of Taormina

Since *Tauromenion* (Greek) or *Tauromonium* (Latin) in history was a magical place, how could its successor not be? The best combination of Sicilian food and wine I've ever tasted was also in Taormina. *Osteria Nero d'Avola* is one restaurant-cum-enoteca where this treasured culinary experience took place. The restaurant on Vico Spuches down from the Corso Umberto is owned by Chef Turi (Salvatore) Siligato. The slightly eccentric but passionate Siligato is an integral advocate of Italy's "Slow Food Movement" (although in reality Sicily never joined the fast food movement). Turi is also a friend of the dynamic California natural food and wine pioneers Alice Waters and Kermit Lynch. The wine came before the meal with fresh crusty bread and local, highly savory virgin olive oil from the Peloritani Mountains to the north. Rarely does a wine light up every possible place in the mouth as much as this particular wine did. It was a 2009 *Syrah* bottled by Tasca Almerita from the production of the Prince of Camporeale's *Sallier de la Tour* winery estate. Tasca Almerita is justifiably known one of the most demanding wine houses in Sicily for highest quality. This wine's aroma was immediately both subtle and complex, like an old friend sharing many intimate memories. On the tongue and palate it seemed to be a softened vintage of many more years than it had, with a rich, accessible tannin. Its long finish was layered with many aftertastes, each giving way to another like archaeological strata, from cherry to chocolate and lastly vanilla. Its viscosity was revealed in legs rolling slowly all the way down the glass.

Turi Siligato's sister Francesca, whom my family has known for years and whose brilliant jewelry boutique, *Kiseki*, right on the Corso Umberto, showcases some of the most elegant and creative work in the world, says her brother is a bit crazy for perfection and so

Fig 7.2 Taormina

passionate about food but that it is possible to understand his dedication only after tasting his artistry firsthand. I believe in his vision after eating his incredible *Tagiatelle con Fungi Porcini, Asparagi e Gamberi*. The pasta was handmade, perfectly *al dente*, and the freshest possible porcini and asparagus were immaculately handpicked that morning. Turi told me the best time to pick both was early in the day and he also showed me from his digital camera at the Hosteria's front desk a photo of the sea bass he had caught that morning right off this Ionian coast that was being lovingly dismembered by the mouthful at another table. His pasta reminded me that when Greek colonists came by ship in the eighth century BCE they were astonished at how quickly wheat germinated in Sicilian earth compared to their rocky homeland.

Semolina wheat pasta from Sicily is still the best in Italy due to the island's broad geological combination of rich volcanic mafic soil from Mt. Etna mixed with great carbonate soil, both full of different nutrients, to create a natural pH balance. The pairing of the 2009 Syrah (Prince of Camporeale's *Sallier de la Tour*) with the fresh pasta was unimpeachable and that was only one of many possible since the hosteria restaurant of Turi Siligato has an enoteca's library of good wines. Due to stronger tannins and higher viscosity than many Italian wines, this wine can have a relatively long cellar life, up to 20 years if stored properly and if the bottle quality is assured with an affidavit of DOCG, more strict than mere DOC.

Beyond merely coupling Turi Siligato's exceptional wine list and delectable table is Taormina's history as a literary topos and an artistic haven. Here Goethe, Lampedusa, T. S. Eliot, Bertrand Russell, Tennessee Williams, Roald Dahl, D. H. Lawrence, and 1955 Nobel Laureate Haldór Laxness wrote, possibly even along with the ancients Homer and Aeschylus and many other poets and writers since. Taormina is also a town of great maiolica decorations everywhere, especially in the artists' quarter, and gardens and trees cascading down to the sea, groves pierced by cypress trees and scented with roses and pelargonium growing from rocks and colorful bougainvillea tumbling from walls. Baron Wilhelm von

Gloeden's infamous photographs even lured Oscar Wilde to Taormina's magical seaside Isola Bella. Despite being the terminus for a century of celebrities and movie stars followed by cruise ships, Taormina somehow remains mostly unspoiled by more touristic visitors ignorant of such longstanding acclaim. Long catering to such literati, connoisseurs, and even royalty like Kaiser Wilhelm II in 1906 whose suite is the core for the luxurious Grand Hotel Timeo (part of the Oriental Express chain), Taormina's wine and food certainly do it justice. Having been there more times than I can count in precious day after day for a dozen years, I'll be in Taormina—back at the Grand Timeo, I hope—every year I can, looking out over the Ionian Sea, the closest locus to Elysium I know on Earth's surface.

Marsala and Sicilian Citrus

Although the region of Roman *Drepanum* (modern Trapani) was active in viticulture in antiquity earlier than Gaul was, its fame for wine and robust economy are due more to modern history, when it became Sicily's largest wine-producing area, especially under the Whitaker Family and Florio Family ventures beginning in the early 19th century as Marsala fortunes were made. *Marsala* is one of Sicily's best-known wines, named after the port of the same name. The original name of the port of Marsala in the northwest of Sicily is *Marsah-el-Allah* from Arabic when Sicily was under Islamic rule from the 9–10th centuries.[11] The wine itself is mostly made from the white gapes Grillo, Inzolio, and Cataratto grapes but fortified with higher alcohol spirit and, if needed, a grape concentrate to make it a sweet red wine, although there are also dry (*secco*) varietals as well. Marsala varieties include *oro*, *ambra*, and the rare *rubico*—color mostly dependent on whether made from white grapes, red concentrate, or red grapes like Nero d'Avola—and the best Marsala is aged a decade before release. More than a few wine lovers say that Marco di Bartoli, "in a league of his own," now makes the best Marsala in Sicily, his aged *Vecchio Samperi*.[12]

Marsala's birthplace is only as recent as the late 18th century when it was blended and fortified for British tastes by its creator John Woodhouse, who landed in Trapani in 1773 but began his Marsala production in 1796. British families like the Whitakers came in 1814 and Italian families like the Florios soon followed. Joseph Whitaker came from Yorkshire to work in his uncle Benjamin Ingham's trade business; Vincenzo Florio began business in 1831 and in 1833 bought the Marsala production of John Woodhouse. Vincenzo Florio even had joint business ventures with Benjamin Ingham in industries like shipping and sulfur exports from Mt. Etna. These families soon controlled the bulk of the fortified wine business in western Sicily and their wealth brought social prominence.

Grand homes like the Whitaker's Villa Malfitano and the Florio's Villina Florio all'Olivuzza hosted visiting artists and writers who then contributed to the intellectual and cultural life of Sicily. When these dynastic families reigned briefly over Palermo's fortunes, the famous Grand Hotel Villa Igiea was recreated between 1899 and 1900 for Belle Epoque dame Donna Franco Florio (1873–1950) née Jacona, wife of Ignazio Florio, on the coast near the Aquasanta port of Palermo. Its suites and gardens hosted almost every royal family of Europe by the early 20th century, and its sumptuous Norman-Islamic style architecture with antique follies, including a faux ruins of columned tholos, was designed by Ernesto

Basile (1857–1932) and matched in the interior by Giovanni Boldini's (1832–1941) Art Nouveau frescoes. This is still the place to stay in Palermo, and I've spent more than a few glorious anniversaries at Villa Igiea, always reflecting on the Florio fortune started in the wine trade.

Unlike the well-known Marsala, so many of Sicily's superb wines are underappreciated or outsold by the more aggressive merchandising of Super-Tuscans and others, but the Sicilians laugh off that perception by saying that means there's more for them and that true cognoscenti who know Sicily love Sicilian wine. Sicily often produces more wine than almost any other Italian province, with 494,000 acres of vineyards and a yield of 264 million gallons per year in 1994, rivaled only by Apulia with 343 million gallons.[13] The wines of the Etna DOC have grabbed attention in the last few years, and rightly so, with over a hundred wineries encircling Mt. Etna on the west side from north to south, with both rich volcanic soils and cooler temperatures at higher altitude. *Carricante* is another Sicilian white wine grape from Etna, and has a lemony brightness.

The varied lemons of Sicily can hardly be described, but they may well be the best in the world. Back in Taormina at his restaurant, Turi Siligato brought around a giant lemon, a *Citron*, (Sicily is famous for its oversize *Citrus medica*[14]) to each table in his restaurant and sliced off a juicy lemon piece plus pith for each of his patrons. Not at all tart or puckering, this little bit of natural *dolci* was a palate freshener as well as sweet enough in itself to be a stand-alone. Better than Meyer Lemon in both texture and taste, pale pith and yellow lemon fruit could hardly be separated, with perhaps more pith than fruit but each almost equally delicious and refreshing. This citrus reminded me of the ancient legends no one who had not been to Sicily believed true: as already mentioned, that this place of unrivaled food prosperity was the Greek spring goddess Persephone's Island, as was said in antiquity by Roman poets like Claudian and revived by writers like Lawrence Durrell in *Sicilian Carousel* (1977) and Mary Taylor Simeti in her understanding of Sicilian cuisine.[15] Of course, it seems that centuries in Sicily hardly count in a land so ancient and magical. It must therefore not be a myth that the fragrance of Sicily is more lemon blossom than bergamot. Sicilians will tell anyone—with no trace of doubt—that unless the lemon is Sicilian, it's not a lemon. But then if you've ever had a Sicilian lemon granita on a hot summer day, it's easy to understand their pride.

Siracusan and Other Sicilian Wines

Other notable Sicilian wines I've tasted on many occasions in Sicily must include some of Barone Pietro Benevento del Bosco's Siracusan wines. At a *degustazione* I shared a few years ago in his magnificent eighteenth century Palazzo Benevento on

Fig 7.3 Chiaramonte and Santagostino 2009

the Piazza Duomo of Ortygia (Siracusa), the baron offered some of his heady *Nero d'Avola*. This wine is named after the black wine of the town of Avola on Sicily's southern tip near Siracusa, and its inkiness is more typical of a syrah. Barone Benevento del Bosco also shared his sweet golden *Moscato di Siracusa 2007* with amaretti cookies. If one can take sweetness to higher levels, many of these wines could be paired with the famed Sicilian cassuto or cannoli, the former possibly with a marmalade jam. The *Santagostino 2009 Nero d'Avola—Syrah* blend I tasted in Siracusa was also a powerful, supple wine, full of sunshine.

Yet another memorable wine that I've tasted in different Sicilian *degustazioni* in Siracusa and also served in the Taormina's Grand Hotel Timeo restaurant is the excellent *Chiaramonte 2009 Nero d'Avola*. Although the Chiaramontes themselves may not have survived to the present winemaking name, the old family presence is easily seen in their late medieval palazzi in both

Fig 7.4 Sallier de la Tour Syrah 2009

Siracusa's old Ortygia and in Palermo's Kalsa next to the Giardino Gardibaldi with its giant ficus trees. The Chiaramontes may have originally come from Clermont in Aragonese France in the thirteenth century, and who would blame the wine-loving French for coming to Sicily and staying? *Nerello Mascalese* is a red wine grape (used in the red wines *Etna Rosso* and *Corvo*) said to originate from Catania, whose name originally meant "Under Etna" (*kat' Etna*) in Greek. Most of the memorable wines I tasted in Sicily in March and April, 2012, were all 2009 so this must have been a great year. I've enjoyed these wines of Sicily each time I come, seemingly an annual sojourn now since 1999, and even though many wines taste better in their homeland than after being bounced around the world, sometimes it is the edge of the romantic ambiente in the place of origin and on many other occasions the fact that so few Sicilian wines are exported.

Back to Sicily's lemons, few realize the more-than-millennial history of citrus here. Roger II (1095–1154) was king of Sicily in the Golden Age praised after the fact by Boccaccio, when Palermo's Palazzo Normanni was nestled in La Conca d'Oro, the Golden Shell. There the whole valley was filled with the perfume of heady lemon blossoms from thousands of citrus trees planted on the advice of the Moorish gardeners, who had carefully tended citrus for centuries, well watered from aqueducts that brought mountain water down to the city. Some remnants of these aqueducts (*qanats* in Arabic) can be viewed in the cloistered garden of San Giovanni degli Eremiti next to the royal palace or where the Arabic fountains of Castello della Zisa—now the Museo d'Arte Islamica—flowed musically into the tiled divan chambers of the Salla delle Fontane.

Here too in Roger's medieval Sicily, vines were cultivated and the wine was exported for other goods.[16] Medieval vineyards at the Abbazia Santa Anastasia on the north central Sicilian coast near Castelbuono under the Madonie Mountains, for example, were producing wine for several centuries after the 1100's, a terrain now recently revived to produce excellent wines again by entrepreneur Francesco Lena and winemaker Riccardo Cotarella, including the rich Santa Anastasia Contempo Nero d'Avola (100% Nero d'Avola)

Fig 7.5 Tenuta Terre Nere Etna Rosso 2011

the acclaimed, high longevity Santa Anastasia Litra, "un grandissimo vino" (100% Cabernet Sauvignon) and the elegant Santa Anastasia Montenero Rosso (Nero d'Avola 60%, Cabernet Sauvignon 20%, and Merlot 20%) grown higher up, around 1,500 ft., under the Madonie foothills. These wines are now beginning to receive the coveted Italian Gambero Rosso Wine of Italy awards.

Of course, universally esteemed Sicilian flagship wines should not be neglected, especially the *Tasca d'Almerita 2010 Cygnus*, unanimous grand winner of the Gambero Rosso "Tre Bicchieri" and noted by Robert Parker and the Concours Mondial de Bruxelles. *Cygnus* is a blend of Nero d'Avola and Cabernet Sauvignon from their famed Regaleali estate, in the family since 1837. For so many years Nero d'Avola was underappreciated, the indigenous ugly duckling of Sicily, but under the best standards as Tasca d'Almerita has represented for generations, it has emerged as the elegant swan of Sicilian varietals, especially in such capable hands.

Remembering Sicily's Moorish heritage, another fabled wine of Sicily and nearby islands is Passito di Pantelleria. Southeast of Sicily on the small island of Pantelleria, the grape called *Zibibbo* in Sicily (known as Moscato d'Alessandria elsewhere) produces this elegant dessert wine. One vineyard there, Marco di Bartoli's Bukkuram (*bukkuram* is an Arabic variant for "father of the vine"), is part of a growing Passito di Pantelleria DOC listed as Sicilian since the island is under Sicilian jurisdiction. The wine is made from dried grapes like its Northern counterpart Amarone; *zibibbo* means "raisin" in Arabic, another relict of Sicily's past, and some say the grape was first brought to the island by the seafaring Phoenicians thousands of years ago.[17] The *Passito di Pantelleria Ben Ryé 2010 Donnafugata* of the Rollo family is another grand winner of the Gambero Rosso Tre Bicchieri.

This last wine also brings me full circle back to Giuseppe Lampedusa since Donnafugata, while not the same estate borrowed into Lampedusa's landmark novel *Il Gattopardo* filled with nostalgia for vicissitudes of Sicilian grandeur. Yet Donnfugata is an old name in Sicily about Habsburg princess Maria Carolina, daughter of Empress Maria Theresa and Emperor Francis I and sister of Marie Antoinette. Maria Carolina came as a "woman in flight" (*donna fugata*) with her husband Ferdinand IV, recently deposed king of Naples, in 1798 to Sicily in a similar time and ethos with Lampedusa's autobiographical novel. The Giacomo Rollo family adopted this historically descriptive name of Donnafugata made immortal by Lampedusa for their great wines whose many international awards continue to remind the world that Sicilian wines can compete with any.

Sicily's idyllic places like Taormina, Siracusa, Agrigento, and the Villa Igiea near Mondello on the coast north of Palermo where wooded Monte Pellegrino has its benevolent influence, are the best places where I can taste sunshine in the most poetic of Sicilian wines, knowing full well that Sicily can be the most seductive island on earth. Perhaps Demeter and her daughter Persephone still bless this fertile island with their graces that shine on the fruit between the dappled vine leaves.

CHAPTER 8

Wine in the Alto Adige

"A madman he who drinking feels melancholy and down at heels."

Rabelais, *Gargantua and Pantagruel*, Book 4

Grown under imposing mountains of the Italian and Austrian Alps, the rolling vineyards produce crisp Alto Adige wines known by connoisseurs. In case anyone thinks this is a new development, this quality has been going on long enough so that even Pliny took notice of Raetic wines. In the first century CE after Romans had expanded their viticultural territory into the Veneto and beyond into the Alps, Pliny said that before Tiberius, "priority at the table belonged to the Raetic grapes."[18]

In June 2011 I spent a week between Verona, Bolzano (*Bozen* in German), and Merano tasting and drinking great local wine. In the Alto Adige under the Alps, Bolzano is that wonderful combination of the best of both Italy and Austria. Annexed to Italy in 1919 from Austria, German culture and language hybridize with Italian language and *amore per la vita* in these lovely mountain valleys with vines growing up the slopes to considerable heights. Above Bolzano, in the evening the "Rosengarten" Dolomites bask in alpenglow to the east. Castles seem to grow out of rocks and the copper-roofed monasteries—of religious orders that still often make their own wines—whose bells ring in almost every valley where conifer forests cascade down the ridges. The spectacular landscape looks almost too good to be true, but it is not artificial, rather the norm for the Tirol where both humans and nature appear in well-tended balance. Perhaps Karen MacNeil has captured the Südtirol best:

> Few wine regions are as stunning as Trentino-Alto Adige, with the Alps for a backdrop, majestic lakes dotting the countryside, and castles, churches and vineyards that are simply immaculate.[19]

On the train from Verona I was amazed how the vertical massive limestone ridges grew higher and higher above the Adige River Valley, finally opening up above Trento but then revealing even more dramatic Alps behind them with almost the entire valley floor covered in vineyard rows like volleys of arrows flying across the landscape.

Fig 8.1 Vineyards around Bolzano

Wine History in the Alto Adige

Surprisingly to some, wine history here not only goes back to Roman times but also before, at least to 500 BCE. Several museums have Roman artifacts including the Museo Archeologico dell'Alto Adige (Südtiroler Archäologiemuseum)—also home of "Ötzi the Iceman," the 5,300-year-old ice mummy—and the Südtirol Museum of Wine in Kaltern. Wine ladles and pruning billhooks (*hippe* in German, *roncola* in Italian)[20] are some of the artifacts in the collections, and locals insist the Rhaetian tribal viticulture was using wooden barrels about 15 BCE when the Romans built roads that connect here, like the Via Claudia Augusta over the *Pons Drusi* (Bridge of Drusus) over the Adige River.

Since Romans like Pliny, Virgil, and Martial all praised Rhaetian (or Raetian) wine, there's a possibility they could have even tasted the early wine of Alto Adige. Centuries later Medieval viticulture was well underway with both Italian passion and Austrian precision, as each culture intertwined together here. Later during Habsburg rule, imperial authority greatly supported quality winemaking in the Alto Adige, which enjoys about 300 days of sunshine per year and cultivates over 20 different grape varieties. Some of the highest summer heat in Italy is in the Bolzano valley—I repeatedly saw 35 °C in late June—which is perfect for ripening grapes. Locals joke that there are 40 vines per every Bolzano resident and that if "Venice floats on water, Bolzano floats on wine."

Modern Viticulture

I can well believe these statements since I saw vines growing everywhere imaginable in every precious square foot of coveted space along the river valleys and climbing the ridges from above Trento through Merano and the Adige Valley, even outside my hotel room in the park of Bolzano's old medieval Luna Mondschein. According to the Alto Adige wine industry and wine lovers who've spent any time here, its quality wines are distinguished in a tiny wine region that stretches less than 50 miles south to north:

> Around five thousand winegrowers tend just 5,300 hectares (13,100 acres) of grape-growing areas in different climatic zones with variable types of soils and at elevations ranging from 200 to 1,000 m. (600 to 3,300 ft.) above sea level—a wide variety that brings forth a considerable dense concentration of top wines. This is confirmed by a quick look at the leading Italian wine guide: for years now, Gambero Rosso has awarded Alto Adige the largest number of top scores ("Three Glasses") in proportion to its total vineyard area.[21]

This is in contrast to Tuscany and Piemonte wines, grown in much larger total areas of viticulture as a wine region but in general with less overall distinction, since more wines (98%) have Italian DOC (*Denominazione di Origine Controllata*) protection appellation here in the Alto Adige[22] than anywhere else in Italy, with diverse microclimates and a complex geology ranging from the eroded limestone soils of the Italian Prealps around Trento to the Venosta sands and Merano shales, mica schists, and phyllites to the porphyry soils of the Dolomites around Bolzano. Yet less than 5% of these wines are even exported to the U.S., with so much (49%) being consumed regionally. Many of the wines are grown on pergolas and high Guyot trellises, whose X-crossbeams can be seen all over the valleys almost from east of Lago Garda northward.

Although Alto Adige white wines are far more famous—Pinot Grigio (also known here as Grauer Burgunder or Ruländer), Chardonnay, Pinot Blanc, Sauvignon Blanc, indigenous Gewürztraminer along with Müller-Thurgau, Sylvaner, Riesling, Veltliner, Moscato Giallo

Fig 8.2 St. Magdalener village

Fig 8.3 St. Magdalener Classico
Leitach 2011

Fig 8.4 St. Magdalener Classico
2010

(Goldmuskateller) and Kerner—making up 55% total volume in the Alto Adige, its red wines (45% total volume) include the indigenous Schiava and Lagrein as well as Pinot Noir, Cabernet Sauvignon, Merlot, Cabernet Franc, and Moscato Rosa, among others. Schiava is also known as Vernatsch in German as well as Trollinger (from Tirol) elsewhere in Germany. A light cherry-red wine, Schiava is blended with the fuller-bodied Lagrein for breadth and depth. More Schiava (22–30%) grapes are grown here than any other grape varietal, with Pinot Grigio a distant second (11%). Many consumers prefer the light Schiava—"berry and almond aromas"—blended rather than by itself. Schiava is also known in Germany as the Black Hamburg grape. Some of the Alto Adige wines can also be designated by the Germanic QbA (*Qualitätswein bestimmter Anbaugebiete*, meaning "Quality wines produced in specified regions") rather than Italian DOC designations.[23]

One of my new Bolzano favorites tasted here is a cuvée blending several red varietals: the Sankt Magdalener (Santa Maddalena) of the village of the same name just east of Bolzano in the hills. Sankt Magdalener unites Schiava and Lagrein in a cuvée percentage depending on the vintner but often around 80% Schiava and 20% Lagrein.[24] I tasted multiple wines, including those of Josephus Mayr, a family making wine since 1568, as well as other red wine blends such as the velvety Lagrein Kretzer Weingut—Erbhof of Josephus Mayr (2009), the memorable Ansitz Waldgries St. Magdalener Classico (2010), the Hans Rottensteiner St. Magdalener (2010) and the St. Justina Leitach St. Magdalena Classico (2011). In his iconic *Sotheby's Guide to Classic Wines*, Molyneux-Berry also highlighted a quality Sankt Magdalener (Oberingram Sankt Magdalener) from Alois Lageder,[25] which was my introduction to this wine. These blended Sankt Magdalener red wines are worth drinking alone for vivid flavor—or paired with the Bolzano cuisine with its distinct Austrian touches of juniper-flavored *speck* (ham) on *schüttelbrot, wurst* with *schwartze trüffel,* and spinach *knödel* dumplings. Of course, you can just as easily have *tagliatelle con funghi porcini* because it is still also Northern Italy.

While Pinot Blanc is the most widely planted white grape here, the Alto Adige also makes an intense sweet dessert white wine from the Goldenmuskateller or Moscato Giallo grape and a semi-sweet to sweet dessert wine from the rosy to ruby Rosenmuskateller or Moscato Rosa grape, sometimes startlingly bold in nectar and whose color is dependent on how much grape skin is used.[26]

Operatic Notes

The Trentino Valley is sufficiently venerable in wine to have a few indigenous grapes, which may include the near-native red Marzemino,[27] made famous—or infamous—not so much for viticultural value but because Mozart's Faustian 1787 opera *Don Giovanni* hails it in the finale of Act II near the last scene of the opera. Don Giovanni calls for a last drink before he disappears in sulfurous smoke down to his dramatic demise in hell. The first Don Giovanni cast in the Prague opera premiere was the famous baritone Luigi Bassi (1786–1825)[28] who was originally from Pesaro down the Adriatic Coast from the Veneto, so he could easily have known the Marzemino wine personally since it also is grown in the Veneto and even Emilia Romagna. More important is that Mozart's librettist Lorenzo da Ponte himself was from the Veneto and was fond of wine.[29] Here is the *Don Giovanni* libretto exchange between Don Giovanni and his servant Leporello:

> *Don Giovanni:*
> Oh, what a flavorful dish!!
>
> *Leporello:*
> ("Oh, what a barbarous appetite! What monstrous bites! I think I'm going to faint.")
>
> *Don Giovanni:*
> "Plate."
>
> *Leporello:*
> "Your Servant. Cheers to the 'Litigants'"!
>
> *Don Giovanni:*
> "Pour the wine!"
>
> (Leporello pours a small glass of wine)
> "Excellent Marzimino!"[30]

There may be more than a bit of satire here given the immediately preceding lines because Marzemino's reputation is spotty and the grapes can go to rot easily, like Don Giovanni himself. The winemakers of Alto Adige themselves often spoof Marzemino since they have so much better in their fantastic white and red wines. Whether or not this operatic hellish fate may be damning to the wine of a rake about to be punished, perhaps it is perfect for a last hurrah. Marzemino also goes by a few other local names, including Balsamina Nera—"Black Balsam"—Ancellata and Uva Tedesco, the last word Tedesco being what Northern Italians often call German style.

Alto Adige and World-Class Wines

Because the finest Alto Adige wines seem to come from the slopes,—which are more difficult to manage and thus more expensive to maintain—than the flat valleys, the esteemed wine of J. Hoffstätter from their Barthenau pergola-trained hill vineyard at Mazon on the eastern side of the valley, especially the *J. Hofstätter Pinot Nero Riserva Vigna Sant'Urbano Barthenau 2000*, is a special find, but mostly unavailable now except in private cellars; their 2008 and 2009 of the same wine can still be found. Equally superb is their *J. Hofstätter Kolbenhof Gewürztraminer 2007* for sheer elegance, and may those gewürztraminer snob detractors—who often think gewurz is for naïve youngsters—never discover this one!

For sheer medieval memorability to all the senses, the old Augustinian monastery abbreviated in German as Kloster Neustift or in Italian as Abbazia di Novacella is located in Varna just north of Bressanone (Brixen). The monastery is one of Alto Adige's stars in the crown, important in the region since the 12th century, founded in 1142 by the Bishop of Brixen at a pilgrimage route junction from the Brenner Pass and established as Augustinian, *regula sancti Augustini*, for the canons regular who still operate it, also providing pastoral service for parishes in the region. Along the Isarco River Valley, Eisacktal in German, at a fairly high elevation of about 2,100–2,900 ft., the monastery produces great wines—a member of the Grandi Cru d'Italia—like the whites Kerner, Sylvaner, and Veltliner and from the vineyards here, also producing red wines like *Praepositus Lagrein* from sunnier fields further south near Bolzano. Their wines are nearly always highly ranked in many lists and almost universally hailed as making some of the best wine in Italy. Their *Kerner Alto Adige Valle Isarco 2009* is one of these, and is 100% Kerner grape, but not as easily found now since it has been snatched up everywhere and cellared by cognoscenti. Good wines not easily exported from the monastery wine cellar can be purchased in the monastery wine shop and tutorial wine tastings are offered with local Südtirol cuisine, including the not-so-austere monastic fare of smoked *Kaminwurzen* sausage with local cheeses. Their sweet Rosenmuskateller is also not to be missed. The Alto Adige Kerner grape, however, is a fairly new hybrid varietal from Germany, bred by August Herold in Lauffen, Württemberg, as a 1929 crossing of red Trollinger and Riesling, which shows the old monastery is up to date in viticulture, and one would hate to see its architecture change, especially its medieval cloister, cathedral, library, museum, and towers. The Abbazia di Novacella rightly claims 850 years of winemaking.

If possible early Roman esteem is not sufficiently modern and current praise too recent, in keeping with the Abbazia di Novacella, Alto Adige wine has also been rightly praised by medieval Tyrolean poets like Count Oswald von Wolkenstein (1377–1445), the feisty nobleman who loved Traminer, and wrote steamy lyrics. Alto Adige wine is even highlighted in the famous frescoes of Brixen (Bressanone) Cathedral. In Bolzano and other towns, decorated with old Gothic script on buildings and wrought iron signs hanging from old

Fig 8.5 Abbazia di Novacella courtyard

shops, you would hardly know you were in northern Italy. Other than a few even older Italian Romanesque campaniles here and there, most of the church towers have Baroque German bronze onion-dome bell towers. After enjoying the sunshine of Bolzano in the vineyards under distant snowy peaks, I totally agree with the poet Heinrich Heine about the Südtirol here:

> *In southern Tyrol, the weather cleared up, the sun from Italy allowed its nearness to be felt, the mountains grew warmer and shinier, I began to see entwined around them wine grapes, and I could begin to lean out of the coach more often.*[31]

If the Alto Adige is not already beautiful enough in greening spring and deep summer or in winter when white snow blankets the stark landscape, its fiery vineyard foliage in autumn when many of the vine leaves flame in vibrant red color may be the best-kept secret of the region. In fall after harvest when the previous year's crisp white crystalline wines fill the palate, the Alto Adige festivals flood the region with harvest greetings over raised wine glasses. Harvest festivals like the October Grape Festival in Merano or the nearby "Vino Culti" in the village of Tirolo north of Merano bring Tiroleans down from the mountain hamlets to celebrate. Not far from either, Naturno is at the foot of the Val Senales emptying into the Adige Valley. Ötzi the Iceman lived 5,300 years ago in the Val Senales and must have also ventured into this river confluence because of the Neolithic site of Juval just above Naturno (Naturns in German). Ötzi's frozen body was discovered high above the valley in the melting Similaun glacier in 1991 and he now resides in Bolzano's Südtirol Museum under deep freeze.

Ötzi was the primary reason I was there in 2011, filming with National Geographic on his mystery and the amazing archaeological finds with him. Ironically, Reinhold Messner—the legendary Austrian Mountain Man whose feats on the world's highest icy mountains are likely unparalleled—lives in Juval where Ötzi may have lived before his death. If Ötzi's clan cultivated or picked any fruit for fermented beverage is unknown, but now in November when all the deciduous trees are bare and the cold wind sweeps down from the icy heights, Naturno holds its Südtirol Riesling Festival. Here the new wines (Nule) fresh from pressing are judged both by respected sommeliers as well as the locals. Locals all across Südtirol call this "Törggelen" Time (Törggel is winepress in the local German), enjoyed outside if possible with roast chestnuts, Klachl fritters, sweet cakes, and of course the wines. Even if only for a short time longer, the sunlit yellow leaves of the Riesling vines glow as much as the golden wines whose alchemy they made.

CHAPTER 9

German and Alsatian Wines

"Wine is the best gift of gods to men." Athenaeus, *Deipnosophistae* 2.37b

Charlemagne's Legacy

Tradition and some evidence have it that Charlemagne (768–814) revitalized the remnant Roman viticulture in his Frankish kingdom, especially in the northern Rhine region and also oversaw its viticultural progress. Alsace has been famous for wine since Roman colonists settled there; some also believe that the Riesling vine derives from the Roman *argitis minor* vine varietal[32] possibly hybridized or cultivated by Carolingian vine-growers under Charlemagne's orders. According to his biographer Einhard, Charlemagne renamed the month of October in Frankish as *windume manuth*, or "wine harvest month."[33] Einhard also makes it clear that Charlemagne himself was extremely temperate:

> *He abominated drunkenness in anybody, much more in himself and those of his household… He was so moderate in the use of wine and all sorts of drink that he rarely allowed himself more than three cups in the course of a meal.*[34]

Charlemagne was one of the prime movers in ending the Dark Ages and the Carolingian Renaissance is named after him for his capable administration that brought back order and learning to Europe after the collapse of the Roman Empire.[35] While the Romans had already established Rhine viticulture in the Mosel (Moselle), Pfalz, Rheinhessen, and Alsace regions,[36] in concert with his other ecclesiastic policies, Charlemagne's *Council of Aachen* in 814 reorganized monastic winemaking practices, recommending the church's canons to grow vines for wine, certainly beyond the needs for eucharist.[37]

Legend suggests that Charlemagne also stimulated viticulture in the area of Schloss Johannisberg and the production of what would eventually become Riesling, but this is difficult to prove, since the Benedictine monastic site is not recorded until 1100 and the name Riesling is not officially recognized until around 1435 near Mainz with a merchant invoice for *riesslingen in die wingarten*; Duke René of Lorraine is credited for connecting Alsace with fine Riesling in 1477 but Riesling is not firmly noted until Hieronymus Bock (1498–1554) in the 1552 edition of his herbal.[38] The date of 1628 is a watermark year for absolute documentary proof of Riesling grapes planted in Alsace. On the other hand, Stolz believes Riesling was introduced as early as 843 in the Rheingau during Carolingian rule under Louis II the German where Riesling may also be the *gentil aromatique* grape.[39] Whatever legacy of Charlemagne and the Carolingian Era can be connected to viticulture, it is both history and the present that should appreciate this great king's commitment to stabilizing civilization and recognizing wine as one of its most important gifts.

Mosel Wine Region

Yhe Mosel (or Moselle in French) River flows mostly north in a wide arc into the Rhine River through France, Luxembourg, and Germany, but it is Germany where its wines are most famous. Starting in the northern Vosges Mountains of French Alsace, the Mosel continues for 338 miles until it enters the Rhine at Koblenz. Most of its German wine territory is in the state of the Rhineland Palatinate.

Decimius Magnus Ausonius (310–394 CE) the Late Roman poet from *Burdigala* (Bordeaux) whose name is known now for a Premier Grand Cru Classé French wine chateau, Château Ausone, spent time in the Moselle, even then a wine region while on German campaigns as an imperial tutor to Emperor Valentinian's son Gratian. Ausonius lived a while in Trier (*Augusta Treverorum*) along the Mosel with the imperial retinue. He wrote a long poem, *Mosella*, in which he describes the river and its viticulture, reminding him of his *Burdigala* home:

> ... the roofs of country houses perched high upon the overhanging riverbanks, the hillsides green with vines, and the pleasant stream of Mosella below with subdued murmuring ... Hail, River ... whose hills are overgrown with Bacchus' fragrant vines ...[40]

That the Mosel region is acknowledged fairly early in history as a wine region is important for tradition, but it is not so easy to know the varietals of the Roman period here as early as the second century CE; only that they were likely to be mostly white grapes in this northern climate zone. Most likely planted for producing garrison wine for the Roman army legions stationed along the borders of *Germania* to lower the cost of importing wine from elsewhere, these Roman wines were light and low in alcohol.

During the Middle Ages when wine villages (*winzerdorfs*) became community hubs, the grape mostly grown in the Mosel area has been the Riesling and it still dominates (around 60%) production, although Müller-Thurgau was brought in the early 20th century because it is easier to grow in the cool climate; now accounting for about 15%, along with Ebling at 7%, and Kerner at 5% of grape yield. The labor-intensive, high-maintenance Mosel region generally has some of the steepest wine slopes in the world—most often necessitating harvesting by hand—on its mostly slate-based geology. South-facing slopes along the Mosel River maximize what possible sunshine helps to ripen grapes, and because so many of the Mosel slopes are fairly steep (the most vertical are at a 65° slope at Bremm), reflected sunlight off the river is extensively used for enhancing ripening. Even if the Riesling grape does not fully ripen, it can still produce a quality wine in Germany under circumstance that could be very challenging to other viticultural regions. Ripeness is not a predictor of quality in Germany. Most of the area's vine rows are vertical, facing downhill for runoff. The rocky slate also heats up doing the day with ambient sunlight and reflects back warmth up into the vines for better ripening. Each year after the rainy season, the slate that washed downhill is carefully retrieved and placed back into vineyards for this reason.

The Mosel wine region—most famous in Germany—is composed today of over 9,000 hectares of vineyards. This also makes it third largest of Germany's wine regions in terms of production, with around 91% given to white grapes, but considerably higher in quality than most German wine regions. Overall in all regions, the simplest German wine ratings are the mostly inexpensive QbA wines and are medium in quality. Understanding German wine nomenclature for the higher-end tiered rankings can be complicated by a unique system. Germany uses the Oechsle Scale, named after pioneer oenochemist Ferdinand Oechsle (1774–1852). Oechsle hydrometry gauges the unfermented harvest grape must density by refractometry and is estimated by refractive index. To make this understandable, at room temperature the refractive index of glass is around 1.5, meaning roughly 1.5 times that of air; that of water at 20 °C is around 1.33 or roughly 1.3 times that of air. The *Qualitätswein* Oechsle numbers measuring grape must density (and generally sugar content) range from a minimum of 51 and a maximum of 72. The alcohol content must be at least 7% but chaptalization—adding sugar to unfermented grape juice—is allowed.

Overall for German *Prädikatswein* tiers, however, chaptalization is not allowed. The usually dry (*trocken*) Kabinett has the same minimum alcohol as a *Qualitätswein* with a minimum alcohol level of 7% and is the lowest level of the *Prädikatswein*, with an Oechsle minimum of 67 and maximum of 82 but in Mosel the minimum Oechsle is 73. The German Spätlese is next up the tier, and literally means a "late harvest" with a minimum alcohol level of 7% and an Oechsle minimum of 76 and a maximum of 90, but in Mosel the mini-mum Oechsle is 85. The German Auslese is next with a minimum alcohol level of 7% and an Oechsle minimum of 83 and maximum of 100, but its Mosel Oechsle minimum must be 95. German Beerenauslese and Eiswein are the next-highest level of *Prädikatswein*. Eiswein is harvested very late after the grapes have frozen, but the Eiswein is usually not affected by botrytis ("noble rot")[41] from *Botrytis cinerea* whereas Beerenauslese is generally affected by botrytis, known as *Edelfäule* in German. The minimum alcohol level for both is 5.5%. The German Oechsle minimum for both Euswein and Beerenauslese is 110 and the maximum is 128, but in Mosel the minimum Oechsle is 125 for both. The highest level of *Prädikatswein* is Trockenbeerenauslese, also affected by botrytis and with an Oechsle minimum of 150 and a maximum of 154, with the same minimum Oechsle number for Mosel Trockenbeerenausle wine. This complicated German wine rating system goes with the turf—German engineering!

Some of the most romantic and highest-quality wine locations in Germany—like the following Rhine region, filled with famous castles—are in the Mosel region, including one of the oldest as well at Bernkastel. Vineyards surround the medieval town on both sides of the Mosel River and vineyards in a five-mile stretch of the river are simply outstanding, especially in what is called the *Mittelmosel* or mid-Mosel district. The Bernkastel name likely derives from an 8th century document where it is named *Princastellum*, possibly because of a 4th century Roman castellum near the remains of Landshut castle. The next version of the local name was *Beronis castellum* from the 12th century. An honored Mosel name long associated with old Bernkastel is *Weingut Dr. Loosen*, just north of old Bernkastel town. One of the consistently highest-rated producers is the Selbach name, especially seen in its *Selbach-Oster 2006 Zeltinger Schlossberg Riesling Spätlese* (rated 91 by Wine Spectator), produced in Zeltingen, the area in the most contorted loops of the Mosel River just north of Wehlen and Bernkastel. Another great Mosel wine, also in the Bernkastel district, is *Joh. Jos. Prüm Wehlener 2010 Sonnenuhr Riesling Auslese Goldskapel.* "Sonnenuhr" refers to huge old sundials placed in certain vineyards for vineyard workers; because the sundials were always put in the sunniest spots, it is no accident that these vineyards became famous and synonymous for some of the best Mosel wines.[42] Prüm's Wehlener Sonnenuhr is produced in Wehlen, also just north of the town of Bernkastel by the Prüm family who have been living here since 1156 and their vineyards are always late harvested, producing wines of great longevity. The *Joh. Jos. Prüm 1949 Wehlener-Zeltinger Sonnenuhr Trockenbeerenauslese* is predicted to last well beyond the publication date of this book. Then there is the *Dr. Loosen Erdener Pralat 2009 Riesling Auslese Goldskapel,* produced in another bend of the Mosel just north of Zeltingen. The best of the rarest Mosel wines can be priceless at auction, equal to any wine in the world, and not for the faint-hearted with an auction paddle.

Rüdesheim and the Rheingau

The Rheingau region of Germany is another area associated with Roman viticulture, since the Romans planted vines nearly everywhere they settled. Roman glass artifacts have been

Fig 9.1 Bromserberg Castle Rudesheim

found around Rüdesheim and a *castrum* was in nearby Bingen across the river as well as a Roman bridge. The tenth century Brümserburg castle was also built over Roman fortifications. Less challenged than many viticultural areas, Rheingau is particularly favorable since the Rhine River runs east to west here and thus vineyards can face south for maximum solar exposure, with Riesling grapes growing in 82% of the area under vine in 1990.[43]

I was in Germany, including the Rheingau and Alsace, lecturing on a Rhine Cruise for Scientific American Travel in April 2012 and tasted a range of Rieslings and Gewürztraminers in Rüdesheim am Rhein, Strasbourg, Colmar, and Wittolsheim. I had been in the Mosel region before, including in Luxembourg; this time I watched the Mosel flow into the Rhine at Koblenz, although we did have Mosel wine on board the cruise ship *Amacello*. Talking with several growers and winemakers and comparing these wines added depth to prior experience, especially satisfying being in the areas noted for production of these wines.

On the ridge above the town of Rüdesheim we were taken to a vineyard tasting (*Weinprobe*) just southwest of the Niederwald-Denkmal monument at the edge of the forest. The old town itself has many *weinstuben*—many on the festive Oberstrasse and Drosselgasse—and their common half-timbered architecture recalls the medieval importance of the town we could see below around the 15th century Pfarrkirche St. Jakobus church.

We started tasting local Rieslings near the Brömserburg Castle ruin with Roman foundations—now a wine museum—and because the buds were just forming before leafing, the rows of the vine parcels were colorful with yellow dandelion flowers. Local winemaker Carsten Hempel explained the local viticulture as we continued tasting with bottles on tables set up along the slope. In our three stops climbing the ridge toward the Klosterlay parcels, among the Rüdesheim wines we tasted were *Weingut Adolf Störzel Kirchenpfad Riesling Kabinett Trocken* 2010 and *Weingut Adolf Störzel Berg Rottland Riesling Spätlese* 2010. Both of these Rieslings were refreshingly light and delicious with 9% alcohol. Hempel also works in Geisenheim, which is home to the prestigious German viticultural school begun in 1872,

the Geisenheim Grape Breeding Institute. This school awards academic degrees in winemaking, the only such institution in Germany, and it also now has graduate degrees administered through Giessen University. This is where Hermann Müller developed the Müller-Thurgau hybrid in the late nineteenth century.

Geisenheim itself just to the east is also adjacent to Schloss Johannisberg, another kilometer further northeast, and the almost-equally famous pilgrim destination's Marienthal Monastery. Since Geisenheim was first mentioned in 772 in

Fig 9.2 Rheingau Rudesheimer Berg Rottland Riesling Spatlese Storzel 2010

Fig 9.3 Schloss Johannisberg

Carolingian documents, the Charlemagne wine connections are not without substance. Rüdesheim's Riesling viticulture has its vertical rows parallel to the slope; that is, like Mosel, vineyards face downward rather than parallel across the topography. The narrow rows also made machine harvesting difficult, so that the majority of picking is done by hand. Every other row is offset with natural growth to retain topsoil and yet limit half the plant competition, an experimental conclusion after a compromise between having every row planted but with a resulting weakening of the wine since sharing the soil's minerals reduced vine vigor. Like all viticultural areas, the geology of the Taunus Massif north of the Rhine directly affects the vines, being high in quartzite and Rüdesheim loess is noted for that acidic high silicate. For geography, it might also be interesting to note that the 50th latitude north runs through Geisenheim vineyards. Recent 2006 statistics also show that the hardy, cold-resistant Riesling with its late-ripening, thick-skinned grape is logically the most planted vine stock in both Germany and Alsace, comprising 21% with over 21,000 hectares (52,000+ acres) and 22% with over 3,300 hectares (8,000+ acres) of all vines in those countries, respectively.[44]

One rising star of Rüdesheim's world-class Rieslings is Johannes Leitz of Leitz Weingut, extolled in the *New York Times* and by Riesling guru Stuart Pigott of *Planet Wine*. Leitz piled up Gold Medals in quite a few categories of the 2010–2012, especially the 2010, International Wine Challenges in London. Leitz was also awarded Gault Millau's 2010 Winemaker of the Year. It would be a real coup if one can obtain the intense *Leitz 2010 Kaisersteinfels, Leitz 2010 Rottland "Hinterhaus"* and *Leitz 2010 Rüdesheimer Berg Schlossberg Riesling "Ehrenfels"* or even the *Leitz 2009 Magic Mountain Riesling* blended from different Leitz parcels. The name *Magic Mountain Riesling* alludes not just to Thomas Mann but also the steep terraces above the Rhine around Rüdesheim in vineyards like Berg Schlossberg, Drachenstein, and Berg Kaisersteinfels, all of which produce superb wine.[45] J. Keller at Weingut Leitz told me that the title "Magic Mountain" (Zauberberg) is also a local reference to the Rüdesheimer Berg, the main ridge above the town. Leitz wines all come from south-facing terraced slopes, the optimum venues for wine with more sun than other directions.

Bingen, across the Rhine from Rüdesheim, was known to Romans as *Bincium*, although Ausonius also names it as *Vincum*, possibly attesting its Roman viticultural prominence. Bingen too is famous for wine in its own right, with a high density of wineries and about 700 hectares of adjacent vineyards. The Dromersheim suburb of Bingen also claims to have discovered Eiswein in February of 1830. Bingen also has its own 11-day wine festival, Fest des Weines, in early September.

To most Rhine River travelers, their river view of Bingen is formed first by the famous Mäuseturm, a small white red-trimmed castle tower straddling a shallow island in the river. "Mouse Tower" has a legend that here in 974 the oppressive Hatto, Lord of Bingen, after cruelly locking up and killing peasants in one of his barns, was imprisoned in his own tower—used mostly to exact punitive tolls from the river, enforced by crossbow bolts— where he met his end. The peasants had revolted over his control of food during famine and so Hatto set fire to the tower, saying, "How they squeal just like mice," as they burned. The imprisoned Hatto was swiftly eaten alive by legions of mice in punishment, as different songs (even in *The Childrens' Hour* by American poet Henry Wadsworth Longfellow) tell the tale of justice from this medieval ditty in translation:

> They whetted their teeth against the stones,
> And then they picked the Bishop's bones;
> They gnawed the flesh from every limb
> For mice were sent to punish him!

Here is Longfellow's allusion:

> They almost devour me with kisses,
> Their arms about me entwine,
> Till I think of the Bishop of Bingen
> In his Mouse-Tower on the Rhine!

Because Romans were here first in what was then a *Franconia* border, Hatto's Mouse Tower is only a later structure—the current one a nineteenth century Prussian remake over medieval and Roman foundations. Nearby too is the Drusus Bridge, rebuilt stone remnant of a first century BCE Roman bridge over the Nahe River in its confluence with the Rhine.

One of the brightest minds in history, Hildegard of Bingen (ca. 1098–1179), medieval polymath abbess, wrote in a wide range from theology to medicine and other sciences, and was also a composer and poet as well as a mystic. She also invented an alphabet and her works fill many volumes, much now collected in the *Dendermonde* manuscript and the *Riesenkodex*. Not surprisingly, she assembled many medicinal wine formulae. Among others, her parsley wine remedies are still used widely in Germany due to her reputation as a healer. Here is one of her poetic maxims:

> Ein Wein von der Rebe, wenn er rein ist,
> macht dem Trinker das Blut gut und gesund.

> A wine from the vine when it is pure makes the drinker's blood healthy and good.

Hildegard's Rupertsberg convent in Bingen is long gone, so I visited her reconstructed peaceful Eibingen Abbey above Rüdesheim, built in Romanesque style and reestablished in modern times under the protection of Karl, 6th Prince of Lowenstein-Wertheim-Rosenberg. The abbey has a Benedictine nunnery and the basilica receives many pilgrims—equal number of men and women—because much of the Roman Catholic Church has acknowl-edged her beatification, although not necessarily her canonization because Hildegard has always had opposition from some male authorities due in part to her uniqueness. Eibingen Abbey is also surrounded by vineyards, some of which are part of its property.

Incidentally, a prominent family in Bingen and Kitzingen had a large impact on California viticulture in the 20th century. The Fromms were a family of successful German-Jewish vintners and wine merchants of several generations when almost 70% of the Jews in Kitzingen were employed in the wine business,[46] most of whom left Germany by 1938. Alfred Fromm co-founded the famous wine traders Fromm and Sichel in the U.S. The Fromm family has been philanthropic in many academic ventures including the bequest for the Fromm Institute in San Francisco. Herbert Fromm—a student of Paul Hindemith—was a conductor and composer in Munich, Bielefeld, Frankfurt, and eventually New York and Boston after emigrating to the U.S.

Heidelberg and the Neckar in Baden-Württemberg

Upriver from Rüdesheim, while Heidelberg along the Neckar does not lie in as famous as a wine-producing area as the Rheingau to the northwest, it is a notable viticultural region al-though its fame lies elsewhere and it is certainly a beer and wine-consuming city, especially

Fig 9.4 Heidelberg from the Castle

at the university and the among what were the thirsty nobles and town burgers as well as guests. On the other hand, Heidelberg's climate is warmer with higher temperatures than many regions of Germany because it is relatively sheltered between the Palatinate Forest in the west and the Odenwald in the east with the Rhine Valley in the middle, into which the Neckar River watershed flows mostly westward at Heidelberg.

Although now Heidelberg castle is mostly an uninhabited romantic ruin, we can gauge the impressive amount of wine stored in what may one of the world's largest "barrels". Deep inside Heidelberg Castle is the *Heidelberg Tun*, made in 1751 and said to have needed the wood of 130 oak trees. This notorious wooden barrel is easily 17 feet high, with a capacity around 228,000 liters (more than 58,000 gallons), no doubt for aristocratic bragging rights in court functions. Debates continue whether it was ever much used, but likely so because Perkeo of Heidelberg was appointed both Court Jester and Castle Guardian of Wine.

The Heidelberg Tun was not the first but rather the fourth huge barrel (also called *Fass*) in a series of great wine tuns at the castle. The list includes others, the Johann-Casimir-Fass (1591), the Karl-Ludwig-Fass (1664), the Karl-Philipp-Fass (1728) and finally this one, the Karl-Theodor-Fass (1751). This large oak tun also has an outside wooden ladder to the balcony on top for a small dancing floor, and if you climb up and stand on it, it emphasizes how small humans are relative to the capacious wine volume inside. The Heidelberg Tun has a somewhat amusing literary history as well, mentioned first in Rudolf Erich Raspe's *Adventures of Baron Munchausen*, Chapter 22

Fig 9.5 Heidelberg Tun

when the baron was seated in Queen Mab's Chariot: "It was a prodigious dimension, large enough to contain more stowage than the tun of Heidelberg …"[47] Similarly, Victor Hugo also mentions the Heidelberg Tun in a macabre passage of *Les Miserables* when Gavroche inspects the interior of the emperor's hollow titanic elephant with the two boys, illuminated by lit pitch-dipped string called a cellar rat:

> Gavroche's two guests looked around and had much such a feeling as any one would have if shut up in the Heidelberg tun, or better still, what Jonas must have experienced in the biblical belly of the whale.[48]

This was an empty Heidelberg Tun, as it mostly has been since the 18th century. Not to be outdone in Romanticism, Washington Irving also includes it in his story "The

Specter Bridegroom" in the Odenwald House of Katzenellenbogen Castle of the Baron von Landshort's preparations for the marriage of his daughter:

> The kitchen was crowded with good cheer, the cellars had yielded up whole oceans of Rheinwein and Fernewein and even the great Heidelberg Tun had been laid under contribution…[49]

In Irving's case, however, the Heidelberg Tun was replete with wine. Jules Verne too references the Heidelberg Tun as a gauge of scale in *Five Weeks in a Balloon* where the company is landing on the beach at Zanzibar:

> They had there fixed upon a convenient spot close to the signal station, near to an enormous [tower] that sheltered them from the east wind. This immense tower, like a tun standing on one end, and compared to which the great tun of Heidelberg is but a small barrel, and was used as a fort, and upon the platforms Baloutchis, armed with lances, kept watch …[50]

Related to the Heidelberg Castle Wine Cellar, on Heidelberg's Haupstrasse at number 75 is a late-nineteenth century hotel and restaurant, the Perkeo Hotel and Kaffeehaus that celebrates Perkeo's celebrated story with a statue of him perched on the outside western corner of the old structure. Perkeo was born with dwarfism and his real name was Pankert Klemens. He became the town mascot and had an enormous appetite for wine. According to Heidelberg legend he was a connoisseur of wine, winning competitions as much for accuracy of identifying varietals as for consumption. Some say he was born Pancratio Clementi to Italian parents who worked in Germany's international immigrant wine-growing community for the Palatine royalty. His nickname Perkeo is also thought to have derived from his comical answer to everything, *perché, no?* ("Why not?"), especially when asked if he wanted another glass of wine. Prince Karl Philip III made Perkeo the Heidelberg Castle wine guardian, only part in jest, when he moved the court to Mannheim. Perkeo seemingly lived healthily into his eighties, and his legend says that he drank only wine—up to five or more gallons a day—until he became ill and his doctor prescribed water. After drinking the prescribed water, he died the next day. The corner statue depicts him in court uniform holding two of his symbols: a huge wine goblet and a large key, possibly to the castle wine cellar. The wine goblet is appropriately raised to his mouth.

Outside Heidelberg and the Neckar Valley in Baden-Württemberg state, the Badische Bergstrasse ("Baden's Mountain Road Region") has a mild climate—sometimes styled as Germany's Riviera—with many days of sunshine promoting viticulture on the steep slopes, including not only white grapes like the expected Riesling, Sylvaner, and Pinot Blanc but also red grapes of Pinot Noir. It is likely these Baden wine districts were started by the Romans as they migrated north along the Rhine River. While local tradition asserts medieval viticulture since the 8th century, the 12th century Lorsch Codex (*Codex Laureshamensis*), in a historic Carolingian minuscule text, documents vineyards here in the Rhein-Neckar region.

One of the local wineries just south of Heidelberg is the Clauer family's shell-rich limestone parcel of 15 hectares producing Riesling, Pinot Blanc, but also taking advantage of sunnier warmth to grow Pinot Noir. In addition, Clauer produces Rivaner (Müller-Thurgau), Pinot Meunier, Chardonnay, and the rare St. Laurent, among others, all from their own Heidelberg vineyards. But another wine region beckons upriver in Alsace, now part of France.

Strasbourg's Treasures

Southward beyond Heidelberg, well upriver along the Rhine in the Alsace, Strasbourg's cathedral towers over the medieval city of canals and nostalgic half-timbered buildings. This is one of the world's most sophisticated cities and a bookish haunt, for several decades home to pioneer printer Johannes Gutenberg whose bronze statue adorns the Place Gutenberg just at the terminus of the Rue Mercière viewing the cathedral portal at its most dramatic approach. Along the Ill River on St. Nicolas Quai very near St. Nicolas Church, I noticed the home of Sebastien Brant (1457–1521), Renaissance Humanist and satirist author in 1494 of *Ship of Fools (Das Narrenschiff)*. He wrote in the style of the biblical Proverbs and drew from Rome poets like Ovid, Juvenal, and Martial. It was illustrated in woodcuts by Durer, among others, and soon painted by Hieronymus Bosch (ca. 1500 and now in the Louvre). Having an original illustrated woodcut from the 1494 satire makes me appreciate Brant all the more.

Although Brant praised Bordeaux, "*Burdeus* has store of wine" and recommended several wines like *Muscadell* (Muscadelle/Moscato) and *Malvesy* (Malvasia/Malmsey), here are a few snippets from Brant's *Ship of Fools* lampooning the world: "Many are those who counsel craftily and show peril that may come to others' sins, but themselves they counsel not: no remedy," "Some look with an angel's countenance, or sad and sober like a hermet… thus hiding their misgovernance." Brant's *Ship of Fools* was influential on Erasmus in his 1509 *In Praise of Folly (Stultitiae Laus)* and the two Humanists knew each other, including from Erasmus' visit to Strasbourg and possibly Brant's visit to Antwerp.

Not all of the city's treasures are literary or historical, but these go well in Strasbourg with other highlights. No folly but instead highly recommended in Strasbourg's famed gastronomy is the perfect pairing of

Fig 9.6 Strasbourg Foie Gras and Mosbach Gewurztraminer 2010

Fig 9.7 Gerard Metz Gewurztraminer Vendages
Tardives

its light *foie gras* and far lighter Alsatian Gewürztraminer. Trying this feat twice in one day—necessarily followed in my case by cycling along the canals to attempt diluting the bloodstream cholesterol—is a huge temptation to which one can easily succumb. In the Place de la Cathédrale (Müensterplatz), the elegant medieval (begun in 1427) restaurant-hotel Maison Kammerzell offered an excellent but not heavy slab of *foie gras* with Gewürz gel and red peppercorns on toast and a green glass of Alsatian *Mosbach 2010 Gew*ürztraminer from Marlenheim, a lunch I couldn't refuse. Just to make sure the pairing deserved its praise, I had a similar second Strasbourg lunch in the Petite France Tanner's District at the chic La Corde à Linge Restaurant in the Place Benjamin Zix. Only slightly extravagant but mostly guiltless, the savory Strasbourg *foie gras* was just as good but this time the bibendum was an even better, a late-harvest Alsatian *Domaine Gérard Metz Gew*ürztraminer Vendages *Tardives* from Itterswiller at the foot of the Vosges Mountains.

To speak only of the gastronomic wealth of the area would be a grave omission, but these products no doubt provided some of the flow of capital to a region also rich in art. A brief word about Strasbourg's Gothic Cathedral (Nôtre Dame de Strasbourg) includes that it was built over a Roman sanctuary in the then-town of *Argentoratum*; later buildings on the site were a gold- and gem-decorated Carolingian church where St. Remigius was buried. The present cathedral also has some of the most beautiful stained glass windows in the world, especially the thirteenth century "Emperor" windows with brilliant secondary colors including the green, purple, and orange more typical for German-crafted hues than medieval French primary colors such as red and blue. Like the rest of the cathedral constructed out of pinkish-red sandstone, the cathedral's north tower pinnacle (circa 1439) was for centuries (1647–1874) the highest in the world at 466 feet, and its 19th c. astronomical clock right of the apse is one of the most precise in history—practically a computer telling equinoxes, leap year, etc.—and along with mythological and zodiacal features, also has a parade of unusual mechanical figures like an hourglass and death figure as well as Christ and the Apostles passing in front of him. Goethe said of this cathedral, "The more I contemplate the façade of the Cathedral, the more I am convinced of my first impression that its loftiness is linked to its beauty." Elsewhere he said it is a "sublimely towering, wide-spreading tree of God."

Colmar

Also in Alsace not far southwest of Strasbourg—about 40 miles—is Colmar, rightly hailed as the City of Art, with "la Petite Venise" canals connecting to the Louch River, a Rhine tributary, and one of the best surviving late-medieval old towns in Europe. Colmar was also the next lovely amble—where I had a glass of Alsace Riesling from nearby Wintzenheim with local Alsatian Bargkass cheese, a tasty combination—in the covered market right before seeing the birth house and statue of artist Martin Schongauer (1448–91) at the Dominican Church. Schongauer's 15th century house is in the old town across from the more picturesque Maison Pfister, and his statue is outside the old 13th century Dominican Church, home to his delicate International Gothic Style 1473 masterpiece *La Vierge au buisson de roses;* the old Dominican Church is now a museum. Schongauer was much admired by Albrecht Dürer, who learned this predecessor's pioneering cross-hatching technique, developing into his own signature style for his famous woodcuts and prints. Colmar is also home to the incredible 1506–15 Isenheim Altarpiece of Mathias Grünewald (c. 1470–1528) in the Unterlinden Museum.

Wines of Alsace

Alsace has been long justly associated with the better Gewürztraminers, derived from the Traminer grape—grown in Alsace since the Middle Ages—adding the descriptive *gewürz* as "spiced," or better "perfumed." Sadly, this wine is often unjustly maligned by snobby "connoisseurs" as made for plebeian palates, deemed over the top for being too heady and richly exotic in both flavor and rosy-lychee fragrance, let alone risible for its pink-hued grape. Late-harvest Gewürztraminers, however, are far more serious wines, not to be dismissed so easily. Broadbent, among many others, has long praised Alsace for its storied wines, especially since World War II—as fascinatingly told in the delightful Kladstrup book *Wine and War,*[51] which I brought along for great reading on this Rhine journey—and Broadbent lists great vintages from famous Alsatian wine dynasties like the Hugel Family and others like Trimbach and Schlumberger, all recognized globally.[52]

Based in Riquewihr north of Colmar in Alsace, the Hugel & Fils family firm has been officially making highly crafted Alsatian wine since at least 1639, although they were known in Riquewihr for centuries earlier. Their Grand Cru Schoenenbourg or Sporen estates have produced many acclaimed *Hugel & Fils Riesling Vendage Tardive* wines (e.g., 1988, 1989, 1995–98, 2001) or *Hugel & Fils Gewürztraminer Vendage Tardive* wines (e.g., 1991, 1997, 2000), both worth every penny. The Hugel Family even drafted the current laws for late harvest in Alsace.

Also in Alsace, equally venerable and even a decade older is the Trimbach House founded in 1626 in Ribeauvillé north of Riquewihr and Colmar. Their *Trimbach Riesling Cuvée*

Frédéric Emile Vendages Tardives (1976, 1983, 1989) and their *Trimbach Gewürztraminer Vendanges Tardives* (1997, 2003, 2005) are exceptional at any price. In 1898, Frédéric Emile Trimbach won the coveted Diplôme d'Honneur at the Bruxelles Concours International, and the Trimbachs have been holding equal court since. The small Clos St-Hune vineyard of Trimbach—entirely Riesling—in Ribeauvillé is often praised as the "Romanee-Conti of Alsace." Chef Christopher Hache at Les Ambassadeurs, Hotel Crillon in Paris, pairs the Trimbach *Riesling Cuvée Frédéric Emile 2005 Vendage Tardive* with crab, and lobster would also be an ideal match.

Domaine Schlumberger was founded in Guebwiller, Alsace in 1810 between Colmar and Muhlhausen, although the family settled in Guebwiller in the 16th century. Schlumbeger's 100 or so hectares of vineyards have produced superb wine since, especially continuing the traditions of the wealthy old Benedictine Murbach Abbey that established viticulture here for a millennium. Schlumberger's "Princes Abbés" cuvées honor that monastic Alsatian winemaking tradition, like their *Domaines Schlumberger 2008 Les Princes Abbés Riesling* produced from their Grand Cru vineyards in Saering, Kessler, and Kitterlé and also from near Bollenberg. Their wines are sought after and often rated in the 90's by *Wine Spectator* and *Wine Enthusiast*, among others.

Other Alsace vineyards of note include Zind-Humbrecht in Turckheim on the Route de Colmar, especially for their Gewürztraminers. The Humbrecht family has been making wine since 1620 and they joined in viticultural vigor with the Zind family in 1959, now producing from 40 hectares across several vineyards, mostly in Turckheim (18 hectares) and Wintzenheim (8.3 hectares) but also one parcel of 5.5 hectares considerably farther south in Thann and another parcel of 6.2 hectares as far north as Hunawihr, below Ribeauvillé. The Zind-Humbrecht Gewürztraminers have been consistently impressive over years of high rankings for Alsatian wines at great prices.

North of Turckheim, on the Alsace Route du Vin is the Faller family's Domaine Weinbach Clos des Capucins under the Schlossberg, approaching the town of Kayserberg from the east where the town is tucked into a curved Vosges Valley. The Capuchin monks began building here in 1612 and the vineyard is a Grand Cru property, along with Furstentum. In addition to their late-harvest Rieslings and Gewürztraminers, Domaine Weinbach began to produce in 1983 a rare botrytized "nectar of nectars," Quintessence de Grains Nobles, but it is not made often and found only in fractions. If you can find *Domaine Weinbach Gewürztraminer Furstentum Quintessence de Grains Nobles Cuvée d'Or, Alsace Grand Cru,* a half bottle (375 ml) is said to be worth its weight in gold.

Wettolsheim Under the Vosges

Just south of Turckheim also in the foothills of the Vosges Mountains we had an Alsatian wine tasting at Wettolsheim for a Grands Vins d'Alsace experience. Although likely not as stratospheric as Hugel & Fils and Trimbach wines, Jacques Mann of Maison Wunsch et Mann, founded in 1763, are very good values for the money. They offered us a winetasting of *Alsatian 2011 Riesling, Alsatian 2010 Gewürztraminer*. Maison Wunsch et Mann proudly display a Gold Medal (Medaille d'Or) in 1994 at the Colmar Grand Concours des Vins d'Alsace for at least seven of their lots, and among others, a Silver Medal (Medaille d'Argent) at the Concours International for a world-class "Riesling du Monde" 2009 for their *Riesling 2007 Grand Cru Steingrubler*, grown on calcareous marl and sandstone and praised by Stevenson.[53] Another Wunsch et Mann Grand Cru is their *Pfersigberg Gewürztraminer*. Perhaps their best-regarded consistent wines are their

Fig 9.8 Wettolsheim Vineyards

Cuvée St. Remy Gewürztraminer and their Steingrubler Riesling. It is worth noting that in both Rheingau and Alsace, the goal is for a low yield of fruit to make the highest quality wines. The Riesling wines Jacques Mann offered certainly filled that high distinction with their dry, crisp acidity. Jacques finished our tasting with a Crémant d'Alsace traditional méthode champenoise sparkling wine. I wandered through the vineyards before leaving, and since it was mid-April, much enjoyed the burst of a sea of red and yellow tulips in the garden. Looking up into the Vosges forest far up the vineyard slope, I wondered how long it would take me to walk into the forest and over the hill until I came down to the vineyards of the Walbach and Zimmerbach villages on the other side.

A few last cultural rather than solely viticultural comments for Rhine contexts, especially places like Strasbourg and Rüdesheim. As the enterprising Romans moved north, bringing vines with them that would adapt to the climate and terrain, they brought civilizing arts, numeracy, and literacy that would leave indelible

Fig 9.9 Wunsch et Mann Winery Door, Wettolsheim

impressions. Despite the lapse of many of the benefits of stability after the Romans left, including a vital economy, the memory of a better time lingered. With renewed viticulture in the Middle Ages came renewed health and trade.

Fig 9.10 Mosel Selbach-Oster 2003
Zeltinger Sonnenuhr 2003
Auslese Riesling

A few other Strasbourg and Rüdesheim residents and visitors deserve note. An antiquarian himself, Goethe was a student at the famed Strasbourg University during one of its German periods and later Louis Pasteur was a professor of chemistry at the university (now the medical school here is named after him). Here too, Albert Schweitzer studied theology and played Bach's profound organ music. Mozart played St. Thomas Church's Silbermann organ in Strasbourg in 1778. Naturally, I was thrilled to visit a vintage secondhand bookseller in Strasbourg's Place Kleber where I purchased a weathered centuries-old leather-bound biography of Mozart, wondering if he had wandered somewhere nearby himself in 1778. Rüdesheim was also a town beloved to Johannes Brahms, who loved to play new piano compositions here on frequent visits to the Rhine Valley, staying with the Beckerath family; there is consequently a Brahms chamber music festival, the Brahms-Tage, here at the Villa Sturm. Below Rüdesheim, of course, is the Gorge of Lorelei and Rhine Maidens made even more famous not just by Wagner but also by Heinrich Heine's lyrics. Thus it should be no surprise that Rhine wines easily accompany music and poetry, other cultural legacies in a place where Romans flourished and revived by the now-vanished but greatly influential court of Charlemagne, who advocated literacy and the arts that followed when the light of civilization blazed again out of Europe.

CHAPTER 10

Swiss Wine, Rhone to Rhine

"He drinks in vain that feels not the pleasure of it."
Rabelais, *Gargantua and Pantagruel*, Ch. 5

C onverse with almost any Swiss person about Swiss wine, and you should observe justifiable national or regional pride, since wine cultivation has been continuing nearly unbroken since the Roman era, nearly 2,000 years, especially around Geneva, Lausanne, and in the Rhone Valley and the upper Rhine Valley. The Romans also began planting grapes in the east in Raetia, and they were in the Rheintal by 13 BCE, building their main Rhine Valley road high above the river along the east side of the valley in Liechtenstein. Sections of this old Roman road now make up the princely *Furstenweg*. But due to several factors including the rugged montane topography and the resulting climate, Roman viticulture was not as extensive along the Rhine Valley in East Switzerland as it was in Western Swiss Rhone regions in what are now Vaud and Valais cantons.

As early as the Late Neolithic around 3000 BCE at St-Blaise in Neuchatel, surviving grape seeds from archaeological sites suggest either consumption or production of wine.[54] Much later after Celtic tribes occupied the region but before the Romans, in the Upper Rhone Valley near Gamsen, grape seeds were found from the La Tène period (450–50 BCE). The earliest ceramic wine "jug" dating to the 2nd c. BCE was found in a lady's tomb south of Martigny near Sembrancher where the Great-St-Bernard Pass route begins its ascent. Later the Romans brought varietals for viticulture and the local Amigne, Arvine, and Humagne varietals grown in Switzerland today probably derive from old Roman parent stock.

While the Swiss today prefer 70% red wine to 30% white wine, they produce only 44% red and 56% white, so the rest of the red wine must be imported to augment their own production. In fact, of their total red wine consumption, they import 74% of additional red wines from Italy, France, Spain, and the New World; likewise for their total white wine consumption, they import 72% of additional white wines. This does not mean premium wines are not produced in Switzerland, because Swiss vineyards yield exceptional local wines as well. The top wine-producing regions in Switzerland are Valais, accounting for almost half of Swiss wines; next is Vaud, accounting for over a third of Swiss wines; Ticino (or Tessin in German) is next with around ten to fifteen percent of Swiss wines; the rest of Swiss wine production is made up of wine regions between Geneva and Neuchatel in the west, and between Zurich and the Rhine Valley in the east.

Valais Canton

The Canton of Valais, also known as Wallis in its eastern German language part, is Switzerland's largest wine region and most Swiss folk there will also affirm Valais is home to their country's best wines. The French name Valais derives from the "Valley" of the Rhone River, a deep glacially carved valley where the river runs mostly west until it bends north around Martigny, ultimately flowing into Lake Geneva in the Canton of Vaud before finally flowing west and south through France into the Mediterranean. Valais wines are either grown on steep south-facing slopes or along the valley floor, and the fairly sheltered location of Valais surrounded by high Alps on two sides gives it a moderate climate relative to other alpine regions of Switzerland, enhanced again by the warming *foehn* wind from Italy. The main wine region of Valais follows the Rhone River westward from Visp to Martigny, and then a smaller, higher viticultural portion of Valais vineyards are found along the south-facing slopes of the Dranse streams near Sembrancher before they flow into the Rhone at Martigny.

Viticulture in Valais has a long history. Historically, the Valais was first Romanized after the Battle of Octodurus in 57 BCE when the 12th legion under Julius Caesar's legate Servius Galba fought local Celtic tribes (Veragri, Aedui, Seduni) in an attempt to open up the Great-St-Bernard pass to Roman traffic. Octodurus was an old Celtic name for what is now Martigny. The Romans, however, did not successfully begin to colonize the Valais until the Salassi tribe, who controlled the southern approach to the pass, was vanquished in 25 BCE. Until the Emperor Claudius, around 50 CE Octodurus was renamed *Forum Claudii Vallensium*, the "Forum of Claudius in the Valley." The town of Martigny today has many Roman archaeological finds and an underlying Roman town.[55] One of the most interesting Roman structures in Martigny is an underground Claudian-period (mid-first century CE) wine cellar discovered and excavated by the Cantonal archaeologist Dr. François Wiblé, evidence of at least strong appreciation for wine and possibly for viticulture, since some of Europe's oldest varietals also have their home here in the Valais, as mentioned. These include the varietals Amigne, Arvine, and Humagne Rouge (also known as Cornalin in Valais). I have been most fortunate to taste local modern Valais wine in Martigny with François Wiblé in this same Roman wine cellar for almost a decade, often wondering about the original Roman wine stewards and what was in this wine cellar two millennia past.

Valais has over 5,300 hectares of vineyards, and while white wine is made in its many independent wineries, especially Chasselas—but going under the name of Fendant in Valais[56]—it is the red wine like Pinot Noir first and Gamay second that Valais produces most. The high concentration of red wine made in Valais—40% of all Swiss red wine—is matched only by the Canton of Ticino's more than 1,000 hectares of Merlot, but this is more in percentage rather than in volume since Ticino produces mostly Merlot red wine. Other Valais red varietals include Gamay as well as Diolinoir—another hybrid created in Switzerland in 1970 by crossing *Rouge de Diolly* and Pinot Noir. Two other Valais red hybrids originating from Gamay include Gamaret, a 1970 Swiss hybrid of Gamay and Reichensteiner, and Garanoir, a lighter version of Gamaret, also from 1970. One additional Valais red hybrid that flourishes in these Rhone vineyards is called Dole, a hybrid of Pinot Noir and Gamay.[57] What the Swiss of Valais call Ermitage is the white Hermitage Marsanne grape of France. The highest-altitude vineyards in Switzerland are in the German-speaking part of Valais on the south side of the Rhone River valley above Visp in the alpine village of Visperterminen, whose old houses are mostly wood and stone. Here west-facing white wine vineyards range around 4,750 feet in altitude. Here can be found the idiosyncratic late-ripening white Savagnier varietal, known in German as the Heida or Paien grape, especially seen in the *St. Jodern Kellerei Heida 2011* wine of Visperterminen.

In the middle of Valais, the Rhone River flows past Sion, another wine haven with its twin hills whose double castles of Valère and Tourbillon rise above the town, the latter mostly a ruin. The Château de Valère has one of the oldest playable organs in the world from 1435. I heard an organ concert there of Renaissance music in the Nôtre-Dame de Valère basilica in 1994. Climbing the steep Valère hill on foot through cobblestone streets will also provide a splendid view of the vineyards surrounding Sion from the castle, especially looking north and west. Sion is named Sitten in German and was the chief town of the Celtic tribe of the Seduni, which gave its Roman name of *Sedunum*. But Sion is far older—its settlements go back to the late Mesolithic around 6200 BCE around the hill's rocky outcrops, with Neolithic farming much earlier than 5000 BCE and the prehistoric necropolis at Le Petit Chasseur, one of the oldest in Europe with megalithic stones from around 3000 BCE. Excellent wines from Sion include the white *Domaine du Mont d'Or Johannisberg Saint Martin 2010* from Domaine du Mont d'Or just west of the town in Conthey and Domaine Cornulus in Savièse above Sion and Diolly on the north slope, especially the *Domaine Cornulus Cabernet Franc Antica 2011* as well as the *Provins Valais Sion Domaine Tourbillon 2009*, a *grain noble*-botrytized late-harvest wine that will easily keep until 2030, made from the Ermitage grape.

Other great award-winning vineyards in Valais include those of Vétroz, Chamosan, Flanthey, Salgesch, Riddes, Le Bioley, Leytron, Nax, Susten, and Sierre. The Grand Prix du Vin Suisse 2012 is well represented in Valais. The pinnacle of these Swiss awards are the Grand Prix du Vin Suisse 2012 Gold Medal winners, including the white *Maître de Chais Petite Arvine de Fully Valais 2011* and the white *Jean-René Germanier Amigne de Vétroz 2011*. The other awarded whites include the *Jean-René Germanier Fendant Balavaud Grand Cru 2011* from Vétroz; the *Cave Nouveau Saint Clément Saint-Léonard 2011* from Flanthey; the *Cave du Crêtacombe Johannisberg Elevé en Amphore 2011* from Chamoson; the *Fernand Cina Petite Arvine Vieilles Vignes 2011* from Salgesch; the *Domaine des Muses Fendant Classique 2010* from Sierre; the *Cave le Tambourin Petite Arvin 2011* from Corin-sur-Sierre; and the Vins des Chavaliers SA Chevalier Blanc 2010 from Salgesch. The awards for rosé include the *Alexis Jacquérioz SA Rosé de Gamay de Martigny 2011* from Martigny. The award-winning reds of Valais noted in the Grand Prix di Vin Suisse 2012 include the *Les Fils Maye Pinot Noir Clos de Balavaud Grand Cru Vétroz 2011* from Riddes; the *Caves des Deux Rives Gamay de Vétroz 2011* from Le Bioley/Brignon; the *Cave du Paradou Gamay*

2011 from Nax; the *Cave la Fournaise Gamay Senteur d'Eté 2011* from Veyras; and the *Gilbert Devayes Merlot 2009* from Leytron.[58]

I love cycling in this steep Rhone River valley around Martigny and have done more than a few circling routes since 1995. I find in summer that it is best to start westward in the morning around Sion because the wind is at your back and returning east in the afternoon, again with a tailwind. The wind changes direction as the Rhone River valley heats up. From the opposite direction around Martigny it's not as easy because it will be a strong headwind going east in the morning and then a possible stronger headwind returning to the west in the afternoon, but cycling through vineyards is especially rewarding when you can add a wine tasting, as I try whenever possible. From Martigny, the Rue de Guercet (becoming the Rue des Villages and then the Rue des Marroniers) on the south side of the valley takes a cyclist through several vineyard and fruit-growing villages, for example, the village of Charrat grows Gewürztraminer grapes along the Rhone valley's south side. There is also a possible dégustation stop for something stronger like Eau-de-Vie à l'Abricot at Princesse Valaisanne in Charrat, since the Martigny region is famous for apricots and the liqueur *abricotin*. Turning left at Avenue de la Gare by bicycle through Charrat-les-Chenes, this road becomes Route de la Gare. Following it, one crosses over the E62 autoroute, then by bridge over the Rhone River to Fully. South-facing Fully is one of the best Valais wine towns with vineyards scaling the slopes on the north side of the valley, taking as much possible advantage of the sun. There are plenty of wine-tasting (*dégustation*) prospects by bicycle in Fully, not the least of which is the Cave du Chavalard. Returning to Martigny by bicycle through vineyards along the Route de Carre and the Avenue de Fully is a rewarding short trip, especially if "bicycle wine dégustations" give the legs time out between negotiating the steep hills of Valais.

Vaud Canton

As mentioned, Roman presence in the West in what is now Vaud was established early, by the end of the first century BCE around Geneva (Roman *Genava*) and Lausanne (Roman *Lousanna* and by 400 CE *Civitas Lousanna*) after the Romans conquered the Helvetian Gauls (Celts) in 58 BCE and set up the *Civitas Helvetiorum* to the north at Avenches (*Aventicum*) in 27 BCE. In addition to their towns at Lausanne and Vevey (*Viveticum*), Roman colonization along Lake Geneva is easily confirmed at places Nyon as well, only 15 miles northeast along Lake Geneva from Geneva. Nyon was called *Colonia Julia Equestris* by the Romans by 45 BCE—reflecting that it was a Julian colony—and like many other towns begun by Gauls, its Gaulish or Celtic name of *Noviodunum* retained the word *dunum*, an old Celtic word for "fort," plus *novio* for "new" before abbreviation in this case to Nyon, its modern name.

One of the best-known medieval wine contexts in Switzerland was at the Cistercian abbey of Montheron north of Lausanne, begun in 1135. The Cistercians found that Switzerland's mountainous topography limited the amount of grapevines that could be sustained in the general climate. As a result they began to plant very steep vineyards above Lake Geneva at Lavaux, southeast of Lausanne about seven miles where the lakeside slope can be nearly vertical. Single vine rows are grown in terraces called *tablars* where some of

Fig 10.1 Lavaux Vaud

the slope is cut out and the base filled up to extend arable terraced land. This continuing viticulture context is also greatly enhanced—like the Mosel River contexts in Germany—by the sunlight reflecting off Lake Geneva that helps to ripen the grapes on their steep slopes.

These honored Lavaux vineyards still produce of some of the best Swiss wines. The current appellation of Dézaley in Lavaux covers 54 hectares and mostly produces wine from the white Chasselas grape and the Lavaux appellation is given the rare Grand Cru status along with its steep neighbor Calamin, although this status refers to the terroir and not the wine from it. The verticality is almost dizzying here if you walk between the single rows and the expense of producing wine per acre is staggering (over $25,000) because so much is done by hand since little to no mechanization is possible with the verticality of the parcels. This location is also intensely picturesque with the breathtaking views of Lake Geneva and beyond to the Alps. I've taken stunning photos of these vineyards on foot and from the train high up on the slope.

Other respected Vaud vineyard subregions include La Côte—meaning its lakeside venue of "the slope"—rich in alluvial gravels just above the city of Geneva and west of the steeper Lavaux and the subregion of Chablais along the eastern edge of

Fig 10.2 Chateau Aigle, Aigle, Chablais, Vaud

Fig 10.3 Fechy La Colombe
2011

Lake Geneva and south of the lake along the Rhone valley that runs north–south here where the Rhone River feeds into the lake. Because the cool subregion of Chablais is overshadowed by the tall mountain ranges of the Alps, it is more conducive to white wines and its soils have a high percentage of glacial moraine as this part of Vaud is clearly located in a classic U-shaped glacial valley. One of the more picturesque spots of Chablais is the wine village of Aigle with its dramatic Savoyard style mostly 12th century classic-walled castle overlooking the village, today housing the Vaud Wine Museum. The crisp and steely whites of Aigle are among my favorite whites, as I stop here every year to visit the wine museum and taste the esteemed *Aigle les Morailles Grand Vin* of Henri Badoux—famous for its lizard motif—en route to alpine fieldwork. Chasselas is the dominant Vaud wine varietal, planted in 2,345 hectares, almost 40% of all Swiss white wine produced.

Some of the best recent Vaud white wines include the *Clos des Abbayes Dézaley Grand Cru 2011,* a Chasselas from Puidou, Lavaux; the *Louis Bovard 'Louis Philippe Bovard' Calamin Grand Cru Ilex 2011,* a Chasselas from Calamin; the *Jean et Pierre Testuz Dézaley Grand Cru L'Arbalete 2010* a Chasselas from Puidou, Lavaux; and the *Domaine La Capitaine Begnins Pinot Gris Vendanges Tardives 2010* a Pinot Gris from Begnins. Vaud wines of note—both white and red—have also received recent prizes in the Grand Prix du Vin Suisse 2012 awarded for 2010–2011 vintages. These include the white *Féchy Grand Cru Domaine du Martheray 2011,* a Chasselas from Féchy, La Côte near Rolles, also a Gold Medal winner; the *Henri Badoux Aigle Lettres de Noblesse 2009*, a rare red blend of Cabernet Franc and Malbec from Aigle; and the *Artisans Vignerons d'Yvorne Varietas Vigne d'Or 2010*, an assemblage of whites from Yvorne.[59] These are just a few of the better Vaud wines in a great Swiss region.

Fête des Vignerons, Vevey

If there is a favorite national wine festival attracting a growing number of more than a million visitors—1999 for example—it is the famous Fête des Vignerons at Vevey in Vaud. Montreux's annual famous jazz festival is held only a few minutes away from Vevey, but Vevey along the Chablais coast of Lake Geneva is home to this summer festival that takes place only a maximum of five times in a century. The last one before 1999 was in 1977 and the next one won't be until 2019. The festival began in 1797, organized by the Confrérie des Vignerons de Vevey (Fraternity of the Vignerons of Vevey) and while most of it centers on the huge Market Square of Vevey by the lake, it also overflows into the town. A large stage area seating 16,000 contains some of the formal organized events, if you dare call a bacchanale formal and organized.

The Fête des Vignerons is also an opportunity to masquerade, since many of the official participants perform in parades, concerts, and revues, some even raucous. Here one can see Bacchus, Silenus, Ceres, Proserpina, and other viticultural myth history characters in intensely colorful, flamboyant costumes in scores of enactments as up to 5,000 official costumed Swiss performers took part in 1999, even orchestras in colorful garb. At Vevey the wine and mirth flow so freely the Swiss, too often thought conservative by others, can hardly be accused of being stodgy, especially during this uninhibited height of summer party that lasts weeks (July 29 to August 15 in 1999) and draws many visitors from surrounding countries as well.

I went in 1999 with an adolescent daughter who first tried to ditch me quickly until she realized we could have more fun together and not just because I was the bank. Everyone was outrageously dressed and I purchased a huge hat that was shaped like a wine barrel even with a small wooden spigot. It blazoned out *Cuvée 1999* and I still have it hanging in my home wine cellar. I wore it during the festival and no one gave me a second look when we ate at the many food stalls or watched dances and performances. In fact, in some of the Vevey events all the visitors can dance as well to a variety of music genres, and if you can catch the big character roles like Bacchus, you might just snag a photo with one or more of them draped around you. My same daughter—who now lives in Switzerland—has since borrowed this Vevey Fête des Vignerons hat more than once for her costume parties.

Swiss Hybrids and Other Varietals

Swiss enologists and botanists have hybridized quite a few hardy varietals for the Rhine region along with other Swiss climatic conditions overshadowed by the Alps, often with considerable rain and frost. André Jaquinet of the Station Fédérale de Recherches en Production Végétale at Changins is responsible for several of these new hybrids. The enology unit at Changins-Wädenswil is part of Agroscope, the Swiss Federal Research Office for Agriculture, and Jaquinet is following the footsteps of the famous enologist Dr. Hermann Müller of Thurgau (1850–1927), the first director of the Swiss unit at Wädenswil. Müller was a pioneer in wine cultivation after whom the worldwide varietal is named since he introduced it in 1882 by crossing Riesling and Madeleine Royal (not Sylvaner). Now over 41,000 hectares (over 100,000 acres) of Müller-Thurgau are cultivated worldwide in mostly cool climates as well as here in the upper Rhine valley.[60]

Another Swiss varietal, Chasselas, may be indigenous. As mentioned, in the Valais it is called Fendant but in the German-speaking eastern half of Switzerland, Chasselas is known instead as Gutedel.[61] Further north around Zurich and grown around the lake, several indigenous Swiss varietals are grown for wine, notably the red Clevner and white Räuschling. Clevner is another older German name for Pinot Noir. While hardly grown today, Räuschling is an old German Traminer vine also known to the Renaissance German vocabulary as *Drutsch* from Hieronymus Bock's (1498–1554) *Kreutterbuch* (Herbal). Räuschling's name may derive from the "rustling" of its leaves in wind because its sturdy thick-leaved foliage is heavy.

In the Rhine Valley between the Swiss cantons of St. Gallen and Graubünden, wine production is small but choice. As is true of Swiss viticulture in general, the best wines of the Rheintal are produced on south-facing slopes rather along the Rhine Valley floor. In fact, it is rare to see any vineyards in the Rheintal or Graubünden anywhere but on these south-facing slopes.

Fig 10.4 Bundner Herrschaft Vineyards

Bündner Herrschaft in Graubünden Canton

Near where two Swiss cantons meet—St. Gallen and Graubünden (or Grisons)—just beyond the border of Liechtenstein and the massive Stockwald limestone ridge that the Rhine River bends around, the small Swiss wine district of the Bündner Herrschaft is nestled in a south-facing curve at the base of the Alps on the east side of the Rhine directly across from the spa town of Bad Ragaz. Above these vineyards the rocky crags of Falknis, Grausptiz, Glegghorn, and Vilan tower over this sheltered valley. At the very top of the range of peaks is Naalkopf, the snowy peak

Fig 10.5 Schloss Salenegg, Maienfeld

that marks the boundary between Liechtenstein, Switzerland, and Austria. Far below and set back on the alluvial talus ledge along the Rhine River, hill vineyards stretch between five villages, the *Fünf Dörfer* of which four are viticulturally important: Fläsch is at the northern arc of the vineyards, and the village of Maienfeld is in the middle, next is Jenins, and last is Malans at the southern end of the viticultural arc.

These are famous Pinot Noir vineyards in the Bündner Herrschaft, but the varietal is mainly known here as *Blauburgunder*, one of the other German names for Pinot Noir.[62] Many other varietals are grown here in the warmest region of German-speaking Switzerland, but Blauburgunder makes up almost 80% of the plantings. The town of Maienfeld is also famous for being the home of Johanna Spyri (1827–1901), author of *Heidi,* so the area is also often called by locals as "Heidiland." Schloss Brandis in Maienfeld lies in the heart of the wine area, and since a pre-Roman cellar was discovered here, it is even possible that local viticulture started under the Celts. With its medieval village under

Fig 10.6 Rutishauser 2009 Pinot Noir Maienfeld

the mountains, Maienfeld is extremely picturesque. In addition to the 13th century castle, Schloss Brandis, in the village center and the nearby Rathaus with its octagonal tower and painted walls, its old buildings include Schloss Salenegg on its northern edge, the latter surrounded by vineyards above and below the 18th century castle. Driving or cycling around Maienfeld is enhanced by tasting its wines while in the village. I found an amazing Rutishauser Maienfeld Bündner Banner 2009 Pinot Noir from Rutishauser Weingut im Herrenfeld to be the perfect companion for a family dinner here. The elegant restaurant in Schloss Brandis is also justifiably famous for its gourmandaise cuisine.

Many have mistaken these Bündner Herrschaft wines for Premier Cru Côte d'Or Burgundies, especially the wine of Chambolle-Musigny, not just because of the Pinot Noir grape but also because of the partly calcareous geology and the warming *foehn* wind from Italy. One famous local wine is even called "Herrschäftler." The late-September harvest festival in Bündner Herrschaft is called the *Herbstfest*, a lively celebration rotated among these four wine villages.

The Grand Prix du Vin Suisse 2012 awarded for 2010–2011 vintages include several prizes for the wines of Bündner Herrschaft. These include several white wine awards: to Weingut Von Salis of Landquart for the *Von Salis Malanser Riesling-Sylvaner 2011*, to Weingut Davaz of Fläsch for the *Davaz Fläsch Riesling-Sylvaner 2011,* and to Weingut Treib (Ueli and Jürg Liesch) of Malan for the *Treib Malanser Chardonnay 2010*. The red wine Blauburgunder

Fig 10.7 Davaz Flasch Pinot Noir
2011

(Pinot Noir) prizes were to Weingut Davaz of Fläsch for the *Davaz Pinot Noir Grond 2010* and to Weingut Thomas Marugg of Fläsch for the *Thomas Marugg Pinot Noir Kruog Barrique 2010.*[63]

Hueb-Sax and the Sennwald of St. Gallen Canton

Although not as famous as the Bündner Herrschaft, another of the lovely Swiss wine districts is a little further north along the Rhine in the upper Rhine canton of St. Gallen, especially the Werdenberg region of eastern Switzerland near and across from the convergence of Austria and Liechtenstein. September 25, 2011 was the *Winzerfest*, the local Wine Festival in the village of upper Hueb-Sax, culminating with its grape harvest as well, and as

Fig 10.8 Brunner Hueb Sax

the grape leaves have been turning festive yellow and red colors, plenty of local wine flowed. These vineyards may be among the most photogenic in Switzerland any time of year—I've found this true in all four seasons, even in snowy winter—with panoramas that stretch across the valley to Liechtenstein's mountains, only a short distance away, and as I found, an easy ride by bicycle across the Rhine River. Feldkirch in Vorarlberg, Austria is tucked away just over the hill to the east. Back in Hueb-Sax again for Christmas, a local pointed out a rocky landmark in the Kreuzberg Range above the town. This vast triple peak and cliff promontory has been called the Angel of Sax for centuries, believed to be standing guard over the commune. After looking for several years, now every time I look up, I see the stone angel with outspread wings high overhead.

In late August 2011 while exploring old Roman roads in the region, I hiked along the Trübliweg southward between Frümsen and Sax, a road winding through the hills, through the Sennwald forest above the Rhine valley floor. The path curves along fragrant alpage grazing pastures all under these towering crags of the Kreuzberg. Cowbells sound out intermittently along with more regular local village church bells. The Hueb-Sax hillside vineyards undulate with the topography because the Swiss tend to use their land so carefully and efficiently, making every square meter count, and few vistas are as satisfying to my eyes as vineyards along hills. While the vineyards are not the dominant landscape feature here, they are nonetheless carefully managed and treasured as a precious resource.

Fig 10.9 Brunner Saxer Diolinoir

Hueb is the hamlet just above the village of Sax, where the road ascending has one of the meticulous vineyards of Herr Brunner, facing south toward far-off Italy and its occasional warm *foehn* wind from far beyond the cantons of St. Gallen and Graubünden, actually deriving from North Africa. Although any view of Italy is blocked by many interim ranges, its distant influence, however small, results in good wine for an alpine region. Brunner has won silver medals in the International Weinprämierungen for his whites, especially his Pinot Blanc, and also for his red *Blauburgunder*. Brunner wisely purchased south-facing hill property in 1981, planted vines two years later in 1983, and continued to expand until he now has 6,000 vines on 1.6 hectares (nearly 4 acres) and produces 10,000 bottles of wine. Nearby, above the town of Sax, are other vineyards and wineries as well, including the Rohner wine production.

Because the region can have good summer heat through early September, Brunner's red wines in addition to his prize-winning *Blauburgunder* also include his *Cabernet Cubin*, *Diolinoir*, and *Gamaret*. Brunner's whites include Sauvignon Blanc, Chardonnay, his prize-winning Pinot Blanc and Riesling Sylvaner. Both Brunner's and Rohner's Sax wines should be valued far beyond the 14–21 Swiss Francs. Brunner's Diolinoir 2009 is one of the silkiest Swiss red wines I've ever tasted, bursting with flavor and character, not at all a lightweight wine but instead superb with a truffle risotto and cheese or just by itself. The bottle I tasted over several days is from his Hemberg vineyard.

On a very warm August evening overlooking the Rhine Valley and Liechtenstein, we all indulged some of this Sax wine in a hillside garden in Hueb-Sax under the Kreuzberg, enjoying it with what may be the best *quarktort* in the world—certainly that evening—a regional dessert made by neighbor Lisel. The deliciously sweet *quarktort* was the perfect combination for balancing a local Sax white wine, Seyval Blanc 2008 (a hybrid often also named Seyve-Villard from some of its French origins, although also called Seibel). Summer warmth made this cooled local wine the most refreshing drink possible.

I also found to my delight that both Goethe and James Joyce appreciated this valley in their travels for varying reasons. Joyce came through this upper Rhine Valley multiple times and has a famous plaque in the nearby train station of Feldkirch, thankful his *Ulysses* was spared in 1915[64]; likewise Goethe has a commemorative plaque in nearby Vaduz, Liechtenstein, from a layover visit in 1788. I do not know if Goethe or Joyce tasted local wines around here, but as they were both fond of good wine, I feel certain they would have enjoyed a foray here at least as much as I have on multiple occasions. From a Christmas visit here, I also suspect Bruegel's 1565 haunting and majestic painting *Hunters in the Snow* has the Hueb-Sax village as a source for at least part of its landscape topography, since he came through this stretch of the Rhine valley in 1553 en route to Rome.[65] For anyone wanting to saturate the senses and the soul with beauty, I heartily recommend a summer Upper Rhine Valley cycling or hiking trip in the Werdenberg region along the Trübliweg (for wine tasting, it's recommended to call Herr Brunner first.[66] Our 2012 alpine archaeology project stayed here in Brunner's Torkel for a week, also bicycling between Switzerland and Liechtenstein across the Rhine River from Sargans to Gothenberg Castle and back to study the age of medieval lichens.

A Swiss wine visit would be my favorite culminating point for the Werdenberg or Bündner Herrschaft, bits of paradise, especially around Hueb-Sax or Maienfeld. The Swiss surely know how to live well in this remarkably beautiful land. As Goethe said in his *Wanderers Nachtlied*, "Über allen Gipfeln ist Ruh," "Over all the mountaintops is peace."

CHAPTER 11

French Bordeaux, Burgundy, and Côte du Rhône Wine Treasures

"It is the wine that makes me talk in this way; wine will make even a wise man fall to singing; it will make him chuckle and dance and say many a word that he had better leave unspoken." Homer, *Odyssey* XIV.463 ff.[67]

France is the wine capital of the world, and many of the world's wines are still mere copies of the grand wines of France. Partly because the French and their lands have been continuously and strenuously engaged in viticulture and the making of good wine for millennia, the rest of the world will be playing catch-up for some time. Whether or not France has the best *terroirs* is another point altogether and not my turf, but the French have been carefully matching their varietals to land longer than anyone else. In keeping with this book, this single chapter does not attempt to be the least bit comprehensive about French wine—others do that much better—nor does it cover many of France's excellent appellations. It only considers a very few regions and somewhat reflectively at that where my own wine journeys have meandered by car, bicycle, train or even on foot, or where I have been lucky to share in dégustations of memorable French wine.

For the sensory side of this—remembering Samuel Johnson's 1755 *Dictionary* where he defines *gustation* as "the act of tasting,"[68] there is an active part to tasting wine in *dégustation* that often requires the literal context of France all around the full experience, sometimes mysteriously unable to be fully captured in places not French. Because taste is the most intimate and personal of all senses and must be the ultimate one engaged, perhaps it is best where the nearby vineyard is part of the tasting in sight, smell, hearing and touch, where the earth itself mothers its wines. I know, this is metaphysically suspect when it comes to tasting French wine, but I try to be in France as often as possible—at least once annually since 1986 when in graduate school—because the perception of mystique is palpable in a land where nuance and subtlety are inextricably bred into all things French. For sure, there is a bit of French blood flowing through my veins and French is my *deuxième langue* but I confess I also love the wines of Bordeaux, Côte du Rhône, and Burgundy because I love the places and people that nurture them.

Bordeaux in Literature

In medieval French literature, *Huon of Bordeaux* is a famous chanson de geste epic with romance elements from around 1240. It influenced many later writers, including Spenser and Shakespeare, and has itself borrowed from the labors of Herakles, among other myths. In the tale, Huon, the young duke of Bordeaux, has killed a son of Charlemagne and must do penance by traveling to Babylon and performing three ordeals, ultimately with both the help and hindrance of Oberon, the fairy king. Oberon has a magic horn called Gloriande endowed by three fairy ladies on the isle of Cafalone, one of whom gifted the horn Gloriande with the magic ability to overcome famine and thirst by wishing to be satisfied:

as though he had drunken his fill of the best wine in all the world.[69]

No doubt the connection between Bordeaux in medieval Gascoigne and wine connoisseurship was already established;[70] even if magic elements are necessary in the above medieval tale of Huon, the real magic of early Bordeaux wine transcended this epic.

Geoffrey Chaucer's father and grandfather were wine merchants; his father even deputy to the king's butler, and at that time Gascony was the best source for wine.[71] The poet of *Canterbury Tales* also received a royal wine stipend, so Chaucer should be expected to recount about wine, as he does in "The Merchant's Tale" where the old knight bolstered himself for amor: "He drank of claret, hippocras, vernage, all spiced and hot to heighten his love's rage." Given the date of England's links to Gascony, Chaucer's "claret" is certainly wine from Bordeaux, whereas "hippocras" was a mulled wine with mostly sugar and cinnamon (similar to modern holiday *glühwein*), and "vernage" was the white Vernaccia most likely of Tuscany.

Although not necessarily about Bordeaux, Rabelais, who celebrated wine as much as any other, joked about the hundred-handed Greek mythological monster, "A butler should have (like Briareus) a hundred hands wherewith to fill us wine indefatigably."[72] Elsewhere, Rabelais has this excerpt of a dialogue between Pantagruel and Friar John:

"Hercules wished to slake the thirst he had acquired while crossing the deserts of Libya ..."

"God's truth!" said Friar John ... "I have heard from several reverend theologians that Tirelupin, butler to your noble father Gargantua, sets aside more than eighteen hundred pipes of wine yearly to make servants and visitors drink before they are thirsty."

"True," said Pantagruel. "But back to Hercules, he did what camels and dromedaries of a caravan do; they drink to slake past, present and future thirst."[73]

Rabelais also tells of Epistemon's visit to Hell before being brought back to life after a battle. In Hell, the peripety of life, everything is reversed: glorious heroes are mere churls and work at mundane tasks. There in Rabelais is Huon of Bordeaux again after his penitent

adventures in Babylon and with the Turks, now reduced to being a cooper who mends wine barrels
by adding their hoops.[74] Rabelais' amusing epic
about giants is no less entertaining about their
appetites.

Samuel Pepys (1633–1703), the London diarist
whose entries are informative about life, wrote a
bit about one particular Bordeaux wine, the first
mention of it. Pepys wrote for April 10, 1683, "Off
to the Exchange with Sir J Cutler and Mr Grand
to the Royall Oak Taverne in Lumbard Street…
and there drank a sort of French wine called
Ho Bryan, that hath a good and most particular
taste that I never met with." Not only is this the
first record of Château Haut-Brion wine, but
Cambridge University's Magdalene College,
Pepys' alma mater and inheritor of Pepys' library,
is commemorating this occasion with an April,
2013 event organized by the Cambridge Wine

Fig 11.1 Clos Fourtet 2000

Society, hoping to also have on hand the 1660 royal cellar book of Charles II since Joseph
Batailhe, wine merchant, supplied the king with 169 bottles of "Hobriono."[75] This is an apt
appropriation of the ancient symposium. Elsewhere Pepys recounts in his diary for August
21, 1666 how some sharp wine dealers in Bordeaux hired a man in a tavern to make so
much noise by pounding thunderously near where the wines were stored, that "saying this
thunder would spoil and turn them, which was so reasonable to the merchant that he did
abate two pistolls per ton for the wine, in belief of that."[76] According to the *Oxford English
Dictionary*, a *pistole* was a French gold coin *louis d'or* issued by Louis XIII in 1640,[77] which
meant a substantial reduction, but the idea of unsettling the wine by loud noise in order to
cheat the wine merchant made Pepys, who had a good cellar, even more unsettled.

Voltaire, whom all might expect to say something witty about the wine of Bordeaux,
famously called wine the "divine juice of September," which is high praise from a skeptic
who didn't believe in very much that was thought to be divine in his day. In *Candide* is the
fictional anecdote of Martin and Candide arriving from El Dorado with a red sheep, and
the Academy of Science of Bordeaux had a prize competition to see who could provide the
most rational explanation for the sheep wool color, although Voltaire only lampoons the
so-called logical process.[78] Elsewhere Voltaire says regarding climate that sacred mysteries could not be celebrated without wine and that climates too cold might not have such
ceremony and he also said regarding the abstinence of wine in the desert, "Mahomet would
not have forbidden wine in Switzerland, especially before going to battle."[79] Right or wrong,
Voltaire was no doubt reflecting how lucky was France.

While others might not consider it literary material, there are also true stories about
Bordeaux that need to be told from contemporary point of view. The Kladstrup book *Wine
and War*, already mentioned regarding Alsace, is a resource that is hard to put down, so full
of memories, many heart wrenching and some amusing, but all written with timeless craft.

Everyone who has visited the region or tasted Pauillac wine from legendary domains like Château Lafite-Rothschild and Château Mouton Rothschild knows the incredible standards there that have lasted for generations. The time of Nazi occupation, while hard on everyone, was particularly hard for the Rothschild families, given both the antipathy toward Jews and how greedy Nazi leaders were for these inimitable wines. Now the mystique continues for the wines of 1945 that defined a century but now almost completely gone, down to the last few cellared bottles.

The riveting Kladstrup narrative tells how immediately after the war in 1945 the small crop was nonetheless astonishing, like a miracle of hope that followed old French anecdotes about incredible vintages at the end of wars. Even when the Bordeaux fields were practically abandoned from dire privations, worker shortage, scanty fertilizer, and near lack of attention, the harvest responded as if heaven blessed a long-sought peace with *l'année de la victoire*. Equally telling is the story about German prisoners of war—using the very soldiers who had occupied the chateau—back at Mouton to repair the war damage at Mouton, for example, filling in internal bullet holes where German soldiers had used even paintings for target practice, ripping out lines of cables since the chateau had been a Nazi communication center, and other tasks of removing signs of their odious presence. Baron Philippe even employed the prisoners of war to create a park with planted gardens and creating a permanent tree-lined wine road linking the Château Mouton property with his Mouton d'Armhailac property. Baron Philippe said later he could never look at the road without thinking of it as the "Route of Revenge."[80]

This is only a fraction of literature where Bordeaux somehow figures as the world's historic nerve center for excellent wine. Although an art achievement rather than literary, Château Mouton's artists labels have been milestones for other reasons. Each year since 1945 when artist Philippe Jullian decorated the label above the Rothschild heraldry with a personal image, in this first case with "1945 Année de la Victoire" and grape tendrils around the large "V," major artists have decorated Mouton labels, often with a ram (*mouton*) or possibly connected with some aspect of viticulture. These *dessins* include some of my favorites: Jean Cocteau (1947) with his satyr-faun-Pan horned ram-like figure holding a grape cluster; Salvador Dali (1958) with a squiggled ram; Pierre Alechinksy (1966) with a ram holding a wine glass; Marc Chagall (1970) with lovers and grapes; Picasso (1973) with a dancing Minotaur and other figures; and John Huston (1982) with a dancing ram. Kermit Lynch wistfully hoped in 1988 that the genius of the Mouton label would not be ultimately compromised with health warnings.[81] These artist *dessin* images only reinforce the pivotal historic role of wine as culture; how deeply connected and inseparable wine is to the civilizing arts.

Bordeaux in History

Some ethnohistorians mark several important timeline points for the historical growth of Bordeaux wines, including the English occupation during the Hundred Years War, and the subsequent religious wars when Protestants (including Dutch) took over the Bordeaux wine trade and its broader distribution from French ports.[82]

To illustrate this development of Bordeaux, the 1152 marriage of Eleanor of Aquitaine to Henry Plantagenet who would become King Henry II of England had forged longstanding ties between Bordeaux viticulture and wine consumption in Britain. Raymond Bertrand de Goth (1264–1314) born in Villandraut, Aquitaine, was Archbishop of Bordeaux in 1297, and soon thereafter, cardinal. In 1305 he was elected Pope Clement V and crowned in Lyon. His strong fealty to French King Philip IV—shown by his dissolution of the Knights Templars—and his move of the papal court to Avignon in 1309 (beginning what Petrarch termed the "Babylonian Captivity") brought even greater prominence to French wine, as the papal court helped to develop viticulture, especially as Pope Clement "enjoyed good wine."[83] Pope Clement V also owned vineyards in Graves that today form part of the wine estate of Château Pape Clément, possibly the oldest name estate in Bordeaux. The Hundred Years War (1337–1453), when Gascony (Gascoigne) was a British holding, brought flourishing trade between Bordeaux and Britain but this abated for a considerable time after the end of the war in 1453, when enterprising Dutch wine traders took up the slack[84] until the British court of Charles II (1630–85) brought French wine back in full favor. The British term for Bordeaux wine, claret, is actually from *clairet*, the name for a medieval blend of the juice from white and red grapes fermented together—although not to be confused with one method of producing modern rosé.[85]

Bordeaux's mostly alluvial soils of the Gironde estuary and the Garonne and Dordogne watersheds include gravels, clays, sands, and limestone slopes, with the best drainage and hence the most preferable terroirs higher up rather than by the river, originally surrounded by marshes. Divided by the Gironde estuary, Bordeaux has two primary designations of "Left Bank" and "Right Bank" appellations, with the in-between region of Entre-Deux-Mers framed by the Garonne and Dordogne watersheds. The Left Bank includes the Médoc and Haut-Médoc of St-Estèphe, Pauillac, St-Julien, and Margaux appellations, with Graves, Sauternes, Barsac, and Pessac-Léognan (just south of the city of Bordeaux)—below the Haut-Médoc and Entre-Deux-Mers. Listrac-Médoc and Moulis are also within the Haut-Médoc. The Right Bank includes the St. Émilion and Pomerol appellations. Other appellations like Bourg and Blaye are across the Gironde estuary from the Left Bank. Fronsac is also across the Gironde estuary but directly north of the Dordogne across from the city of Libourne where the Dronne-Isle watershed has its confluence with the Dordogne.

The Left Bank 1855 Gironde Classification was the first Bordeaux rating system because Napoleon III requested this official ranking from wine brokers for the Exposition Universelle de Paris of that year. The Right Bank was classified much later, mostly in the 20th century; for example, Cheval Blanc was rated in 1954.

The best Bordeaux single-bottle prices consistently transcend $1,000, and not just in banner years like 2000 and 2005, thought to have been classic years and rare in any century. Just in the past few years, the 2010 and 2011 Bordeaux releases promise even higher ratings. According to *Wine Spectator*, the *Château Lafite Rothschild Pauillac 2009* was priced at $1,800 and rated at 98 points; *Château Latour Pauillac 2009* was priced at $1,600 and was rated at 99 points in 2012; *Château Mouton Rothschild Pauillac 2009* was priced at $1,000 and rated at 98 points; *Château Margaux 2009* was priced at $1,250 and rated at 96 points; *Château Haut-Brion Pessac-Léognan 2009* was priced at $1,000 and rated at 98; and *Château La Mission Haut-Brion Pessac-Léognan 2009* was priced at $885 and rated at 96 points. Such is the cachet of "first growths" and others highly rated in 1855 or in the case of Mouton-Rothschild at a later date. But in the same *Wine Spectator* rating, Pomerol's *Château Petrus 2009* hit \$4,000 and was rated at 99; *Château Cheval Blanc 2009 St. Émilion* was priced at \$1,300 and rated at 98.[86]

Wine connoisseurs in France usually trace Bordeaux wine pedigrees to a few generations before the 1855 classification. But in reality the *Bituriges* tribe of Gauls (or Celts as Herodotus named them), who ultimately occupied the Garonne estuary in the centuries before Julius Caesar's armies came, already had an appreciation for good wine. One Roman wine varietal in the region was even known by Pliny as *biturica* and is probably the origin of *vidure*, which became the parent of Cabernet. The modern city of Bordeaux derives its name from the Roman town of *Burdigala* and was an important municipality even then, with its first vines apparently planted between 40 and 60 CE, but the *Burdigala* region was mostly established in the second century for commercial viticulture.

Decimius Magnus Ausonius (ca. 310–ca. 394 CE) already mentioned in Mosel, was an aristocratic Roman poet, imperial tutor—a *grammaticus*—and statesman. A native of *Burdigala*, he trained there for law as a *rhetor* but found teaching and writing more to his liking. Despite frequent stints in imperial Roman cities like Constantinople and Trier (*Augusta Treverorum*) and eventually appointed as a Praetorian Prefect of Gaul and layer as a Consul, it was his home in Bordeaux where he was happiest and to which he retired around 380, which he writes about in his poem "Mosella": "The elegance of shining Bordeaux with its pleasing aspect." Ausonius also describes Bordeaux in his poem "De herediolo" where he described growing vines on his inherited land and also claimed that his region of *Burdigala* was already an important place for viticulture.

Although east of modern Bordeaux and ancient *Burdigala* by some 25 miles, some of the old Roman property of Ausonius—he owned about 67 acres—are claimed to be part of the present esteemed Château Ausone wine estate in St. Émilion, and a large Roman villa

Fig 11.2 Chateu Les Grandes Murailles, St. Emilion

has been found outside St. Émilion that may correspond to the property of Ausonius,[87] although others suggest the estate of Ausonius was at Bazas by the Garonne.[88]

Château Ausone itself, first named in 1781, is a rare first growth (Premier Grand Cru Classé A) in St. Émilion, situated on only about 17 south-facing acres on the steep west side of the village appellation and generally produces about 50% Cabernet Franc and 50% Merlot on its fairly unique sand and clay soil on a limestone base, with a small but much-sought-after yield of only about 2,000 cases annually, therefore with a premium price per bottle of around $1,800 for the *Château Ausone St. Émilion* and $750–800 for the 2011. The Grand Cru wine estate of Château Figeac of St. Émilion is also built over the remains of a Roman villa from the 2nd century CE belonging to the Gallo-Roman *Figeacus* family.

One of my favorite visits to Bordeaux was to the "Right Bank" in 2010, when we stayed near St. Émilion at Château Grand Barrail, surrounded by vineyards on the Rue de Libourne a little west of the village, with vines just outside our patio door and birds singing to wake us at breakfast time. The medieval village of St. Émilion rising on its hill above the vineyards with its Gothic churches, ecclesiastic ruins, wine merchants, underground cellars, and winding streets may be about the most charming in Bordeaux. Most of its commercial activity promotes wine and wine visitors and its medieval and later history is also well preserved as a UNESCO World Heritage site. Despite Roman presence here for almost two millennia, the village is named after a legendary wandering hermit Émilion who lived in a cave in the limestone rock of the village. The medieval wines were produced by monks who built on the saint's legacy in the monastic houses here in the village, and ruins like the Cordeliers Cloister adjacent to the west side of the village show some of this dual activity of viticulture and religious maintenance of Jacobins, Benedictines, and other orders.

Perhaps unique for the region, under the village is the *Église Monolithique*, Europe's largest underground church. Benedictine monks carved the church and its catacombs over the course of several centuries out of the limestone rock, close to the hermit saint Émilion's own cave.

The entire St. Émilion appellation covers only 5,200 hectares, one of the smaller Bordeaux regions, yet its production is probably the largest in Bordeaux,[89] and its diverse geology of sand, gravel, clay, and limestone soils are best for a blend that combines mostly Merlot and Cabernet Franc, making wines that are softer and more accessible earlier in the aging process than many other Bordeaux wines, even though their longevity is also good. First classified in 1958, with reclassifications in 1969, 1985, 1996, 2006, and 2012, this appellation has recently been involved in dispute and legal wrangling over recent declassifications.[90] The nomenclature of Grand Cru in St. Émilion can

Fig 11.3 Chateau Pavie 2003

Fig 11.4 Chateau Cheval Blanc

be confusing to novices because Grand Cru Classé is the term that carries more weight as a classified growth since Grand Cru here refers only to unclassified growths.

Dégustation at wine chateaux in St. Émilion is fairly easy, but the best chateaux require more effort, sometimes wine-industry connections, and almost always must be arranged in advance. Some of these highly regarded producers are

Château Ausone and Château Cheval Blanc, another Premier Grand Cru Classé A—spared by the infamous late 19th century phylloxera epidemic that destroyed so many Bordeaux vines—and Château Angelus and Château Pavie. In 2003 I gave a custom wine tour to a single VIP, who bought a case of *Cheval Blanc 1970* from a French merchant on our itinerary. To best understand the value of Cheval Blanc, Christie's in 2010 at their Geneva auction sold an *Imperial* (6 liters) bottle of 1947 *Cheval Blanc* for $304,375.00. We ended up carting this special case of wine around for a few days before we could get it to Paris. Each night we would have the hotel staff carefully bring the case of wine in from the vehicle to the VIP's hotel suite; I always joked the wine was worth at least double the value of our expensive new

Fig 11.5 Chateau La Conseillante

rental vehicle. Contrary to what the cinema character of Miles seemed to scorn in the 2004 movie *Sideways* when he derogated Merlot, his cult wine Cheval Blanc is generally a blend of around 40% Merlot, with the other 60% Cabernet Franc, although drinking it out of a paper cup seems pointless in the movie unless this is part of the comedy, although French and international devotees of Cheval Blanc could find this cinema caricature blasphemous. The average price for either a Cheval Blanc 2009 or 2010 hovers around $1,200 and even the most searing critics at *Wine Spectator* pegged the 2009-high rating at 98.[91]

The local St. Émilion wine shops also provide an enormous selection, especially of very good wines not exported outside Bordeaux but reasonably priced. The available caves and cellars are also extensive, including those of Clos de Menuts, the St. Émilion Grand Cru of the Rivière family. Many

Fig 11.6 Chateau Grand Mayne

stairs are involved to get into the deepest underground caves but worth every moment to see even a portion of the Clos des Menuts medieval cellars storing well over 20,000 visible bottles produced from their 30 upper-slope hectares west of the village. Critic James Suckling, no longer at *Wine Spectator,* independently rated the *Clos des Menuts l'Excellence 2010 St. Émilion* with 92–93 point rating as "outstanding," and I purchased several other vintages, averaging around a reasonable $50, from these cellars, with the 1990 averaging $100, to be brought back home to California. Other St. Émilion visits included Château Grand Mayne on the gradual slope west of the village and at Château La Grave Figeac on the edge of Pomerol, the adjoining Bordeaux village with more good wine to buy and ship home. Pomerol wine visits on this same trip included the estates of Château La Conseillante, between Château Cheval Blanc on the edge of St. Émilion and Château Petrus in Pomerol, and Château La Fleur du Gay.

In the interim between annual France visits, my account at Berry Bros. & Rudd, the wine merchant established in 1698 at 3 St. James Street, London, records obligatory purchases of their house "claret," and sometimes it is easier to pick up excellent Bordeaux in London since it is my usual stopover to the continent. I keep Berry Bros. price lists indefinitely; for example, the October 1998 book confirms what every list has said about the legendary 1982 Bordeaux vintage: possibly the best for decades since 1961 and whose bottles are now very hard to find.[92]

Another London wine merchant I frequent is Corney & Barrow—established in 1780—first in an old rectory on Helmet Row but now near Tower Bridge and with various London shops, including Kensington Park Row in Notting Hill. I also keep my Corney & Barrow wine list books, since this wine merchant is the agent for Château Petrus, among other fine estates.

In Pomerol, the unique terroir of Petrus is geologically fascinating on its almost 11.4 hectares (29 acres): its soil is blue-grey clay on gravel over iron pan clay subsoil called *crasse de fer* on a slightly elevated mound in Pomerol; another hallmark is the unique Petrus wine signature of mostly one varietal, 95% Merlot, 5% Cabernet Franc.[93] Several notes of distinction are that Petrus' previous owner Madame Loubat gifted a case of Petrus to Queen Elizabeth II's coronation in 1953, having it specially shipped to Buckingham Palace; also that some versions of Agatha Christie's *Death on the Nile* have Hercule Poirot drink Petrus; and, of course, it is a "must have" important stock for the most important state dinners in the French Presidential Palace in Paris, Elysée Palace on the Rue du Faubourg Saint-Honoré.[94] Whether or not Petrus is France's most Olympian Bordeaux, the perception of it being at the pinnacle of taste has certainly made its price out of reach for most.

Union des Grands Crus de Bordeaux

Sometimes one doesn't have to go to France, because the Unions des Grands Crus de Bordeaux (UGCB) and their 132 grand cru estates also come to San Francisco's Palace Hotel. Here I met Jean-Marc Giraud, the Director of UCGB at the organized tasting for 100+ Grand Crus, who graciously wrote back to me the day after the organized tasting in response to my personal thanks as a member of the press invited by Grand Cru hosts. The best producers at this dégustation usually include owners or vignerons, and most recently the 2010 vintage was showcased in San Francisco. My favorite reds at the event, while not from every appellation hosted, caught attention for various reasons. Not necessarily in order, my notes mention *Château Rauzan-Gassies 2010 Margaux*, 65% Cabernet Sauvignon, 25% Merlot, and 5% each of Petit Verdot and Cabernet Franc, as it made a strong impression for being gracefully balanced as a ballerina between the soaring flight of its fruit and the gravity of its tannin. I also much enjoyed the *Château Prieuré Lichine 2010 Margaux*, 55% Cabernet Sauvignon, 40% Merlot, and 5% Petit Verdot. Also notable was the *Château Leoville Barton 2010 Saint-Julien,* especially darkly rich, aromatic of nose, and yet still accessible with its 74% Cabernet Sauvignon, 23% Merlot, and 3% Cabernet

Fig 11.7 Prince Eudes D'Orleans, Chateau du Fargues Sauternes 2010

Fig 11.8 Aline Baly of Chateau Coutet at Union des Grands Crus de Bordeaux

Franc. President of Leoville Barton, Barton family's Lillian Barton-Sartorius' generosity made the dégustation a highlight by her warm conversation as we discussed the fine Kladstrup 2001 book *Wine and War*, in which the authors told the Barton story. *Château Clerc Milon 2010 Pauillac* was astonishingly complex with many layers in its 49% Cabernet Sauvignon, 37% Merlot, 11% Cabernet Franc, 2% Petit Verdot, and 1% Carmenère, perhaps the most profound for velvety complexity but it also promised a very long future as its tannins did not overpower up front but appeared only after the long finish.

Of the Sauternes at this dégustation, to which I went back many times over an afternoon, two stood out beyond all others. The *Château de Fargues 2010 Sauternes* was a taste of heaven for its sublime nectar and flowers, full of liquid gold at 80% Semillon

Fig 11.9 Chateau Coutet Sauternes-Barsac 2010

and 20% Sauvignon Blanc, from a property in the Lur-Saluces family for half a millennium. The host for this Sauternes was Prince Eudes d'Orleans, Directeur Général of Château de Fargues, impeccably courteous with a smile as noble as his sweet wine yet paradoxically full of humility: I could hardly imagine him in a modern setting as his dignity was that of someone who wore it naturally. Then there was the *Château Coutet 2010 Sauternes-Barsac,* a first growth (Premier Grand Cru Classé) in 1855[95] and made more for angels than humans with 75% Semillon, 23% Sauvignon Blanc, and 2% Muscadelle. At this dégustation it was most unlikely if any one person could be more hospitable than Aline Baly, one of the family owners of Château Coutet. Her genuine care for her nectar and the people who joyfully drink it made the most indelible impression of any Bordeaux experience I've ever had. The welcome invitation to return to Bordeaux and to these Sauternes estates by both Prince Eudes d'Orleans and Aline Baly will be accepted as soon as possible.

Early Rhone Valley

How early did human ancestors collect wild grapes in Europe, especially France? According to France's Institut National de Recherches Archéologiques Préventives (INRAP), Paleolithic evidence is secure for wild grapes although not necessarily of the same *Vitis vinifera sylvestris* ancestor or even the *Proles pontica* family:

> In southern France, the site of Terra Amata, near Nice, dated 400,000 years ago, has yielded many seeds, which can certify that Lambrusco grapes were

already harvested and collected from the Palaeolithic between 500,000 and 120,000 years.[96]

If true, this find may establish the oldest grape seeds in the archaeological record, but harvested rather than cultivated by what may be as old as the human ancestor *Homo heidelbergensis*, whose materials were also found at Terra Amata.

Although the Greek Phocaean colony of *Massalia* (Marseilles) were transporting imported Greek wine from across the Mediterranean for Celtic consumption up the Rhone Valley, the claim that they also had significant vineyards is not yet fully verified but appears valid for several hundred years before a Roman presence. The founding legends of Massalia from 600 BCE tell of a marriage between Phocaean Greek explorer named Photis who wed a local Ligurian princess named Gyptis and that the ceremony included a wine exchange. Based on amphorae and shipwrecks in and around the Lacydon harbor, Greek wine was certainly arriving in bulk from at least 500 BCE, and the Celts (Gauls) were eager for wine as a trade good. A few meters from Marseilles' old port (Vieux-Port) has turned up ample Greek pottery of wine drinking, including early red-figure skyphoi ca. 500 BCE that also have representations of wine vessels painted on them. Again, INRAP, sponsor of many archaeological excavations, also has sufficient evidence for viticulture at Lattes (*Latara*),[97] Herault, near Montpelier in the form of grape seeds circa 500 BCE, a site associated with the Volcae tribe on the Lez River near the Rhone étangs and later incorporated into the Roman civitas of Nimes. So viticulture in France seems to have started long before the Romans.

Celts and Wine in the Rhone Region

That wine was highly desirable by Celtic tribes in Gaul from at least the 6th c. BCE is seen in amphorae finds spread across the entire southern coast of France and inland across Langeudoc and Provence along river routes like the Rhone, Saone, and Seine, especially from the third century BCE onward.[98]

But seminal single artifacts also evidence early wine imports. Perhaps the most famous wine vessel in history was found in 1953 by Pierre Jouffrai. Now in the local museum at Chatillon-sûr-Seine, it was excavated from the ca. 525 BCE grave of a Celtic princess from Vix near Mount Lassois in central France, a Celtic *oppidum* fort and cemetery identified as being on the route bridging the Rhone-Saone and Seine watersheds, which suggests the control of the ancient wine trade here. This enormous highly decorated bronze wine krater 1.63 meters (about 5'4") in height and weighing 450 lbs. (200 kg)—the largest known krater anywhere and the single largest metal find from antiquity—was an important burial good as her ticket to celebration in the afterlife, ensuring she would be well-received in the halls of the gods with such a divine gift for eternal vintages. While most likely Rhodian Greek in its make, the huge Vix wine krater holding 1,100 liters (290 gallons) of wine was also buried with many Greek Black figure vessels, amphorae, and Etruscan wine vessels for immediate use.[99] Inspired by the composite cultural imagery of Greek and Gaulish synthesis, I published a poem in 2009 on this Vix krater, which I wrote for Bruno Racine, President of the Bibliothèque National of France in Paris; he wrote back his thanks shortly afterward.

Princess of Vix

Looking for new markets overseas
Greeks traded lordly wine to Gauls,
amphorae dragged from long ships
to far domains where Celtic bards
praised such potent juice. Gaulish kings

drank with elation but were assured
mortals could only handle so much
of this divine gift, but with no such limits
in the next life. Plus, it would make
their sunless world less dark.

This is why one wise princess of Vix
took to her Celtic grave a giant krater,
bronze masterpiece made in distant Rhodes.
But it wasn't treasured for its craft:
it held enough wine for a fête in Elysium,

assuring her a welcome there, sufficient
to twice fill over seven hundred cups
and make every farmer's well echo
under fields of Chatillon-sûr-Seine
with drinking songs for centuries.

Some scholars have long theorized that wine itself was a primary vehicle for establishing the status of the Celtic warlords and chieftains—somewhat mirroring pre-democracy Greek aristocrats with symbolism of the krater mentioned earlier on Greek wine.[100] These chieftains could convene social events for their vassals around feasting and wine consumption with distribution to "civilize" as well as confer favor through this luxury good, as shown on Celtic bronze *situlae* like the late 7th c. BCE *Benvenuti Situla* from Este.[101]

The Celts probably consumed thousands of tons of wine via this social mechanism between 500 and 100 BCE, and according to Pliny, apparently preferred wooden casks to clay amphorae. Possibly several million liters of wine were imported every few years (or annually) to Gaul from the Greek world to the east given the quantities of amphorae found both on land and in shipwrecks.[102] As Cunliffe noted about the Celtic feast as a potlatch distribution, "the consumption of huge quantities of expensive imported wine, of which the Celts were inordinately fond, was another form of public wealth destruction."[103] By the second century BCE, there is both strong viticultural and textual evidence that the Celts of the Allobroges tribe in Vienne were among the first to plant vineyards in France's Rhone Valley; Pliny even notes this antecedent of full Roman control in his *Natural History* XIV.26 when the Celtic tribes still kept their old names.

Romans Along the Rhone

Gallia Narbonensis was one of the first Roman colonies outside Italy, spreading across what is now Languedoc and Provence, as established by the late second century BCE. Even the modern name "Provence" derived from this Roman *Provincia*. Roman cities like Arles (*Arelate*), Nîmes (*Nemausis*), Orange (*Arausio*), St. Rhemy-en-Provence (*Glanum*), and Vaison-la-Romaine (*Vasio Vocontiorum*) were some of the early Roman cities here, filled with veterans who acquired farmland through distribution after their service ended. One of the first reasons for early provincial viticulture here was to provide the Roman legions with a needed wine ration, but soon a vast commercial enterprise with villa estates using slave labor accompanied private farming. Pliny mentions viticulture in Gallia Narbonensis at Alba Helvia, near modern Viviers-sûr-Rhône just south of Montélimar.[104]

The Avignon Papacy and Châteauneuf-du-Pape Evolution

In the medieval period until the early 14th century, local viticulture around Avignon was promoted by the Bishops of Avignon but it was during the "Babylonian Captivity" beginning with Pope Clement V (Raymond Bertrand de Gothe, a Frenchman) in 1308–9 that Rhone wine—especially to the north in Burgundy—saw its first great period of growth; but a French papacy also stimulated local winemakers to produce wine for the burgeoning bureaucracy in Avignon. Clement's successor Pope John XXII created a specific papal market for the local "Vin du Pape" and built a village castle, "new castle of the Pope" (*Châteauneuf du Pape*) that became the focal point of the local wine industry. Even though the "legitimate" Avignon papacy lasted until only 1376, a series of Avignon "illegitimate" prelates continued to claim the papacy until 1403. One of the oldest documented Châteauneuf-du-Pape properties—Château Mont-Redon—has been making wine as early as 1334.[105] Meanwhile the local wine industry flourished and after some abatement continued to develop viticulture in the Provence region through the next centuries, partly at first because of British wine imports from France through Gascony during the Hundred Years War (1337–1453), falling thereafter but rising again through Dutch trade in the late 16th century and beyond. It is unlikely that any of these early Rhone wines had the distinction and quality that now makes them outstanding; in fact, a lot of wrangling, fraud, and debate accompanied the making of what would eventually become Châteauneuf-du-Pape until the 20th century, with resolution coming only after 1923 with Appellation Contrôlée rules.

What started as "Vin du Pape" then became Châteauneuf-Calcenier for centuries, known for producing "Vin d'Avignon" and only gradually evolved into the strict Châteauneuf-du-Pape after 1923, can now include up to 13 traditional varietals (14 if you count both red and white Grenache)—although 18 are legally possible in 2009—and this famous wine is today dominated by Grenache, along with Mourvèdre and Syrah as principal varietal blends with incremental amounts of the other varietals, including Cinsaut, Carignane, Counoise, Muscardin, Piquepoul Noir, Terret Noir, and Vaccarèse, among others.

Some of the most highly regarded Châteauneuf-du-Pape wines include those of Château de Beaucastel, Domaine du Vieux Télégraphe, Château Rayas, Château de Beaurenard, Château La Nerthe, Clos des Papes, and Le Vieux Donjon, among others.[106] The most famous

Châteauneuf vineyard is La Crau where much of Domaine du Vieux Télégraphe commands the hill. Château de Beaucastel, which began its documented vineyard history around 1549, is the only great vineyard to grow and blend the legislated full 13 varietals allowed to make up the traditional Châteauneuf-du-Pape.

In the vineyards around the famous village of Châteauneuf-du-Pape are the millions of characteristic rocks that cover much of the appellation vineyards, the *galets roulés* or "pebbles" of weathered quartzite left over from glacial episodes. These stones reflect solar heat into the vines as a ripening agent, although not all the vineyards have these rocky surfaces.

Fig 11.10 Hermitage

Great Production Subregions in the Rhône Valley

The principal or greatest Rhone subregions run from the north to south along the Rhone. First, the northern Rhones are Côte-Rôtie (red, mostly Syrah), Condrieu (white, Viognier), Saint-Joseph (red, Syrah; white, Marsanne or Roussanne), Hermitage (red, mostly Syrah; white, Marsanne or Roussanne), Crozes-Hermitage (red, mostly Syrah; white, Marsanne or Roussanne), and Cornas (red, mostly Syrah). The southern Rhone subregions are Châteauneuf-du-Pape (already mentioned), Gigondas (red and rosé, 80% Grenache, with 15% Syrah or Mourvèdre, the rest being Cinsaut or another red), and Vacqueyras (mostly red with Grenache but with higher Syrah than in Gigondas). These last two are on the edge of the Rhone Valley considerably east of the river. Last but not least, the Côtes-du-Rhône subregion—with freedom to use nearly any of the Rhone varietals—is spread around the southern edges of this region as well as north to the west of Valence across the river and downriver of Valence just above the Drôme confluence with the Rhone. Côtes-du-Rhône, however, has been mostly concentrated between Orange and Avignon with more vineyards on the west side of the river. It is important to note that more than 75% of all Rhone wines are classified Côtes-du-Rhône and Côtes-du-Rhône-Villages, from over 140,000 cultivated acres.[107]

Other Rhone *vins nobles* less known outside France but often just as worthy include the rare but precious *Château-Grillet* white wine from Viognier, located between Condrieu and Hermitage; also the subregion of Saint-Péray just west across the Rhone River from Valence is known for its sparkling wine, especially the wine of *Domaine Chaboud* where grapes have been harvested since 1778, they also make Roussanne and Marsanne in single bottlings. Other notable wines are found within the Lirac, Tavel, and Muscat de Beaumes-de-Venise subregional productions. Tavel is most known for its rosé wines made by the *saignée* method where maceration with the red skin continues for a short time period until the suitable pink color is attained, not a blend of red and white. The Muscat de Beaumes-de-Venise is a singular *vin doux*, a sweet Muscat wine. Wine may have been made here since Roman times in the village of Beaumes-de-Venise.[108] The old monastic *Domaine des Bernardins* is one of the few traditional Vaucluse producers of this old-style Beaumes sweet wine that is mostly forgotten or overshadowed by its powerful red counterparts in the Rhone Valley.

Three family names have dominated Rhone wines for decades both as negociants and for making wine: Guigal, whose more than 20 wines are almost all of the highest quality although they are especially famous for their Côte-Rôtie; Jaboulet who are especially known for Hermitage La Chapelle although they also produce other remarkable Rhone wines; and Chapoutier who are also especially known for Hermitage but also produce other fine Rhone wines.

I usually spend some time in the Rhone Valley annually but seemingly always about the peak of the year's heat in July or August. From my first trip decades ago to the late 1990's, Provence was on my itinerary for various reasons including Roman archaeology at Arles, Nimes, Orange, St. Rhemy, Vaison-la-Romaine, Vienne, and Valence. Especially recently when I should have been cooling off in a swimming pool, I seem instead to have been sweating on long bicycle journeys up the Rhone, often with Stanford students as we tracked the route of Hannibal. Our teams have cycled from Beaucaire to Avignon to Orange to Pont-St-Esprit.

Although I had long ago discovered Châteauneuf-du-Pape in solo trips, one of my favorite forays was in 2007 with 32 Stanford students between Avignon and Orange and the quietest and safest road—although not most direct—for our peloton of bicycles. We followed the D976 bridge out of Roquemare across the Rhone River, continuing along to the D72 and wheeling through Châteauneuf-du-Pape vineyards on one of the hottest days of the year when heat shimmered through the vineyards. We had to make a rest stop with a dégustation—the students were all over the age of 21—at Domaine de Châteaumar before turning north toward Orange along the D68. The students were excited to be in a famous wine region where they could cycle past vineyards but also taste wine from them. I remember soaking my face, neck, and arms in water troughs at Châteaumar multiple times between tasting different wines, then especially enjoying the rich Châteauneuf-du-Pape from their 5 hectares near the village grown in red clay and large *galets* pebbles. Because that day we had so many bicycles with handlebar packs, we were able as a group to purchase and cycle away with three dozen bottles of excellent Châteauneuf-du-Pape individually carried to Orange, ending our cycling that day at the Roman Arc deTriomphe in the old city. Most of the split-up cases of 36 bottles went to student hosts on that trip or home to parents, all of whom appreciated the gifts of excellent wine. On following summers my wife and I spent other days in Provence, selfishly and indulgently revisiting familiar Châteauneuf-du-Pape haunts by ourselves and having these wines over long dinners at dusk when we hear the cicadas singing about the day's heat around the old castle.

Burgundy's Côte d'Or

Miles of vineyards stretch to the horizon in each direction, from the Plain of Saône in the east to the line of limestone hills in the west and north to south as well between some of the greatest wine villages in the world. Between Dijon in the north and Beaune in the south is one of France's greatest natural treasures, the heart of Burgundy's wine region called the Côte-d'Or, a 30-mile stretch of some of the greatest vineyards in the world for Pinot Noir and Chardonnay. It is composed of the Côte de Nuits to the north and the Côte de Beaune to the south with the city of Beaune somewhat between the two areas although within the southern half. Generally, the higher up the slope these Côte d'Or vineyards stretch, the better the wine. These higher parcels produce the Grand Cru and Premier Cru wines, and these vineyard parcels are all found west of the Route National D974 that runs parallel to the limestone scarp of hills. While the best Côte de Nuits wines are elegant red wines made from Pinot Noir, the best Côte de Beaune wines are rich white wines made from Chardonnay.

Well known to archaeology, the Rhone valley itself and ultimately Burgundy were colonized for Roman wine growth, which, according to Jasper Morris, editor of the *Journal of Wine Research*, may even account for the name domaine of La Romanée alongside Roman and Burgundian archaeological sites, so named in 1651 "presumably on account of Roman finds being found nearby".[109] A section of old Roman road is also preserved between Dijon and the Forest of Cîteaux south of the abbey. Remains of Gallo-Roman vineyards from the first century BCE were also found in Gevrey-Chambertin, possibly the oldest in Burgundy.

Many historians have written[110] how the medieval monastic orders like Cluniacs and the Cistercians of Cîteaux saved viticulture from full decline and restored the vineyard lands with both their own monastic workforce along with village laborers, often serfs under prelate aristocrats whose church sinecures included land and those who worked it. These monks, especially the literate ones who also preserved and studied Roman agricultural texts like Columella and Pliny, hybridized vines to fit the terroirs and set up the original *clos* "walled" system of walls separating vineyard parcels. Extant vineyard names in Burgundy today preserve many monastic parcels: Clos de Vougeot, Clos de Tart, Clos des Meix, Clos-de-Bèze, Clos du Chapître, Clos des Mouches, Clos des Ursules, and Clos Saint-Jacques are just a few of these monastic remnants, and some of Burgundy's old wine families descend from the same vineyard workers who labored for the church. After 1791 and the French Revolution when the dissolution of much Church property nationalized the vineyards, many of these same families who had never left Burgundy gradually became owners, at first of minuscule parcels, but some prospered and their vineyard lands grew along with their wealth.

The Côte-d'Or was my first visceral exposure to a French wine region and is still my favorite. Although I knew its reputation and had experienced its elegant wines, I personally discovered and explored it while driving between the Alps and Paris en route homeward late one summer and have returned annually since the early 1990's, often while traveling in both directions before and after archaeological fieldwork. I have now also brought at least ten groups of people through Burgundy in different seasons, ranging from Stanford students to experienced adult wine connoisseurs.

The mostly Jurassic limestone escarpment of this great wine region runs from southwest to northeast in Burgundy, roughly passing through 33 villages or towns along the Route des Grands Crus, along which are thirty Grand Cru vineyards in the Côte-d'Or. While the Romans were here two millennia ago, the Burgundians followed as the Roman world diminished. Later, Cluniac and Cistercian monks helped to develop vineyards in this region in the 12th century, forming many small-walled enclosures or *clos* that still exist. Charlemagne was a seminal force in between Romans and the Church.

In 775 Charlemagne gave a precious vineyard to the Abbey of Seaulieu. It was on the famous hill of Corton above the village of Aloxe-Corton in the heart of this wine country, a vineyard that carried the king's name since as *En Charlemagne* and *Le Charlemagne*, producing a great Grand Cru wine called Charlemagne with its neighboring Grand Cru known as Corton-Charlemagne. The Church owned this vineyard until 1791 when it was confiscated during the French Revolution; soon thereafter the Bonneau-Véry Family purchased this vineyard. Only three owners have owned this land since 775 and today the Domaine Bonneau du Martray remains on this hill above the village of Aloxe-Corton.

From the medieval walled city of Beaune to Aloxe-Corton, Nuits-St-Georges, Vosne-Romanée, Vougeot, the legendary Route des Grands Crus follows the French national road D-974 (Route National 74) until it turns at Flagey-Échezaux and continues higher along the base of the slope through the villages and vineyards of Chambolle-Musigny and Morey-Saint-Denis to Gevrey-Chambertin. Beyond this the national road D-974 again passes by Fixin and Marsannay-la-Côte en route to Dijon.

Aloxe-Corton in the Côte de Beaune is the only village in this prestigious region of the Côte d'Or to produce both red and white Grand Crus, one reason I spend as much time as possible in Aloxe-Corton. These Grand Crus include the opulent reds Le Corton, Corton le Clos du Roi, Corton-les-Bressandes, Corton-Renards, Corton Clos des Meix (monopole), Corton-Le Rognet and the already-mentioned white wine loved by Charlemagne, the Grand Crus known now as Charlemagne or Corton-Charlemagne. These Grand Cru reds are produced from 250 acres and the Grand Cru whites from 121 acres. The Corton hill—its crest thickly covered with the Bois de Corton—rises between the villages of Aloxe-Corton on the east and Pernand-Vergelesses on the west and generally the best wines are from the slopes, although excellent Premier Cru wines are also found around the village of Aloxe-Corton.

Fig 11.11 Corton Hill

Several excellent producers of wine in this lovely village, perhaps not considered by many as exclusive as Domaine Bonneau du Martray, but nonetheless superb wines, especially at Domaine Comte Senard, Cave Louise Perrin and Pierre André, the latter in the large winery Château Corton André at the north end of the village, especially known for their *Château Corton André Grand Cru Chevalier Montrachet, Grand Cru Bonnes Mares,* and *Grand Crus Corton-*

Fig 11.12 Saturday market Beaune

Charlemagne, among others. The Premier Crus of Aloxe-Corton are La Coutière, Les Chaillots, Clos du Chapître, Les Fournières, Les Maréchaudes, Les Paulands, and Les Valozières, produced from about another 100 acres (about 40 hectares) of red wine. Corton André is owned by Ballande, which also owns Château Prieuré Lichine in Margaux. Domaine Comte Senard not only has exceptional wine like their showcase *Domaine Comte Senard Clos des Miex Grand Cru Monopole* but also five other marvelous Grand Crus reds (Corton-Bressandes, Corton Clos du Roi, Corton Les Paulands), along with several Grand Cru whites (Corton Blanc and Corton-Charlemagne) and excellent Premier Crus and even offers a wonderful lunch with dégustation.

The Côte d'Or city of Beaune is one of the richest in France for art and culture, especially with the Hôtel-Dieu of the Hospices du Beaune and its tapestries and the huge polyptych of Rogier van der Weyden's (ca. 1400–1464) *Last Judgment* circa 1448. Beaune hosts many orchestral concerts, and preserves stained glass windows and tapestries in the Collégiale Nôtre-Dame de Beaune; many wine shops, regional specialties, and

Fig 11.13 Hotel Le Cep and Loiseau des Vignes, Beaune

Fig 11.14 Bouchard Pere et Fils, Beaune

antiques also fill the walled city. I know how lucky I am to have spent almost annual stays in the city of Beaune, especially because of the available wine dégustations at producer-négociants like Bouchard Père & Fils since 1731, who own 320 acres (130 hectares) of which 30 acres (12 hectares) are Grand Cru and 132 acres (74 hectares) are Premier Cru. Beaune also has gourmet restaurants like Loiseau des Vignes (Group Bernard Loiseau) at Hôtel le Cep, Le Bénaton, and Clos de Cèdre; I have feasted at the first two and await a repast at the third. If instead in Aloxe-Corton, the restaurant Le Charlemagne is only a 15-minute walk away around the hill of Corton in Pernand-Vergelesses. Each of these restaurants has one Michelin star. When in Beaune I have always stayed at either Hôtel Le Cep or Hôtel de la Poste. In addition to the great Burgundian producer-négociant family in Beaune of Bouchard Père & Fils, the two other equally important producer-négociant families are also based in Beaune; these are Maison Louis Jadot since 1859 and Maison Joseph Drouhin since 1880.

As much as Beaune is an exciting town for so many cultural reasons, my favorite wine villages are Aloxe-Corton and Vosne-Romanée mostly because of hospitable vigneron friends in those villages with whom I've spent the most time. Véronique Perrin owns Villa Louise in Aloxe-Corton;[111] she is seemingly an angel who decided to stay on earth. The 17th century manor house is situated in the village, its gardens look out on the hill of Corton and it features not only the most peaceful, restful ambience with the best vineyard views in Burgundy but also likely the best *petit-déjeuner* with homemade compotes and the most gracious hostess. I've known Véronique for over a dozen years and her son Leopold also visited us when he was a young student at Stanford. Many times I've sat in the family's private parlor with a glass of the *Cave Louise Perrin Grand Cru Corton-Bressande* or *Corton-Renards* and I remember so well the rare 1985 and 1996 vintages of those wines brought up from the cave, although these vintages are probably long gone. Other times I've walked the quiet small road at night north out of the village with family members where the stars are blazing overhead or by moonlight with cricket music just before *vendange*. Some of my most vivid memories of France are framed by stays in the Villa Louise where the generosity and hospitality know no end. It's also a short bicycle ride from Villa Louise to Savigny-lès-Beaune's wine dégustations to the southwest—a local motto says that Savigny-lès-Beaune wines are *théologiques, nourissants et morbifuges*, "theological, nourishing and making death flee." I've cycled and hiked over several years with Leopold, my own family, and others around the many small country vineyard roads like the D-115, D-18, and D-20 between Beaune, Ladoix, Magny-lès-Villars, Échevronne, Chorey-les-Beaune, Pernand-Vergelesses, and Aloxe-Corton, often for local dégustations. Véronique Perrin's family has been making wine in the region for centuries, and while her vigneron parents were based in the neighboring village of Ladoix, it seems this old vigneron

Fig 11.15 Vosne Romanee

family has its likeliest roots in the Cluniac viticulture since the 12th century and knows the land better than anyone else with roots so deep here.

Any mention of other superlative Côte d'Or wine villages have to include Vosne-Romanée, which was my introduction to Burgundy in 1996 and a tough one to follow. The Vosne-Romanée Premier Cru wines (about 15 or so) are produced on about 140 acres (57 hectares); the Grand Crus (6) are produced on about 168.5 acres (68 hectares). What this means is that there is more Grand Cru total vineyard area in Vosne-Romanée than Premier Cru, which doesn't happen anywhere else in the world, making this the pinnacle of wine exclusivity.

While passing through or staying nearby, I have dropped in on more than a few Vosne-Romanée vignerons over the years, including the always hospitable Rion and Gros families. But the one vigneron family there with whom I've been most acquainted were the G. Noellats and M. Cheurlins (George Noellat's family), especially Marie-Thérèse Noellat on the Rue des Chaumes, who often invited me for a meal or a jaunt through her vineyards. More recently her grandson Maxim Cheurlin has taken over much of the vigneron duties and is equally committed to making the best Burgundy. The most recent times I've been there, Maxim is running the operation with aplomb, keen taste, and energy with high standards. I've met four generations of this Noellat and Cheurlin family and eaten with them while relishing their Grands Crus and Premier Crus. From their back patio overlooking the Les Chaumes vineyards on the edge of town, I could throw a stone into La Tâche if I wanted to, but I wouldn't dare even if it might be the dead of winter when it wouldn't hit a vine laden with precious grapes, because the vines themselves are so valuable. G. Noellat's best wines are their *Grand Échezaux Grand Cru* and their *Vosne-Romanée Premier Cru Les Chaumes* or *Les Beaux Monts* and I often brought some of their *G. Noellat Grand Échezaux Grand Cru* to the then-Abbé-Prévot Msgr. Benoit Vouilloz of the Grand-St-Bernard Order at the Monastery Hospice du Grand-St-Bernard high in the Alps. I also took many bottles of the G. Noellat Grand and Premier Crus home over the years, including the 1996 and

2002, both mostly now unavailable. Their wines now command very respectable prices in the hundreds of dollars. The wine villages of Vosne-Romanée is perhaps the premium viticultural context in the prestigious Côte-d'Or—or maybe all of France—in the heartland of Burgundy, with a lion's share of great monopole reds with Grand Cru distinction from the famous Domaine de la Romanée-Conti. Here some of the world's most esteemed wines—often costing several thousand dollars for a single bottle.[112]

Vosne-Romanée's peerless Domaine de la Romanée Conti, or DRC as it is abbreviated, is a family affair now between the Villane and Leroy clans. Domaine de la Romanée Conti can easily claim 1,500 years of history from late Roman times onward, later existing for centuries as a property of the Abbey of Cluny. In 1760, the parcel of La Romanée belonged to the 18th century Bourbon prince, Louis-François de Bourbon, Prince of Conti, but it was confiscated decades later during

Fig 11.16 Romanee St. Vivant

the French Revolution. Its six renowned vineyard parcels above the village include *Romanée-Conti, La Tâche, Richebourg, Échezaux, Grands Échezaux*, and *Romanée-St-Vivant*, and each one can seem astronomically priced relative to almost all other wine in Burgundy. Both Romanée-Conti and La Tâche are monopoles. I've been lucky to taste each of these at different times thanks to generous friends and acquaintances and have even purchased one of the lesser stars on occasion. Outside the village down in the south end of Côte de Beaune, DRC also produces one great Grand Cru white, *Le Montrachet,* between the villages of Puligny-Montrachet and Chassagne-Montrachet. The DRC wines most often set the standards by which all other Burgundy wines are measured. On occasion Marie-Thérèse Noellat has walked me through one of her parcels to the end because her row of Grands-Échezaux near the border of Vougeot continues into DRC's parcel. I must admit I cannot see any difference between the vines or the soil, although DRC's starts only slightly higher up the slope. In fact, when I lived in London some years ago, I remember a Christie's London Auction where a single bottle of *La Tâche 1945* went for close to $7,000.00; a Sotheby's 2008 New York auction sold a single bottle of *La Tâche 1945* for over $11,700 and a rare bottle of this wine might still be available for a relative bargain at $12,000.00 if one looks hard enough in less glamorous urban contexts than Paris, Geneva, New York, Hong Kong, or London.

The other Côte de Nuits villages also produce their fair share of esteemed Grand Crus, including Vougeot's Clos de Vougeot; Chambolle Musigny's Bonnes Mares; Morey-St.-Denis' Clos de Tart (monopole), Clos de la Roche, Clos des Lambrays, Clos St.-Denis, and Bonnes Mares. Over time I've explored these villages as well and their wines, and as already mentioned, the frequency of the word *Clos* (walled) in Côte d'Or reminds that the Church once owned most of these vineyards, especially the wealthy Cluniacs and the Cistercian monks of Cîteaux.

In Clos de Vougeot is also the famous Château du Clos de Vougeot, begun in the 12th century as a wine farm by monks from Abbey of Cîteaux and you can still see their farm implements and towering wine presses in the oldest barns. It was enlarged and aggrandized as a chateau in the 16th century but since 1945 it is home to the Confrérie des Chevaliers du Tastevin as the seat of this august wine order, with many

Fig 11.17 Chateau Clos de Vougeot

worldwide chapters (*Sous-Commanderies*). Its causes are noble for Burgundy: "To hold in high regard and encourage the use of the products of Burgundy, particularly her great wines and her regional cuisine," "To maintain and revive the festivities, customs and traditions of Burgundian folklore," and "To encourage people from all over the world to visit Burgundy,"[113] which are not hard to hold dear. Every fall when the vines are splendidly colored in brilliant autumn hues, like a fairy tale, the Confrérie hosts a Gargantuan harvest feast with elaborate old regalia of a bygone age and the pouring of incredible wines that flow almost all night. Of course, Rabelais would be proud, but perhaps who can eat or drink much for a week after this celebration?

Last but not least in Côte de Nuits is Gevrey-Chambertin, where I've also spent many days cycling or driving in search of dégustations. Gevrey-Chambertin with its 770 acres (310 hectares) of vineyards also has distinguished Grand Cru red wines, including Le Chambertin, Chambertin Clos-de-Bèze, Chapelle-Chambertin, Charmes-Chambertin, Griotte-Chambertin, Latricières-Chamberin, Mazis-Chambertin, and Ruchottes-Chambertin. There is a small stone gateway on the Route des Grands Crus at Latricières-Chambertin where over the years every member of our family has been photographed.

In such a large appellation, Premier Crus are also well represented in Gevrey-Chambertin, including but not limited to

Fig 11.18 Gevrey Chambertin

Les Cazetiers, Les Clos Saint-Jacques, Lavaut Saint-Jacques, Combe au Moin, Petit Cazetiers, Les Goulots, Champeaux, Craipillot, Champonnet, Les Verroilles, Poissenot, Fonteny, Bel-Air, Les Corbeaux, La Perrière, Clos Prieur-Haut, Cherbaudes, Champitenois, Ergot, Au Combottes, among others.

Recently the Masson Family sold the singular Château du Gevrey-Chambertin, but this artistic family of actors, pianists, academics, and vignerons made a colorful contribution to the village for several hundred years. At several points I discussed with various Masson family members a possible research excavation of the extensive remains of the large 13th century Burgundian castle, partly because many brown and yellow exquisite medieval floor tiles were once part of the castle—perhaps a quantity and quality equal to the medieval abbey tile collections at the Louvre in Paris or Ashmolean Museum in Oxford—with pilgrims, dragons, knights, and other motifs. These splendid tiles may be originally from the old Cluniac priory originally here from the 12th century. In addition, I was shown Celtic artifacts like bronze fibulae originally found between rows of vines around the remnants of Château du Gevrey-Chambertin, which may have occupied similar fortified areas adjacent to a nearby Celtic *oppidum* fort here before the Romans came, possibly somewhere around the Lavaut St-Jacques, Les Cazetiers, or Clos St-Jacques parcels or above them in the forest. Equally interesting are the times I've been in Gevrey-Chambertin the weekend before its *vendange*. One of my best recollections in the village was when I once attended the service of *vendange* mass at the Église St. Aignan de Gevrey-Chambertin, the village church above the Rue de Lavaux, with the homily dedicated to St. Vincent, patron of viticulture. Most of the village women were inside singing the old plainsong—much of the music retaining those singular French medieval melodies; most of the men were outside the main sanctuary, remaining in the narthex talking about the upcoming harvest. But just before the priest began the blessing of the harvest, on cue all the village men hurriedly returned inside with a lot of scuffling but with bowed heads to guarantee inclusion of their parcels in the blessing. This was a serious business as the church was suddenly packed and the priest almost grew a foot taller from added relevance.

There is an old medieval story in France that St. Martin (another a saint of viticulture) was once an itinerant cleric and happened to tie up his donkey in a vineyard to a vine. To his horror when he returned, the hungry donkey had eaten most of the vine, cropping almost all its tendrils back to the nub. All thought the vine was severely damaged by this misfortune, but the next spring the plant grew back so vigorously and was so healthy with the best grapes ever, that the monkish vignerons realized the donkey's work was the best possible thing, and they adapted this to all vineyards as the practice of pruning back the vines to encourage their best grape production. Greeks and Romans, of course, have similar stories with different participants including Silenus, yet the donkey is the same agent of pruning, so clearly an amusing old myth has been refurbished.

The picturesque Côte d'Or town of Nuits-St-Georges also has a considerable weight of excellent wines from its vineyards, including 41 Premier Crus. The town is also home to many respected négociants and wine merchants and has its own wine auction for the Hospice du Nuits charities. Premeaux-Prissey to the south along the D-974 is also often considered a satellite of Nuits-St-Georges with some shared Premier Crus between them. Some of the most well-known Nuits-St-George Premier Crus include *Domaine Faiveley*

Fig 11.19 Chateau de Meursault, the author and his wife

Les Porets-Saint-Georges; *Nuits-Saint-Georges Premier Cru 2002, 2005, 2009*; as well as *Domaine Meo-Camuzet Aux Murgers*; *Nuits-Saint-Georges Premier Cru 2002, 2005, 2009*; and *Domaine Leroy Les Boudots Nuits-Saint-Georges Premier Cru 2002, 2005*, and *2009*. Some Côte d'Or vigneron names are so highly regarded that even the wines not Premier Cru are just as desirable, like the late Henri Jayer's *Henri Jayer Nuits-Saint-Georges*, often selling for over $1,000.00.

South along the D-974 between Ladoix and Nuits-St-Georges are some of France's most important quarries around Comblanchien. This noble, faintly honey-hued stone is named *Pierre de Comblanchien*. In the best stone layers of its Bathonian Jurassic deposition, its creamy golden or beige color is slightly marbled with rosy pink and occasional slender veins of translucent calcite. Because it is so durable and fine-grained it can take a polish. It has been used in some of France's most loved monuments, including the gleaming floors of L'Opéra in Paris. Its fame has even brought it to California where it now graces the beautiful floors of the new Bing Concert Hall of Stanford University.

Along its southern flank, the Côte de Beaune is more

Fig 11.20 Caves Chateau de Meursault

Fig 11.21 Bouchard P&F Pommard les Pezerolles, a la Fred Concklin

renowned for its white wines. As mentioned, Aloxe-Corton in the northern part of Côte de Beaune is certainly part of this heritage but also has its magnificent reds—especially south of Beaune, are the villages of Pommard on the slope and Meursault lower along the valley. While excellent wines—especially the Premier Crus from Meursault—are worth every accolade, it is the white wine villages of Puligny-Montrachet and Chassagne-Montrachet that bring the Côte d'Or its deserved crown for white wine like Bâtard-Montachet, Chevalier-Montrachet and at the pinnacle, Le Montrachet. I recently picked up a most reasonable bottle of *Domain Jomain Bâtard-Montrachet 2006 Grand Cru* but this appellation wine is never a bargain. Other excellent wine villages like Volnay and Auxey Duresse lie between Pommard and Meursault and produce some Premier Crus, and while like Ladoix they do not always have the recognition of the other villages, they are generally great bargains. Near the southern edge of the limestone scarp of the Côte d'Or ridge are other subregions and valleys producing some excellent Premier Cru wines from villages like Santenay. Never to be forgotten is the best vintage I recall for several years, the *Bouchard Père & Fils Pommard Les Pézerolles 2009*, especially wonderful paired with the local handmade cheese of Alain Hess, Delice de Pommard with its brown mustard grains and black truffles. One of my favorite stops in Meursault

Fig 11.22. Comte Alexandre de Lur-Saluces with author

has always been the serene Château de Meursault, whose viticultural origins hark back to the 11th century. Its extensive caves below ground are also replete with thousands of bottles and its grounds around the old chateau are lovely to stroll around, venues for more than a few family photographs. I much enjoy *Château de Meursault's Meursault 1er Cru* from their nearby Meursault Charmes and Meursault Perrieres vineyards.

But exploring the Côte Chalonnaise south of the Côte d'Or around Chagny and Rully is also more and more pleasurable, especially after eating incredibly well on three different occasions at Lameloise in Chagny where each evening a different sommelier recommended Rully. It was the Domaine Jacqueson Rully 1er Cru "Grésigny" and was so ethereal that I soon drove out to the domaine with two of my daughters and purchased several bottles personally from Mr. Paul Jacqueson. His Rully was light and subtle as anything I'd ever tasted, as perfect as it was through several courses at Lameloise and almost a dessert by itself.

Vintage Burgundy like the inimitable years of 1985, 1990, and now 1996 and even 1999 and sometimes 2002, are often hard to find, and becoming increasingly so. But in years when the wine is made to last like the DRC's matchless vintages, the wine of Burgundy may reach a profound elegance that seems impossible outside of France. Like this wine, I don't claim to be getting old now, just increasing in vintage. The best wine that lasts like this reminds me of what Jesus said in *Luke* 5:39: No man having drunk old wine wants new right after, for he says, "The old is better."

CHAPTER 12

Champagne and Bubble Physics

"You love your brilliant champagne from Reims ..." Voltaire[114]

Napoleon is often credited with saying, "In victory you deserve champagne, in defeat you need it." Whether he did say it or not doesn't really matter, since he readily comes to mind as one who knew both sides of epic battles. Champagne comes with certain illusions naturally, like Madame de Pompadour thought, "Champagne is the only drink that leaves a woman more beautiful after drinking it." No wonder champagne has the glamorous right of celebration over any other beverage.

Vintage champagne collectors had a wonderful frisson of profound excitement a few years ago: in July 2010 a Baltic shipwrecked schooner was found that had been 50 meters deep in very cold water for 170 years just south of Fasta Aland Island. Divers had revealed and brought up a cargo of champagne, more than a few still sealed and in possibly excellent shape. When initially brought up to the surface where pressure was much less, one bottle's cork had popped from the change in pressure; tasting the open bottle, the first diver Christian Ekstrom found it good and so the salvage operation began. Much of the champagne survived for many reasons: the bottles were lying horizontally as if still racked; the Baltic water was very cold; being so far north, the nearly six months of darkness; and the protection of water deep enough to be almost fully dark the other half of the successive years, ,and little disturbance from tides or storms. The Finnish authorities originally recovered total 168 bottles of champagne, but many were broken or contaminated. Opening up several intact bottles with a few journalists to record the event in Mariehamn on Fasta Aland, the champagne was still good, sweet as tastes dictated nearly 200 years earlier.[115]

The producers of most of the Baltic shipwreck bottles were Juglar—since absorbed into Jacquesson in 1829—and Clicquot (now Veuve Clicquot), with the circa-1829 ship destination likely being St. Petersburg and the Czar Nicholas I's imperial cellars and other Russian princely houses or grand merchants. Initially expecting up to a possible $135,000 total, the lot of 11 surviving champagne bottles (6 Juglar, 4 Clicquot, and 1 Heidsieck) were later

Fig 12.1 Veuve Clicquot

auctioned almost a year later in June, 2012. The separate bids brought up the auction to over $156,000 and one bottle of Clicquot brought 15,0000 euros. One of the buyers was French magnate François Audouze and wine collector who owns 40,000 of the world's best wines, many over a century old and over a quarter of his collection has a vintage of over 50 years. Audouze bought two of the intact salvaged bottles, including one of the 1828 Juglars. Andouze had previously tasted in a London cellar a bottle of 1690 wine.[116]

I well remember my first time in Épernay. My rate of driving slowly up the Avenue de Champagne was directly proportional to the level of awestruck excitement I felt at seeing the houses of many Champagne grand marques I was passing by. These were mid-nineteenth century palaces behind their wrought iron gates, including Moët & Chandon, Perrier Jouët, Heidsieck, Mercier.

I could easily remember the first time I had tasted each of these legendary champagnes. Although other greats like Pol Roger were only a street away and other towns like Ay were home to Bollinger and Deutz and the city of Reims housed Roederer, Krug, Ruinart, Veuve Clicquot, Taittinger, G. H. Mumm, Henriot, and Pommery, the town of Épernay seemed to claim at least half the dual crown shared with Reims for the capital of Champagne.

I found substantial reason to have utmost respect for French champagnistes a few years ago. I was just returning from an annual Alps expedition, eventually making my way to Paris.

Fig 12.2 Billecart-Salmon

Having several days, I had stopped that morning en route in Old Annecy—that tangle of canals in the medieval old town—to pick up some favorite saucisson from the charcuterie Chez Abel, le Petit Saloir—before taking the busy autoroutes northwest. I brought with me an assorted lot: several of each, including *saucisse avec cèpes, saucisse avec du fromage beaufort, saucisson de sanglier sauvage, saucisse fumée, saucisse au fenouil,* among others. The Beaufort cheese–cured sausage had little nougats of aged cheese and the sausage with cèpe mushroom had a liberal number of small cubes interspersed. I was having a wine dinner with French vignerons of the Noellat and Cheurlin families that night at their home in Vosne-Romanée. I wanted to bring something comestible and figured my modest contribution would be the appetizer viands before the actual meal, which also promised fine wines. It turned out that my vigneron friends' son, Mr. Cheurlin was a champagniste himself from Cheurlin-Noellat in Bar-sür-Seine in the Aube region of Champagne and now visiting his ancestral home in Burgundy with his children for Grand-Maman to spoil.

Setting my prizes on the outdoor table where the family was gathering, it already looked promising that Mr. Cheurlin loved saucisson as much as I did or maybe more. To begin with he had a grand moustache that would have made a Gallic chieftain proud and above it a great nose looking like it belonged to a man triple his size. It was a fine nose in other respects as well. Although I'd had no intention of testing him, after I had peeled off all the labels, he was easily able—with his eyes shut and in a deeply religious voice suited for a liturgy—to immediately identify every saucisson with a happy sigh, just from the bouquet. My nose may not be a parfumier's but I could have identified some of them blind too, like the smoked one and maybe the fennel one, but the others I would know only by taste like the gamy wild boar, whereas Mr. Cheurlin could hold a small slice four inches from his moustache-brushed nose and still get it right as if there was some semi-divine message wafting subtly through the evening air, "Ah, Beaufort. Oui, Sanglier." To me that olfactory feat signaled a rare gift and decades of intensive training.

Champagne Geology

The legal right to use the word Champagne is closely watched around the world and vigorously protected, justly so and not just for tariffs. Such quotes as "The word 'Champagne' is so full of meaning, so desirable that it has always provoked envy," spoken by a member of the CIVC (The Comite Interprofessionel du Vin de Champagne), France, makes perfect sense. Watchdogs for France are vigilant, and outside the Champagne region, international trade laws are in place to compel acquiescence with malediction followed by full court fury. Of course, *méthode champenoise* is fully acceptable even if little difference may actually be found except in the terroirs.

Fig 12.3 Bollinger

The rolling French countryside between Epernay, Reims, and especially along the Vallée de la Marne and the underlying strata have a unique geological combination of limestones, chalks, and clays across several hundred million years of Jurassic and Cretaceous sedimentary deposits with some of the most brilliantly white calcaire in the world, all fairly alkaline in soil chemistry under the surface. Once the ocean receded some 70 million years ago, leaving behind residual chalk deposits, great wrenching seismic events pushed the old marine layers to the surface for erosion. The Champagne Plain of the Paris Basin is not reproduced anywhere else like this. The name Champagne is merely the Gallic version of Southern Italy's Campania and Central Italy's eastern Campagna of Rome because the same Latin word sources each: *campania* for "open country."[117]

Why Bubbles?

Staring at the bubbles in a champagne glass isn't necessarily a sign of being under the influence. Poets, however inspired, have described champagne bubbles metaphorically as cabuchon gold or pearl gems, as in the above image. Nor is the physics of champagne merely a guaranteed interesting table conversation topic. Not to be outdone by poets, physicists have studied the bubbles in champagne and sparkling wine for more than a century and a half, where the behavior of carbon dioxide follows a regular pattern of gases in a liquid. Who hasn't watched the bubbles rise in golden chains though a flute, increasing in size as they rise to the surface, wondering why the bubbles grow as they ascend? That's one effect that champagne seems to have on both poets and physicists.

One scientist in particular appears to have studied these kinds of questions and their history more assiduously than almost anyone else, possibly suggesting not only that he is connoisseur of champagne but one of its most informed consumers. Gerard Liger-Belair at the Université de Reims in the heart of France's champagne country is just that highly

Fig 12.4 Champagne Dom Perignon 1988

regarded bubbles expert, judging by only a selection of his publications below. Many people assume that champagne was "discovered" in the late 17th century and perfected by the Abbey of Hautvillers monk cellar master Dom Pierre Pérignon sometime after 1670, but it was more likely that he merely began to tame the rogue bubbles. The Church wanted to rein in the effervescence in what was called the "Devil's Wine" because so many bottles exploded in their monastic cellars in the region, and Dom Pérignon was tasked to reduce effervescence. It was mostly a physics problem whose solutions had to be practical. As Liger-Belair relates in his fascinating book *Uncorked: The Science of Champagne* (Princeton 2004), a famous anecdote is that Dom Pérignon reputedly exclaimed, "Come quickly, brothers, I am drinking stars!" True story or not, another poetic metaphor is born. But at first there were more negatives than positives in the up-and-down story of champagne. No less informative on the fluctuations of champagne, including gutsy wartime survival of heroic champagnistes, is Don and Petie Kladstrup's excellent book, *Champagne: How the World's Most Glamorous Wine Triumphed Over War and Hard Times* (Harper, 2006). One Kladstrup factoid reinforcing the danger of exploding bottles was the requisite iron grill facemask worn on early cellar visits.

Fig 12.5 Dom Perignon

Boyle's Law and Champagne

Stronger bottles—including thicker glass and a deep punt "dimple" in the base—and more reliable ways of keeping the cork secure, eventually a wire cage called a *muselet*, were two evolving fixes. Comparing the wider-base cork from a bottle of champagne or sparkling wine to the straight cylindrical cork of normal wine shows another solution applied to this higher-pressure fermentation product known as champagne. These physics fixes didn't happen overnight but rather over decades and even at least a century between the late 17th and 18th centuries. It must not be a coincidence that these pragmatic improvements happened during the Enlightenment when burgeoning science also came to grips with Boyle's Law on the behavior of gases and Lavoisier's later identification of oxygen. How timely is it that Robert Boyle published his law in 1662, the same year other champagne milestones occurred, discussed below? Boyle's Law essentially states that the relationship between the absolute pressure and volume of a gas is inversely proportional if the temperature is kept at a constant within a closed system. Sounds like either Boyle was studying champagne or others applied his published experiments to champagne! This is exactly the problem champagnistes were encountering with fluctuating temperature from winter to spring in Champagne's refermentation cycle. So there is a directly proportional relationship between Boyle's Law and champagne!

Roman Bubbly?

I was back in Épernay in 2010 at Moët & Chandon in conversation with the champagne house communication department representative Stephan Jacquemin. We were musing about the earliest history of sparkling wine, possibly before Dom Pérignon.[118] Many have suggested the Romans had a natural sparkling wine with inevitable but unpredictable carbonation. If true and Roman vintners ever achieved something close to a tight seal for even a short period, the carbonation pressure must have shattered more than a few clay amphorae. Although much debated and not necessarily desirable or sought after, some evidence for this Roman antecedent is often posited in the Latin word *spumatio* and its source verb *spumo*,[119] speculating that Italian spumante wine derives from a much older Roman tradition.

But it is important to remember that sparkling wine would not have necessarily been a contrived effort but instead merely a natural by-product of carbonation from yeast. Jancis Robinson clearly explains in *The Oxford Companion to Wine* that "bubbles form because a certain amount of carbon dioxide has been held under pressure dissolved in the wine until the bottle is unstoppered, in which case the wine is transformed from the stable to the meta-stable state."[120]

As mentioned, the natural yeast's carbonation produced undesirable results for centuries, including bursting bottles, since the cold French winters halted fermentation and warmer spring kick-started fermentation again. It was touch and go until stronger bottles were specially made to withstand the internal pressure. That the Romans were in and around Reims is clear from the chalk mines that now comprise some of Pommery's and others' champagne caves converted from chalk pits, called *crayères*, around 30 meters (about 100 feet) underground.[121] I visited these ancient chalk pits over a decade ago and noted the abundant intact Roman artifacts on display in the adjacent mines sharing space with champagne racks.

Widow Clicquot's Legacy

Tastes changed radically after the sparkling wine from the region of Champagne was introduced at the Louis XIV's Versailles court by Marquis de Sillery. It was the exiled Marquis Charles de St-Évremond who seems to have presented champagne to London around 1662. Christopher Merret had even read a paper in 1662 before the Royal Society in London about how to make sparkling wine. Since our London-based historian daughter had introduced us to Tilar Mazzeo's recent book *The Widow Clicquot: The Story of a Champagne Empire and the Woman Who Ruled It* (Harper, 2008), our family duly trooped in pilgrimage through the countryside to see Madame Clicquot's neo-Gothic chateau in Boursault overlooking the

Marne. Madame Clicquot retired here after almost single-handedly building the supply-and-demand global champagne market by 1840, making it an elegant commodity by her merchandising genius. Thanks to Veuve ("Widow") Clicquot (née Barbe Nicole Ponsardin), champagne today is a status beverage whose orderly bubbles confer even more elegance on grand ladies, especially the ambience of an excellent champagne. The international LVMH (Moët Hennessy—Louis Vuitton S.A.) Group is well represented not only in Épernay but anywhere wealth and celebration meet. Although LVMH has a stable of thoroughbred perfume and fashion houses like Louis Vuitton, Fendi, Dior, Givenchy, and even a 20% stake in Hermes, it controls many of the world's best names in the world of wine and spirits. In addition to Hennessy cognac and the great Sauterne of Château d'Yquem as two of its holdings, its Champagnes are Dom Pérignon, Moët & Chandon, Veuve Clicquot, and Krug.

Fig 12.6 Chateau de Boursault Veuve Clicquot

California Sparkling Wines and Méthode Champenoise

As I frequently present lectures on the history of ancient wine in wineries and for vintners in California wine country, I did so to the Napa Valley Vintners Association a few years ago at Meadowood, St. Helena, and met makers of several excellent sparkling wines, also tasting these California sparklings on many occasions. More than a few of these sparkling producers are offshoots of great French houses transplanted to California. For example, Chandon's parent is also LVMH, and Domaine Carneros' parent is Taittinger, whose La Rêve is arguably just about the best in California. Mumm Napa's top sparkling is DVX, named after founder Guy deVaux who left France in 1960 and Mumm Napa is owned by the French company Pernod Ricard, which also owns G. H. Mumm & Cie and Perrier-Jouët champagne. On the other hand, California has its own quality sparkling producers independent of international French companies with a stake in California. Schramsberg is also often touted as the best sparkling wine in California and vintner Hugh Davies continues the Schramsberg legacy that started in 1862.[122] Some primary differences of *méthode champenoise* in California are that the blend is primarily Chardonnay and Pinot Noir, rarely Pinot Meunier, and of course the California terroir is completely different and rarely a limestone chalk base. One other distinction may be the amount of time spent being racked, where California sparklings may be generally released somewhat earlier at 18 months to 6 years for the best, instead of 3 years minimum for vintage and *prestige cuvée* of 7 years for the French grand marques. Otherwise the best California sparkling wines mentioned above are becoming known for finesse that must be acknowledged worldwide since the 1980's.[23]

Now given the enormous worth of the global champagne industry since Barbe Nicole Ponsardin-Clicquot (in France 322 million bottles of champagne were sold in 2008, with at least $3.5 billion or more in sales[124]), champagne bubbles and their non-French effervescent cousins—sparkling wine—are entirely worthy of the scientific study they can easily afford.

Bubble Physics

After initial natural fermentation when fruit sugar and yeast mix in the air, champagne requires secondary yeast and sugar in addition to what nature puts in, producing carbon dioxide pressure from the CO_2 gas trapped in the liquid. The volume of trapped carbon dioxide begins its release when the wide-based cork is popped from its high-pressure wired-tight contact with the champagne bottle's enlarged rim.

Flutes produce a better aroma of bursting bubbles than wider-rim glasses partly because they increase the distance bubbles rise, and therefore the kinetic energy of the bubbles, and concentrate the surface area; indeed the whole liquid surface of a concentrated champagne flute participates in the bubble-bursting at a greater rate, which enhances the champagne aroma, especially of a great champagne.

As Liger-Belair informs, people often assume the higher quality of a champagne based on a smaller size of individual bubbles. The old adage "the smaller the bubbles, the better the wine" is partly true aesthetically as well as physically. Smaller bubbles "rise more leisurely … and consequently create the wine's characteristically lingering sort of effervescence and delicate inner glow." But better, vintage champagne is also usually older, meaning that it has lost some carbon dioxide and presents a lower bubble rate.[125]

The bubbles in champagne and sparkling wine may start out at around 20 micrometers in size from nucleation sites on the glass but can grow to 1 millimeter just before reaching the surface. The bubbles increase in size mostly because of the decrease in surrounding liquid pressure as they approach the surface.

The velocity of migration of champagne bubbles upward in a column is such that only the top of a bubble rises above the surface. Then the liquid around the bubble crown drains downward in a time span of from 10 to 100 milliseconds and the bubble crown is reduced to a thickness of 100 nanometers, too thin to sustain itself and it ruptures. The collapsing liquid rushes inward, collecting itself in such a way as to send a tiny jet upward that breaks into droplets. These droplets traveling several meters per second can also reach a height above the liquid of a few centimeters, which can be felt on the face if the champagne flute is full.

According to Philip Ball from the research of Vandevall et al., the popping sounds of champagne bubbles are in fact like avalanches where each bursting bubble seems to affect the others. There is a mathematical relationship—described as a power law—not only where the duration of a bubble's "life" is unpredictable but so is the time gap between bubbles bursting. As champagne bubbles burst, they unpredictably compel other bubbles to change shape and possibly pop as well, but it is at a so-far-unknowable rate. If you bend down and listen to the champagne fizz or feel it on your face, someone will probably jump to the conclusion you've reached your limit unless you can convince people you're a scientist like Liger-Belair.

Some say there are up to 50 million mesmerizing bubbles in a bottle of champagne,[126] but if you try counting more than a few, you're probably beyond the state of Russia's Peter the Great (à la Kladstrup) who nightly took—along with other more warm curves—four bottles of champagne to bed. Perhaps those are the kinds of parabolas Archimedes could have only dreamed to measure in Elysium.

BIBLIOGRAPHY

Leslie Adkins and Roy A. Adkins. "Vinalia" in *Dictionary of Roman Religion*. New York: Facts on File, 1995, 232–4, 240.

Hamish H. Aird. "Assyria" and "Greece" in Jancis Robinson, ed. *Oxford Companion to Wine*. Oxford: Oxford University Press, 1994, 61, 463 ff.

Maxwell L. Anderson. "Pompeian Frescoes in The Metropolitan Museum of Art." *The Metropolitan Museum of Art Bulletin*, 45.3 (Winter, 1987–88) 17–36.

Lew Andrews. "Botticelli's Primavera, Angelo Poliziano and Ovid's Fasti." *Artibus et Historiae* 63 (XXXII) 2011, 4 & ff.

Marcus Gavius Apicius. *De Re Coquinaria* I. (Epimeles) II.1–8.

W. Arrowsmith. *Petronius' Satyricon*. University of Michigan, 1959.

Athenaeus: The Deipnosophists, vol. 1 (Books 1–3.106e). C. B. Gulick, tr. Cambridge, MA: Loeb Classical Library 204/Harvard University Press, (1927) 1961 rev.

Leora Auslander. "When Champagne Became French: Wine and the Making of a National Identity." *The American Historical Review* 110.1 (2005) 232–33.

Raphaëlle Bacqué. "Elysee Aromatic—Journey onto the Wine Cellar of France's Presidential Palace." *Le Monde*, Dec 27, 2012.

Philip Ball. "The Fizz-ics of Champagne." *Nature: International Journal Weekly of Science (Science Update)* (Jan. 8, 2001).

Hellmut Baumann. *The Greek Plant World*. Portland: Timber Press, 1993.

Elizabeth Belfiore. "Wine and Catharsis of Emotions in Plato's Laws." *Classical Quarterly* 36.2 (1986) 421–37.

Nicholas Belfrage. *The Finest Wines of Tuscany and Central Italy: A Regional and Village Guide to the Best Wines and Their Producers*. Berkeley: University of California, 2009.

J. S. Bergsma and Scott Hahn. "Noah's Nakedness and the Curse on Canaan (Genesis 9:20–27)." *Journal of Biblical Literature* 124.1 (2005) 25–40.

Lesley Beaumont. "Mythological Childhood: A Male Preserve? An Interpretation of Classical Athenian Iconography in Its Socio-Historical Context."*Annual of the British School at Athens* 90 (1995) 339–61.

Robert Blumberg and Hurst Hannum. *The Fine Wines of California*. Third Edition. New York: Doubleday, 1984.

John Boardman. *Athenian Black Figure Vases*. London: Thames and Hudson, 1974.

_____. *Athenian Red Figure Vases: The Archaic Period*. London: Thames and Hudson, 1975 repr.

Hieronymus Bock. *De stirpium commentariorum libri tres*, Strassburg (Strasbourg), 1552. Note also his *Neu Kreütter Buch von underscheydt, würckung und namen*. Strassburg (Strasbourg), 1539.

Fiora Bonelli. "Pestarole etrusche nel castello: I segreti del vino al Potestino." *Il Tirreno-Grosseto*. Jan. 14, 2011.

Larissa Bonfante, ed. *Etruscan Life and Afterlife: A Handbook of Etruscan Studies*. Detroit: Wayne State University Press, 1986.

Jessica Bordoni. "I Top Hundred 2011 di Paolo Massobrio e Marco Gatti." *Civiltà del Bere*, Sept. 16, 2011.

Philippe Borgeaud. "Dionysos, the Wine and Ikarios: Hospitality and Danger" in Renate Schlesier, ed. *A Different God?: Dionysos and Ancient Polytheism*. Berlin: Walter de Gruyter, 2011, 161–72.

Jean Bottero. *Everyday Life in Ancient Mesopotamia*. Baltimore: Johns Hopkins University Press, 2001.

Ewen Bowie. "Wandering Poets, Archaic Style" in Richard Hunter and Ian Rutherford, eds. *Wandering Poets in Ancient Greek Culture: Travel, Locality and Pan-Hellenism*. Cambridge: Cambridge University Press, 2009, 135–36.

Michael Broadbent. *The Great Vintage Wine Book*. New York: Knopf/Christie's, 1991.

Jean-Pierre Brun. *Archéologie du vin et de l'huile de la préhistoire à l'époque hellénistique*. Paris: Editions Errance, 2004.

_____. "Le Tecniche di Spremitura dell'Uva: origini e Svi-Luppo dell'Uso del Torchio nel Mediterraneo Occidentale." *Archeologia della Vitivinicoltura nel Mediterraneo Occidentale*, 2007.

Walter Burkert. *Greek Religion*. Cambridge, MA: Harvard University Press, 1985.

Sylvie Cazes and Jean-Marc Giraud, eds. *Union des Grands Crus de Bordeaux, 2012–13 ed.* Bordeaux: UGCB, 2011.

Zeffiro Ciuffoletti and Paolo Nanni, eds. *Un vino di Maremma. Il Morellino di Scansano*, Pitigliano: Editrice Laurum, 2002.

Barbara Clinkenbeard. "Lesbian Wine and Storage Amphoras: A Progress Report on Identification." *Hesperia* 51.3 (1982) 248–68.

Clive Coates. *An Encyclopedia of the Wines and Domaines of France*. Berkeley: University of California 2001.

_____. *The Wines of Burgundy*. Berkeley: University of California, 2008 rev.

Columella, *de Re Rustica* 5.4.1 & 5.5.16.

Alexander Conison. *The Organization of Rome's Wine Trade*. Ph.D. Dissertation, University of Michigan, 2012.

Andrew Dalby. *Food in the Ancient World: From A-Z*. London: Routledge, 2003.

Stephanie Dalley. *Mari and Karana: Two Old Babylonian Cities*. Piscataway, NJ: Gorgias Press, 2002.

Stephanie M. Dalley, tr. *Myths from Mesopotamia: Creation, the Flood, Gilgamesh and Others*. Oxford: Oxford University Press, 2009 rev. ed.

Michal Dayagi-Mendels. *Drink and Be Merry: Wine and Beer in Ancient Times*. Jerusalem: The Israel Museum, 1999.

B. C. Dietrich. "A Rite of Swinging During the Anthesteria." *Hermes* 89 (1961) 36–50.

E. R. Dodds. *The Greeks and the Irrational*. Berkeley: University of California Press, 1951.

Stefan K. Estreicher. *Wine: From Neolithic Times to the 21st Century*. New York: Algora Publishing, 2006.

H. Rushton Fairclough, tr. *Virgil I. Eclogues, Georgics Aeneid 1–6*. Cambridge, MA: Harvard University Press / Loeb Classics Library 63, 1999 rev. ed.

Ferdowsi's *Shahnameh: The Persian Book of Kings*. Dick Davis, tr. New York: Penguin Books, 2007.

John Forsdyke. "The 'Harvester' Vase of Hagia Triada." *Journal of the Warburg and Courtauld Institutes* 17.1/2 (1954) 1–9.

Karen Pollinger Foster. "Dionysos and Vesuvius in the Villa of the Mysteries." *Antike Kunst* 44 (2001) 37–54.

Christopher Foulkes. *Larousse Encyclopedia of Wine*. Paris: Larousse, 2001.

J. A. A. de la Fuente. "Some Thoughts on Etruscan *math-* '(Honeyed) Wine.'" *Historische Sprachforschung* Bd. 120 (2007) 305–10.

Deutscher Wein Statistik, German Wine Institute, 2008.

Louis Forest. *Monseigneur Le Vin, Paris, 1927—Wine Album*. New York: Metropolitan Museum of Art, 1982.

Barbara Hughes Fowler, tr. *Love Lyrics of Ancient Egypt*. University of North Carolina Press, 1994.

P. Galet and L. T. Morton. *A Practical Ampellography*. Ithaca and London: Cornell University Press, 1979. *Genesis* 9:20–23 NSRV.

Douglas Gerber, tr. *Greek Iambic Poetry: From the Seventh to the Fifth Centuries BC. (Archilochos, Semonides, Hipponax)*. Cambridge, MA: Loeb Classical Library 259/Harvard University Press, 1999.

Margarita Gleba. "Archaeology in Etruria 2003–09." Council of the British School at Athens. *Archaeological Reports* 55 (2008–2009).

J. B. Gough. "Winecraft and Chemistry in 18th-century France: Chaptal and the Invention of Chaptalization." *Journal of Technology and Culture* 39.1 (1998) 74–104.

Joseph A. Greene and D. P. Kehoe. "Mago the Carthaginian on Agriculture: Archaeology and the Ancient Sources." *Actes du IIIème Congrès International des études phéniciennes et puniques*, II, Tunis, 1991, 110–17.

O. R. Gurney. *The Hittites*. London: The Folio Society (Penguin, 1952), 2002 (sixth printing).

T. M. Hickey. *Wine, Wealth and the State in Late Antique Egypt: The House of Apion at Oxyrhynchus*. Ann Arbor: University of Michigan Press, 2012.

Stephanie Holmes. "'World's Oldest Champagne' Found on Baltic Seabed" *BBC News*, July 17, 2010.

Mack P. Holt. "Wine, Community and Reformation in Sixteenth Century Burgundy." *Past & Present* 138 (1993) 58–93.

Homer. *Odyssey* IX.119, 142–3 (Robert Fitzgerald translation).

Horace. *Odes and Epodes*. Niall Rudd, tr. Cambridge, MA: Harvard—Loeb Classical Library, 2004.

Patrick Hunt. "Summus Poeninus in the Grand-St-Bernard Pass." *Journal of Roman Archaeology* XI (1998) 265–74.

_____. "A Roman Refuge in the Plan de Barasson: Field Reports for 1998–2000." *Vallesia: Chronique du découvertes archéologiques dans le canton du Valais* LIV (Sion, 1999) 300–08.

_____. "Triptolemos and Beyond in the Stanford Kleophon Krater." *Journal of the Cantor Center for Visual Arts, (Stanford Museum Journal)* (Winter, 2001, 3–8.

_____. "Bronze Tabulae Ansatae at Roman Summus Poeninus in the Roman Alps." *Acta: From the Parts to the Whole, vol. 2, Proceedings of XIIIth Int'l. Bronze Congress*, Harvard University Art Museums, *JRA Suppl.* 2002.

_____. *Caravaggio*. Life & Times Series. London: Haus Publishing, 2004

Henry R. Immerwahr. "New Wine in Ancient Wineskins: The Evidence from Attic Vases." *Hesperia* 61.1 (1992) 121–32.

Jonathan I. Israel. *Dutch Primacy in World Trade 1585-1740*. Oxford, 1989.

Ronald S. Jackson. *Wine Science: Principles and Applications*. London and Burlington, MA: Academic Press/Elsevier, 2008 third ed.

M. K. James. *Studies in the Medieval Wine Trade*. Oxford: Clarendon Press, 1971.

Ian Jenkins and Kim Sloan. *Vases and Volcanoes*. British Museum Press, 1996.

Hugh Johnson. *Vintage: The Story of Wine*. New York: Simon and Schuster, 1989 (also see 2006 ed.).

Hugh Johnson and Jancis Robinson. *The World Atlas of Wine*. London: Mitchell Beazley, 6th rev. ed. 2007.

Don and Petie Kladstrup. *Wine and War: The French, the Nazis, and France's Greatest Treasure*. Broadway/Coronet, 2001.

_____. *Champagne: How the World's Most Glamorous Wine Triumphed Over War and Hard Times*. New York: Harper Books, 2006.

K. Kotsakis. "Viticulture in Prehistoric Macedonia: The Evidence from Toumba." *Proceedings of the workshop on viticulture*, Athens 1998.

Kostas Kotsakis and Maria Mangafa. "A New Method for the Identification of Wild and Cultivated Charred Grape Seeds." *Journal of Archaeological Science*, 23.3 (1996) 409–18.

K. Kristiansen. *Europe Before History*. Cambridge: Cambridge University Press, 1998.

Giuseppe Tomasi di Lampedusa. *The Siren (Il Professore e la Sirena) and Selected Writings*. London: Harvill Press, 1995.

D. H. Lawrence. *Etruscan Places*. London: Martin Secker, 1933 (Leiserson Press, 2007 repr.).

Stephanie A. Layton. "Etruscan Bucchero Pottery from Cetamura del Chianti." *Etruscan Studies* 12.1 (2009) 21–60.

Karl Lehmann. "Ignorance and Search in the Villa of the Mysteries." *Journal of Roman Studies* 52 (1962) 62–68.

Peter Leithart. "Nabal and His Wine." *Journal of Biblical Literature* 120.3 (2001) 525–7.

Leonard Lesko. *King Tut's Wine Cellar*. Berkeley: B.C. Scribe Publications, 1978.

_____. "Egyptian Wine Production in the New Kingdom" in McGovern et al., 1995, 215–30.

Alexis Lichine. *Alexis Lichine's Encyclopedia of Wines and Spirits*. London: Cassell, 1987 ed.

Gérard Liger-Belair. "The Science of Bubbly." *Scientific American* (December, 2002).

_____. *Uncorked: The Science of Champagne*. Princeton University Press, 2004, 3, 8, 59 & ff.

_____. "The Physics and Chemistry Behind the Bubbling Properties of Champagne and Sparkling Wines: A State-of-the-Art Review." *Journal of Agricultural and Food Chemistry* 53.8 (2005) 2788–2802.

Lexicon Iconographicum Mythologiae Classicae, "Dionysos," vol. III. Zürich, Münich, Düsseldorf: Artemis and Winkler Verlag, 1988, 478–82, plates 376–81.

François Lissarague. *The Aesthetics of the Greek Banquet: Images of Wine and Ritual*. A. Szegedy-Maszak, tr. Princeton: Princeton University Press, 1991.

Alan B. Lloyd. *A Companion to Ancient Egypt*, vol. 1. Wiley, 2010.

Paul Lukacs. *Inventing Wine: A New History of One of the World's Most Ancient Pleasures*. New York: W. W. Norton, 2012.

Joanna Luke. "The Krater, Kratos and the Polis. *Journal of Greece & Rome* xli.1 (1994) 23–32.

Kermit Lynch. *Adventures on the Wine Route: A Wine Buyer's Tour of France*. New York: North Point Press/Farrar, Straus and Giroux, 1995 ed.

Jenny March. *The Penguin Book of Classical Myths*. London: Allen Lane, 2008.

B. Margalit, "The Ugaritic Feast of the Drunken Gods: Another Look at RS 24.258 (KTU 1.114)," *Maarav* 2.1 (1979–80) 65–66.

Tilar Mazzeo. *The Widow Clicquot: The Story of a Champagne Empire and the Woman Who Ruled It*. New York: Harper-Collins, 2008.

Patrick E. McGovern. "Wine for Eternity." *Archaeology* 51.4 (1998).

_____. *Ancient Wine: The Search for the Origins of Viniculture*. Princeton: Princeton University Press, 2007.

_____. *Uncorking the Past: The Quest for Wine, Beer and Other Alcoholic Beverages*. Berkeley: University of California Press, 2009.

Patrick E. McGovern, Stuart Fleming, and Sol H. Katz, eds. *The Origins and Ancient History of Wine*. Philadelphia: Gordon and Breach, 1995.

Patrick E. McGovern, D. L. Glusker, L. J. Exner, and Mary M. Voigt. "Neolithic Resinated Wine." *Nature* 381 (1996) 480–481.

Patrick McGovern, Armin Mirzoian, Gretchen Hall, and Ofer Bar-Josef. "Ancient Egyptian Herbal Wines." *Proceedings of the National Academy of Sciences* 106.18 (2009) 7361–66.

Karen MacNeil. *The Wine Bible*. New York: Workman Publishing, 2001.

Carole P. Meredith. "Science as a Window in Wine History." *Bulletin of the American Academy of Arts and Sciences* 56.2 (2003) 54–70.

Jon D. Mikalson. *Ancient Greek Religion*. Blackwell Ancient Religions Series. Oxford: Wiley-Blackwell, 2010, 2nd ed.

Naomi F. Miller. "Sweeter Than Wine? The Use of the Grape in Early Western Asia." *Antiquity* 82 (2008) 937–46.

Marc Millon. *Oz Clarke's Wine Companion to Tuscany*. London: Webster's International Publishers, 1997.

David Molyneux-Berry. *The Sotheby's Guide to Classic Wines*. New York: Ballantine Books, 1990.

Jennifer Moore. *A Survey of the Italian Dressel 2-4 Wine Amphora*. M.A. Thesis. McMaster University, 1995.

Mark P. O. Morford and Robert J. Lenardon. *Classical Mythology*. New York: Oxford University Press, 2007 ed.

Michael G. Mullins, Alain Bouquet, and Larry E. Williams. *Biology of the Grapevine*. Cambridge: Cambridge University Press, 1992.

Mary Anne Murray. "Viticulture and Wine Production" in Paul Nicholson and Ian Shaw, eds. *Ancient Egyptian Materials and Technology*. Cambridge: Cambridge University Press, 2000, 581–7.

Bill Nanson. *The Finest Wines of Burgundy*. Berkeley: University of California Press, 2012.

Roland De Narbonne. *Château du Clos de Vougeot*. Paris: Société d'Édition Régionales, 1995.

Nonnos, *Dionysiaca* 47.

Remington Norman. *Grand Cru: The Great Wines of Burgundy Through the Perspective of Its Finest Vineyards*. New York: Sterling Epicure, 2011.

John F. Nunn. *Ancient Egyptian Medicine*. London: British Museum Press, 2006.

Gloria Olcese and Stefania Giunta. eds. "I. Ischia: Le anfore greco italiche di Ischia: archeologia e archeometria." *Immensa Aequora: Ricerche archeologiche, archeometriche e informatiche per la ricostruzione dell'economia e dei commerci nel bacino occidentale del Mediterraneo*, 2012, 21–22.

Kerin O'Keefe. *Brunello di Montalcino: Understanding and Appreciating One of Italy's Greatest Wines*. Berkeley: University of California Press, 2012.

William C. O'Neal. *Archeology of the Christopher Buckley Winery*.

Livermore Valley Museum Wine Project. Livermore: TAS. 1986.

Kirk Ormand. *A Companion to Sophocles*. Blackwell Companions to the Ancient World. Oxford: Blackwell-Wiley, 2012.

James Owen. "Earliest Known Winery Found in Armenian Cave." *National Geographic News*, January 10, 2011.

Alessandro Papo, Gianluca Citi, and Letizia Marini. "Vini etruschi e anfore di Calafuria." *Il Relitto Etrusco di Calafuria*. Nibbiaia, Rosignano Marittimo (Livorno): Gruppo Archaeosub Labronico, 2006.

Robert C. T. Parker. "The Anthesteria and Other Dionysiac Rites." *Polytheism and Society at Athens*. Part II, Chapter 14. Oxford: Oxford University Press, 2007.

Robert M. Parker. Jr. *Burgundy: A Comprehensive Guide*. New York: Simon and Schuster, 1990.

Jeremy Paterson. "Salvation from the Sea: Amphorae and Trade in the Roman West." *Journal of Roman Studies* 72 (1982) 146–57.

_____. "Classical Rome" in Jancis Robinson, ed., *Oxford Companion to Wine*, Oxford, 1994, 819–20.

_____. "Wine" in Simon Hornblower and Antony Spawforth, eds. *Oxford Companion to Classical Civilization*. Oxford University Press, 1998, 775.

D. P. S. Peacock and D. F. Williams. *Amphorae and the Roman Wine Economy*. London: Longman, 1986.

Thomas Pellechia. *Wine: The 8,000-Year-Old Story of the Wine Trade*. Philadelphia: Running Press Books (Perseus), 2006.

Lisa Pieraccini. "The Wonders of Wine in Etruria," in N. T. de Grummond, I. Edlund-Berry, eds. *The Archaeology of Sanctuaries and Ritual in Etruria*. JRA [Journal of Roman Archaeology] Supplementary series, *81*, 2011, 127–38.

_____. "Food and Drink in the Etruscan World" in *The World of the Etruscans*, ed. Jean Turfa. New York: Routledge, 2013.

Pliny. *Natural History* XIV.6.8

Guillaume Polidori, Philippe Jeandet, and Gérard Liger-Belair. "Bubbles and Flow Patterns in Champagne: Random Effervescence." *American Scientist* 97.4 (July–August 2009) 294.

Marvin A. Powell. "Wine and the Vine in Ancient Mesopotamia: The Cuneiform Evidence" in Patrick E. McGovern, Stuart Fleming, and Sol H. Katz, eds. *The Origins and Ancient History of Wine*. Philadelphia: Gordon and Breach, 1995, 96–124.

N. Purcell. "Wine and Wealth in Ancient Italy." *Journal of Roman Studies* 75 (1985) 1–19.

François Rabelais. *Gargantuan and Pantagruel*. Jacques LeClercq, tr. New York: Heritage Press, 1942.

Jancis Robinson. *The Oxford Companion to Wine*. Oxford: Oxford University Press, 1994.

Jancis Robinson, Julia Harding, and José Vouillamoz, eds. Wine Grapes. *A Complete Guide to 1,368 Vine Varieties, Including Their Origins and Flavours*. London: Penguin/Ecco Books, 2012.

Alexander Rofé. "Naboth's Vineyard: The Origin and Message of the Story." *Vetus Testamentum* 38.1 (1988) 89–104.

H. J. Rose. *A Handbook of Greek Mythology*. London: Routledge, 1991 ed. (Methuen, 1928).

Brigette Ford Russell. "Wine, Women and the *Polis*: Gender and the Formation of the City-State in Archaic Rome." *Journal of Greece & Rome* 50.1 (2003) 77–84.

David Sacks, with revisions by Oswyn Murray and Lisa Brody. "Dionysus" in the *Encyclopedia of the Ancient Greek World*. New York: Facts on File, 2005 rev. ed.

Bruce Sanderson. "Heaven on Earth." *Wine Spectator,* May, 2010, 49.

Klaus Schmidt. "Göbekli Tepe, Southeastern Turkey: A Preliminary Report on the 1995–1999 Excavations." *Paléorient* 26 (2001) 45–54.

Richard Seaford. *Dionysos*. London: Routledge, 2006.

Desmond Seward. *Monks and Wine*. New York: Crown Publishers, 1979.

Ian Shaw and Paul Nicholson. *The Dictionary of Ancient Egypt*. London: British Museum Press, 1995.

Mary Taylor Simeti. *On Persephone's Island: A Sicilian Journal*. Random House, 1986.

Susan Sontag. *The Volcano Lover*. Farrar, Straus and Giroux, 1992.

Nigel Spivey. *Etruscan Art*. London: Thames and Hudson, 1997.

M. Stephen Spurr. "Agricultural Writers" in Simon Hornblower and Antony Spawforth, eds. *Oxford Companion to Classical Civilization*. Oxford University Press, 1998, 19.

_____. "Roman Agricultural Implements" in Simon Hornblower and Antony Spawforth, eds. *Oxford Companion to Classical Civilization*. Oxford University Press, 1998, 18.

Tom Standage. *A History of the World in 6 Glasses*. New York: Walker Publishing, 2006.

Richard C. Steiner. "On the Rise and Fall of Canaanite Religion at Baalbek: A Tale of Five Toponyms." *Journal of Biblical Literature* 128.3 (2009) 507–25.

T. Stevenson. *The New Sotheby's Wine Encyclopedia*. New York: Dorling Kindersley, 2001.

Stephan Steingräber. *Abundance of Life: Etruscan Wall Painting*. R. Stockman, tr. Los Angeles: J. Paul Getty Museum Publications, 2006.

David L. Stone. "Culture and Investment in the Rural Landscape: the North African *bonus agricola.*" *Antiquités africaines* 34 (1998) 103–13.

Strabo, *Geography* VI.3.102.

David Stronach. "The Imagery of the Wine Bowl: Wine in Assyria in the Early First Millennium B.C." in Patrick E. McGovern, Stuart Fleming, and Sol H. Katz, eds. *The Origins and Ancient History of Wine*. Philadelphia: Gordon and Breach, 1995, 181–203.

George M. Taber. *Judgment of Paris: California versus France and the Historic 1976 Paris Tasting That Revolutionized Wine*. New York: Simon and Schuster, 2006.

Daniel Thomases. "Campania" in Jancis Robinson, ed. *The Oxford Companion to Wine*. Oxford: Oxford University Press, 1994, 183–4.

Jonathan N. Tubb. *Canaanites*. Peoples of the Past Series. London: British Museum Press, 1998.

James Turnbull. *Rhone Valley: The 90 Greatest Wines*. Paris: Hachette, 1999.

James Turnbull. *Bordeaux: The 90 Greatest Wines*. Paris: Hachette, 2006.

P. Timothy H. Unwin. *Wine and the Vine: An Historical Geography of Viticulture and the Wine Trade*. London: Routledge, 1996.

N. Vandevalle, J. F. Lentz, S. Dorbolo, and F. Brisboi. "Avalanches of Popping Bubbles in Collapsing Films." *Physical Review Letters* 86 (2001) 179–182.

Varro, *De Rerum Rusticarum*, Libri III, Bk. I.

Richard Vines. "World's Oldest Champagne Tastes Sweet After 200-Year Shipwreck." *Bloomberg News*, Nov. 17, 2010.

Virgil's *Georgic* 2.60.

Karen Vitelli. "Were Pots First Made for Food? Doubts from Franchthi." *Journal of World Archaeology* 21.1 (1989) 17–29.

Eva-Lena Wahlberg. *The Wine Jars Speak: A Text Study*. M.A. Thesis, Dept. of Archaeology, Ancient History, Egyptology, Uppsala University, 2012.

Ruth Nagle Watkins. "Baalbek, Ancient Heliopolis, City of the Sun." *Art Journal* 24.2 (1964–5) 130–33.

Gong Weiying. "A Historical Survey of Chinese Wine Culture." *Journal of Popular Culture* 27.2 (1993) 57–73.

F. C. White. "Love and Beauty in Plato's Symposium." *Journal of Hellenic Studies* 109 (1989) 149–57.

François Wiblé. *Martigny-la-Romaine*. Martigny: Pro Octodure/Fondation Pierre Gianadda, 2008.

Dyfri Williams. *Greek Vases*. London: British Museum Press, 1999, 2nd ed.

James Wilson. *Terroir*. Berkeley: University of California Press, 1999.

E. Yarshater. "The Theme of Wine Drinking and the Concept of the Beloved in Early Persian Poetry." *Studia Islamica* 13 (1960) 43–53.

William Younger. *Gods, Men and Wine*. Wine and Food Society (in association with World Publishing, Cleveland, 1966.

ENDNOTES

Preface

1. Plato, *Laws* 2.666ab.

Notes to Chapter 1

2. Dr. Patrick McGovern is preeminent in this research. Fritz Maytag was the first to suggest this to me well over a dozen years ago, *pers. comm.*, from his participation in ventures with Patrick McGovern. Fritz Maytag is himself legendary and his personal role in beverage history was secure long before his distinguished James Beard Foundation Lifetime Achievement Award in 2008. The seminal 1995 Napa Valley conference co-chaired by McGovern followed by the 1995 McGovern/ Fleming/Katz book noted in footnote 8 along with McGovern's co-authored 1996 *Nature* article and many other publications are the pioneering texts. Utilizing Sumerian and Akkadian cuneiform texts with ancient Near Eastern scholars, among many other ancient historical beverage questions he has examined, Fritz Maytag has pioneered the scientific study of reviving the crafting of Sumerian beer with Prof. Sol Katz of University of Pennsylvania—see S. H. Katz and Fritz Maytag. "Brewing an Ancient Beer" *Archaeology* 44 (1991) 24–33; he has also supported reconstructive paleochemistry of beverages with Dr. Patrick McGovern of University Museum (also U. Penn). Plus Fritz Maytag has also worked closely with oenologists and historians at the Robert Mondavi Institute at the University of California, Davis, where he was honored as Commencement Speaker in 2010. Also see Patrick E. McGovern. *Ancient Wine: The Search for the Origins of Agriculture*. Princeton: Princeton University Press, 2007. Also note the work of A. M. Negrul and Michael Mullins and Larry Williams, the latter both enologists at one point at University of California, Davis.
3. Robinson, Harding, Vouillamoz, 2012, xxii.
4. Patrick McGovern. *Uncorking the Past: The Quest for Wine, Beer and Other Alcoholic Beverages*. Berkeley: University of California Press, 2009, esp. Preface, x–xii and ch. 1, 26& ff; Hans Barnard, Alek N. Dooley, Gregory Areshian, Boris Gasparyan, and Kym F. Faul. "Chemical evidence for

wine production around 4000 BC in the Late Chalcolithic Near Eastern highlands. *Journal of Archaeological Science* XXX (2010) 1–8, esp. 1.

5. Karen Vitelli. "Were Pots First Made for Food? Doubts from Franchthi." *Journal of World Archaeology* 21 (1989) 17–29, esp. 27. I had my first archaeology publication in this same year volume, and this has long been a personal question as well from my first course in ceramic technology in 1986 at the Institute of Archaeology, London.

6. *pers. comm.*, 2012. Prof. Dr. Rainer Vollkommer is the Director of the Liechtenstein LandesMuseum, Vaduz. Our most recent conversation on this topic was at the museum in December 2012.

7. Klaus Schmidt. "Göbekli Tepe, Southeastern Turkey: A Preliminary Report on the 1995–1999 Excavations." *Paléorient* 26 (2001) 45–54.

8. Daniel Zohary, "Domestication of the Grapevine *Vitis vinifera* L. in the Near East" in Patrick E. McGovern, S. J. Fleming, and Sol H. Katz, eds. *The Origins and History of Wine*. Philadelphia: Gordon Breach, 1995, 23–30; Jean-Frédéric Terral, Elidie Tabard, Laurent Bouby, Sarah Ivorra, Thierry Pastor, Isabel Figueiral, Sandrine Picq, Jean-Baptiste Chevance, Cécile Jung, Laurent Fabre, Christophe Tardy, Michel Compan, Roberto Bacilieri, Thiery Lacombe, and Patrice This. "Evolution and History of Grapevine (*Vitis vinifera*) Under Domestication: New Morphometric Perspectives to Understand Seed Domestication Syndrome and Reveal Origins of Ancient European Cultivars." *Annals of Botany* 105.3 (2010) 443–55, esp. 443 & ff.

9. Jancis Robinson, Julia Harding and José Vouillamoz. *Wine Grapes: A Complete Guide to 1,368 Varieties, Including Their Origins and Flavours*. London: Penguin/Ecco Books, 2012, xxvi.

10. Michal Dayagi-Mendels. *Drink and Be Merry: Wine and Beer in Ancient Times*. Jerusalem: Israel Museum, 1999, 10.

11. I had brief communication with Gregory Areshian on this. Again see Hans Barnard, Alek N. Dooley, Gregory Areshian, Boris Gasparyan, and Kym F. Faul. "Chemical Evidence for Wine Production Around 4000 BC in the Late Chalcolithic Near Eastern Highlands." *Journal of Archaeological Science* XXX (2010) 1–8; also see Gregory E. Areshian, Boris Gasparyan, Pavel S. Avetisyan, Ron Pinhasi, Keith Wilkinson, Alexia Smith, Roman Hovsepyan, and Diana Zardaryan. "The Chalcolithic of the Near East and South-Eastern Europe: Discoveries and New Perspectives from the Cave Complex Areni-1, Armenia." *Antiquity* 86:331 (2012) 115–30.

12. Michael G. Mullins, Alain Bouquet, and Larry E. Williams. *Biology of the Grapevine*. Cambridge: Cambridge University Press, 1992, 31 & ff. This research follows that of A. M. Negrul; also see Ronald S. Jackson. *Wine Science: Principles and Applications*. London and Burlington, MA: Academic Press/Elsevier, 2008 third ed., 26 & ff.

13. Liman Tepe, partly underwater, may date back 6,000 years to the Chalcolithic, as Ekem's Akurgal's finds suggest from the 1950's. See Beverly N. Goodman, Eduard G. Reinhardt, Hendrik W. Dey, Joseph I. Boyce, Henry P. Schwarcz, Vasif Sahoğlu, Hayat Erkanal, and Michal Artzy. "Multi-Proxy Geoarchaeological Study Redefines Understanding of the Paleocoastlines and Ancient Harbours of Liman Tepe (Iskele, Turkey)." *Terra Nova* 21.2 (2009) 97–104.

14. According to oenologists, the Turkish varietal known as *Sultaniye* seems to be the *Sultana* grape, better known in the U.S. as Thompson's Seedless for being an edible table grape.

15. Robinson, Harding, Vouillamoz, xxxiv.

16. William Cocke. "First Wine? Archaeologist Traces Drink to Stone Age." *National Geographic News*, July 21, 2004.

17. G. Algaze, ed. *Town and Country in Southeastern Anatolia*, Vol. 2: *The Stratigraphic Sequence at Kurban Höyük*. Chicago: The Oriental Institute, 1990.

18. O. R. Gurney. *The Hittites.* London: The Folio Society (Penguin, 1952), 2002 (sixth printing) 79.

19. Trevor Bryce. *Life and Society in the Hittite World.* New York: Oxford University Press, 2004, 92, 176.

20. Trevor Bryce. *The Kingdom of the Hittites.* New York: Oxford University Press, 2006, 141, 421.

21. Jean Puhvel. "Balm and Barm, Hittite Style." *Journal of Cuneiform Studies* 63 (2011) 103–104.

22. Hugely influenced by such visionaries but not to be outdone, iconic Terry Gilliam's epic Monty Pythonesque 1988 movie *The Adventures of Baron Munchausen*'s stellar cast includes the late John Neville as the Baron, Eric Idle as the fleet manservant Berthold, Uma Thurman as the goddess Venus, Jonathan Pryce as the Right Ordinary Horatio Jackson, Robin Williams as the King of the Moon, Oliver Reed as Vulcan, Peter Jeffrey as the Sultan, and Sarah Polley as Sally Salt, among many other stars in a box office bomb ($46.5 million budget, a mere $8 million box office at the time) but now cult movie without peer. In Terry Gilliam's own words about this film: "The clash between the Baroque and the Newtonian view of the world is my message in a bottle. Films are like flares fired from a lifeboat to see if anyone else is out there."

23. Rudolph Eric Raspe. *The Adventures of Baron Munchausen.* Rockville, MD: Wildside Press, 2010, 123–8 ff.

24. *Memoirs of Lorenzo da Ponte.* Elizabeth Abbot, tr., Charles Rosen, preface. New York: New York Review of Books Classics, 2000, 155.

25. David Sacks, with revisions by Oswyn Murray and Lisa Brody. "Dionysus" in the *Encyclopedia of the Ancient Greek World.* New York: Facts on File, 2005 rev. ed., 114.

26. Jancis Robinson, ed. *The Oxford Companion to Wine.* Oxford: Oxford University Press, 1994, 995.

27. Lisa Kealhofer, ed. *The Archaeology of Midas and the Phrygians: Recent Work at Gordion.* Philadelphia: University of Pennsylvania Museum of Archaeology and Anthropology, 2005.

Notes to Chapter 2

28. Samuel Noah Kramer. *The Sumerians.* Chicago: University of Chicago Press, 1963, 53–4, 149–51, 111, 206, 220–23.

29. Jean Bottero. *Everyday Life in Ancient Mesopotamia.* Baltimore: Johns Hopkins University Press, 2001, 72–3 & ff.

30. Stephanie M. Dalley, tr. *Myths from Mesopotamia: Creation, the Flood, Gilgamesh and Others.* Oxford: Oxford University Press, 2009 rev. ed., 111.

31. B. Margalit, "The Ugaritic Feast of the Drunken Gods: Another Look at RS 24.258 (KTU 1.114)," *Maarav* 2.1 (1979–80) 65–66.

32. P. Timothy H. Unwin. *Wine and the Vine: An Historical Geography of Viticulture and the Wine Trade.* London: Routledge, 1996, 34.

33. Alan B. Lloyd. *A Companion to Ancient Egypt,* vol. 1. Wiley, 2010, 38.

34. Patrick McGovern, Armin Mirzoian, Gretchen Hall, and Ofer Bar-Josef. "Ancient Egyptian Herbal Wines." *Proceedings of the National Academy of Sciences* 106.18 (2009) 7361–66.

35. T. G. H. James. "The Earliest History of Wine and Its Importance in Ancient Egypt" in McGovern et al., 1995, 197–213; Dayagi-Mendels, 16.

36. John F. Nunn. *Ancient Egyptian Medicine.* London: British Museum Press, 2006 repr., 18.

37. Leonard Lesko. *King Tut's Wine Cellar.* Berkeley: B.C. Scribe Publications, 1978, 15.

38. T. G. H. James in McGovern et al., 1995, 212.

39. Ian Shaw and Paul Nicholson. *The Dictionary of Ancient Egypt.* London: British Museum Press, 1995, 22.

40. Dayagi-Mendels, 16.

41. T. G. H. James in McGovern et al, 1995, 211.

42. Shaw and Nicholson, 102, 108.

43. Lesko, 1978, 15.

44. Nunn, 72, 140, 148

45. *ibid.*, 158.

46. *ibid.*, 161.

47. *ibid.*, 195.

48. Shaw and Nicholson, 209.

49. Lesko, 1978, 2 & ff.

50. Heidi Jauhiainen. *Do Not Celebrate Without Your Neighbors: A Study of References to Feasts and Festivals in Non-Literary Documents from Ramesside Period, Deir el-Medina.* Ph.D. Dissertation of the University of Helsinki, Institute for Asian and African Studies 10, 2009, 304.

51. Herodotus, *History* 2.42.2: "For no gods are worshipped by the whole of Egypt except only Isis and Osiris, whom they say is Dionysus."

52. Shaw and Nicholson, 245.

53. Mary Anne Murray. "Viticulture and Wine Production" in Paul Nicholson and Ian Shaw, eds. *Ancient Egyptian Materials and Technology.* Cambridge: Cambridge University Press, 2000, 581–7 ff.

54. *Athenaeus: The Deipnosophists*, vol. 1 (Books 1–3.106e). C. B. Gulick, tr. Cambridge, MA: Loeb Classical Library 204/Harvard University Press, (1927) 1961 rev.

55. Eva-Lena Wahlberg. *The Wine Jars Speak: A Text Study.* M.A. Thesis, Dept. of Archaeology, Ancient History, Egyptology, Uppsala University, 2012, 3, 15, 77.

56. Miriam Lichtheim. *Ancient Egyptian Literature,* vol. I. Berkeley: University of California Press, 1973: 192.

57. Barbara Hughes Fowler, tr. *Love Lyrics of Ancient Egypt.* University of North Carolina Press, 1994, 52, 68 ff.

58. Miriam Lichtheim. *Ancient Egyptian Literature,* vol. II. Berkeley: University of California Press, 1980: 210.

59. Patrick E. McGovern, D. L. Glusker, L. J. Exner, and Mary M. Voigt. "Neolithic Resinated Wine." *Nature* 381 (1996) 480–481.

60. Stefan K. Estreicher. *Wine: From Neolithic Times to the 21st Century.* New York: Algora Publishing, 2006, 75; Patrick E. McGovern. *Ancient Wine: The Search for the Origins of Viniculture.* Princeton: Princeton University Press, 2007, 40–48.

61. Dayagi-Mendels, 15.

62. Patrick Hunt. "Gudea, King of Lagash." *The Ancient World: Great Lives from History*, vol. 1, 2004, 366–69.

63. Dayagi-Mendels, 16.

64. Stephanie Dalley. *Mari and Karana: Two Old Babylonian Cities.* Piscataway, NJ: Gorgias Press, 2002, 15, 33–4.

65. Marvin A. Powell. "Wine and the Vine in Ancient Mesopotamia: the Cuneiform Evidence" in Patrick E. McGovern, Stuart Fleming, and Sol H. Katz, eds. *The Origins and Ancient History of Wine.* Philadelphia: Gordon and Breach, 1995, 96–124, esp. 111 & ff.

66. Dalley, 2002, 72–4.

67. *ibid.*, 90.

68. *ibid.,* 26, 29.
69. David Stronach. "The Imagery of the Wine Bowl: Wine in Assyria in the Early First Millennium B.C." in Patrick E. McGovern, Stuart Fleming, and Sol H. Katz, eds. *The Origins and Ancient History of Wine.* Philadelphia: Gordon and Breach, 1995, 181–203, esp. 181–3.
70. Hamish H. Aird. "Assyria" in Jancis Robinson, ed. *Oxford Companion to Wine.* Oxford: Oxford University Press, 1994, 61.
71. Stronach in McGovern et al., 1995, 200–203.
72. Jonathan N. Tubb. *Canaanites.* Peoples of the Past Series. London: British Museum Press, 1998, 91.
73. *ibid.,* 42–6. Tubb is the principal excavator of Tell es-Sa'adiyeh since 1985 for the British Museum.
74. *ibid.,* 102, 132.
75. Herodotus, *History* I.133. Although few doubt Herodotus' comment about Persian love of wine, others debate the veracity of Herodotus on the decisions of state when both drunk and sober.
76. Strabo, *Geography* XV.3; Athenaeus *Deipnosophistae* I.28
77. Ferdowsi's *Shahnameh: The Persian Book of Kings.* Dick Davis, tr. New York: Penguin Books, 2007, 431, 605, 624–6, 637 & ff. Translator poet Dick Davis and I have shared wine at Stanford and at dinner at my house, where we also crowned him as a laureate with a *Laurus nobilis* wreath. See Patrick Hunt, "Re-Grafting 'Apollo's Laurel Bough': Byroniana at Gennadeion." *Akoué*, American School of Classical Studies at Athens, June, 2009, 7–8.
78. Simon B. Parker, ed. *Ugaritic Narrative Poetry.* Atlanta: Society for Biblical Literature, 1997 (the actual text is my mine here from the Ugaritic; Parker's reads: "Day long they pour the wine … must-wine, fit for rulers. Wine, sweet and abundant, select wine … the choice wine of Lebanon, Must nurtured by El.").
79. Richard C. Steiner. "On the Rise and Fall of Canaanite Religion at Baalbek: A Tale of Five Toponyms." *Journal of Biblical Literature* 128.3 (2009) 507–25.
80. Ruth Nagle Watkins. "Baalbek, Ancient Heliopolis, City of the Sun." *Art Journal* 24.2 (1964–5) 130–33, esp. 132–3.
81. Athenaeus, I.29
82. Joseph A. Greene and D. P. Kehoe. "Mago the Carthaginian on Agriculture: Archaeology and the Ancient Sources." *Actes du IIIème Congrès International des études phéniciennes et puniques,* II, Tunis, 1991, 110–17; David L. Stone. "Culture and Investment in the Rural Landscape: the North African *bonus agricola.*" *Antiquités africaines* 34 (1998) 103–13, esp 111.
83. Alexander Rofé. "Naboth's Vineyard: The Origin and Message of the Story." *Vetus Testamentum* 38.1 (1988) 89–104. Rofé points out the legal principles of inheritance that even a king should not contravene, 90.
84. e.g., Peter J. Leithart. "Nabal and His Wine." *Journal of Biblical Literature* 120.3 (2001) 525–7.
85. "Wine-bibber" is the King James Version word choice; most newer translations use the word "drunkard."
86. Voltaire, *Philosophical Dictionary*, vol. IV, Part II, end of Section I on Cromwell.

Notes to Chapter 3

87. Plato, *Laws* I.649de, end of Book I, Benjamin Jowett, tr.
88. John Forsdyke. "The 'Harvester' Vase of Hagia Triada." *Journal of the Warburg and Courtauld Institutes* 17.1/2 (1954) 1–9.
89. H. J. Rose. *A Handbook of Greek Mythology.* London: Routledge, 1991 ed. (Methuen, 1928), 149–59.

90. Douglas Gerber, tr. *Greek Iambic Poetry: From the Seventh to the Fifth Centuries BC. (Archilochos, Semonides, Hipponax).* Cambridge, MA: Loeb Classical Library 259/Harvard University Press, 1999, 3-4, 14-70ff.

91. *ibid.,* 3.

92. Quoted from Athenaeus, *Deipnosphistae,* excerpt 120 in Gerber, 161.

93. Richard Seaford. *Dionysos.* London: Routledge, 2006, 5.

94. Walter Burkert. *Greek Religion.* Cambridge, MA: Harvard University Press, 1985, 4.

95. Gerber, 3.

96. H. G. Liddell and R. Scott. *A Greek-English Lexicon.* Oxford: Oxford University Press, 1996 repr., 1998-99.

97. Dyfri Williams. *Greek Vases.* London: British Museum Press, 1999, 2nd ed., 80-1.

98. John Boardman. *Athenian Black Figure Vases.* London: Thames and Hudson, 1974, 218; John Boardman. *Athenian Red Figure Vases:: The Archaic Period.* London: Thames and Hudson, 1975 repr.; "Dionysos" in *Lexicon Iconographicum Mythologiae Classicae,* vol. III. Zürich, Münich, Düsseldorf: Artemis and Winkler Verlag, 1988, 478-82, plates 376-81; Lesley Beaumont. "Mythological Childhood: A Male Preserve? An Interpretation of Classical Athenian Iconography in Its Socio-Historical Context." *Annual of the British School at Athens* 90 (1995) 339-61, esp. 341-2.

99. E. R. Dodds. *The Greeks and the Irrational.* Berkeley: University of California Press, 1951, 76.

100. Jon D. Mikalson. *Ancient Greek Religion.* Blackwell Ancient Religions Series. Oxford: Wiley-Blackwell, 2010, 2nd ed., 88-91 ff.

101. Seaford, 27-31.

102. Liddell and Scott, 1809.

103. Dodds, 76.

104. Burkert, 90-2, 161-7, 237-42, 287-8.

105. Robert C. T. Parker. "The Anthesteria and Other Dionysiac Rites." *Polytheism and Society at Athens.* Part II, Chapter 14. Oxford: Oxford University Press, 2007.

106. F. C. White. "Love and Beauty in Plato's Symposium." *Journal of Hellenic Studies* 109 (1989) 149-57, esp. 151-2.

107. Thomas Pangle. *The Laws of Plato.* Chicago: University of Chicago, 1988, 405.

108. Theognis, *Fragment 643;* Pindar, *Nemean Ode* 9.49.

109. Elizabeth Belfiore. "Wine and Catharsis of Emotions n Plato's Laws." *Classical Quarterly* 36.2 (1986) 421-37, esp. 426.

110. Joanna Luke. "The Krater, Kratos and the Polis. *Journal of Greece & Rome* xli.1 (1994) 23-32, esp. 24-6.

111. H. G. Liddell and R. Scott. *Greek-English Lexikon.* Oxford: Clarendon Press, 1996 rev. ed., 990-1.

112. e.g., Plutarch's *In Genio Socratis* 27-34 explores the connection between the Theban tyrants and their drunkenness, which leads to their assassination when the conspiracy of revelers who only appear to also be wining and dining come to kill them.

113. Walter Leo Hildberg. "Apotropaism in Greek Vase Paintings." *Folk Lore Magazine* 57 (1946) 154-78; Burkert, 104.

114. Liddell and Scott, 566.

115. Nonnos, *Dionysiaca* 47.

116. Philippe Borgeaud, "Dionsyos, the Wine and Ikarios: Hospitality and Danger" in Renate Schlesier, ed. *A Different God?: Dionysos and Ancient Polytheism.* Berlin: Walter de Gruyter, 2011, 161-72, esp. 165 ff.

117. Pseudo-Apollodorus 3.14.7

118. B. C. Dietrich. "A Rite of Swinging During the Anthesteria." *Hermes* 89 (1961) 36–50, esp. 42–3.

119. "Kabirion, Boiotia, Greece" in Richard Stillwell, William L. MacDonald, and Marian Holland McAllister, eds. *The Princeton Encyclopedia of Classical Sites*. Princeton: Princeton University Press, 1975.

120. Seaford, 25

121. *ibid.,* as quotation.

122. Jenny March. *The Penguin Book of Classical Myths*. London: Allen Lane, 2008, 476–7.

123. Plutarch. *Life of Antony* 24.3, 60.3, 75.3–4.

124. *ibid.,* 4.1 (or "shapely beard" in the 1920 Loeb translation)

125. Examining numismatic evidence, T. J. Buckton bridles at any likeness between Dionysus and Marc Antony. "Marc Antony as Bacchus" in *Notes and Queries*, London, July 4, 1868, 115 [Oxford Journals archives, W. J. Thomas and Dr. John Doran, eds.].

126. H. J. Rose, 61.

127. Kirk Ormand. *A Companion to Sophocles*. Blackwell Companions to the Ancient World. Oxford: Blackwell-Wiley, 2012, 171.

128. H. J. Rose, 265; Mark P. O. Morford and Robert J. Lenardon. *Classical Mythology*. New York: Oxford University Press, 2007 ed., 605–7.

129. Patrick Hunt. "Titian's Bacchus and Ariadne 1520–23." *Renaissance Visions: Myth and Art*. Ariel Books: New York and San Diego: University Readers, 2008, 41–60, esp. 48–9. It is worth reminding that the intended commissioner Duke Alphonse d-Este of Ferrara probably had "pet" cheetahs in his estate menagerie, as both Erwin Panofsky and Charles Hope had already long noted in 1969 and 1980, respectively.

130. Jenny March, *pers. comm.* 1990; also see Hunt, 2008, 45–6 and n93, 130.

131. Seaford, 32.

132. Hunt, 2008, 46–7.

133. Cantor Center for the Arts, Stanford University, 80.5 x 65 cm, Acc. #1971.37.

134. Athenaeus, *Deipnosophistae* 2.6.

135. Kostas Kotsakis, *pers. comm.*, when in residency at Stanford University, 2001–02 as Visiting Professor. See K. Kotsakis. "Viticulture in Prehistoric Macedonia: The Evidence from Toumba." *Proceedings of the workshop on viticulture*, Athens 1998; also see K. Kotsakis and M. Mangafa. "A New Method for the Identification of Wild and Cultivated Charred Grape Seeds." *Journal of Archaeological Science*, 23.3 (1996) 409–18.

136. Hamish Aird. "Greece" in Jancis Robinson, ed. *Oxford Companion to Wine*, 1994, 464 ff.

137. Homer, *Odyssey* 24.341–3.

138. *De Causis Plantarum* 11.1–4 for matching vines to soil and climate; 11.5–13.4 for optimal vine planting and training; 14.4–15.5 for optimal seasonal pruning and how to do it.

139. Sidney P. Noe. "The Mende (Kaliandra) Hoard." *Numismatic Notes and Monographs* 27 (1926). New York: American Numismatic Society, 33 and Plate IX #82.

140. Athenaeus, 1.28, 1.51.

141. MacNeil, 604.

142. Hellmut Baumann. *The Greek Plant World*. Portland: Timber Press, 1993, 55.

143. Barbara Clinkenbeard. "Lesbian Wine and Storage Amphoras: A Progress Report on Identification." *Hesperia* 51.3 (1982) 248–68.

144. Jotham Johnson. "Review of Nino Lamboglia (et Fernand Benoit). *La nave romana di Albegna, Revue d'Etudes Ligures* XVIII (1952)." *Latomus* 15.4 (1956) 703–5, esp. 704.

145. MacNeil, 607.

146. Jancis Robinson, ed. *Oxford Companion to Wine*, 1994, "Malmsey", 593.

147. MacNeil, 610.

148. *ibid.*, 606.

149. Quoted, translated, and discussed in Ewen Bowie, "Wandering Poets, Archaic Style" in Richard Hunter and Ian Rutherford, eds. *Wandering Poets in Ancient Greek Culture: Travel, Locality and Pan-Hellenism.* Cambridge: Cambridge University Press, 2009, 105–36, esp. 117.

Notes to Chapter 4

150. D. H. Lawrence. *Sketches of Etruscan Places and Other Italian Essays.* Simonetta de Filippis, ed. Cambridge: Cambridge University Press, 2002, 19.

151. D. H. Lawrence. *Etruscan Places.* London: Martin Secker, 1933 (Leiserson Press, 2007 repr.), Ch. 3 "Painted Tombs of Tarquinia," 63–102.

152. J. K. Anderson, ed. *Funerary Symbolism in Apulian Vase-Painting.* Classical Studies, vol. 12. Berkeley: University of California, 1976.

153. Lawrence, 83–4.

154. Nigel Spivey. *Etruscan Art.* London: Thames and Hudson, 1997 (fig. 154) 166.

155. Spivey, (figs. 75–6) 90–1; this sarcophagus is even the cover image. Also see 172–3 (figs. 162–65) of other sarcophagi.

156. Dr. Lisa Pieraccini, U.C. Berkeley. "The Ever-Elusive Etruscan Egg." Annual Raubitschek Memorial Lecture, Stanford Archaeological Institute of America, May 18, 2012; Jean Macintosh Turfa. "Evidence for Etruscan-Punic Relations." *American Journal of Archaeology* 81.3 (1977) 368–74, esp. 373 on the 7th c. Populonia Lamp; also see Gregorian Etruscan Museum, Vatican Museum Collections, Room II; also see Diane L. Carroll. "A Classification for Granulation in Ancient Metalwork." *American Journal of Archaeology* 78.1 (1974) 33–39, esp. 34–5. Dietrich von Bothmer. "An Etruscan Pectoral." *Bulletin of the Metropolitan Museum of Art, New York* 24.9 (1966) 261–79 & ff.

157. In Larissa Bonfante, ed. *Etruscan Life and Afterlife: A Handbook of Etruscan Studies.* Detroit: Wayne State University Press, 1986, 67.

158. I had several conversations about early Etruscan oenology and viticulture with Larissa Bonfante and Helen Nagy at Archaeological Institute of America (AIA) Annual Meetings. Elsewhere I've discussed this topic with Lisa Pieraccini and Gretchen Meyers, both lecturing at Stanford for the AIA.

159. *Ab Urbe Condita* 1.57. I worked on Livy's Lucretia narrative for the Danish Royal Theater (Det Kongelige Teater) and their Britten opera production of *Lucretia* in March 2009, also giving a paper for the international symposium in Copenhagen at that time.

160. According to David Way, in Zeffiro Ciuffoletti and Paolo Nanni, eds. *Un vino di Maremma. Il Morellino di Scansano*, Pitigliano: Editrice Laurum, 2002.

161. Lisa Pieraccini. "The Wonders of Wine in Etruria" in N. T. de Grummond, I. Edlund-Berry, eds. *The Archaeology of Sanctuaries and Ritual in Etruria. JRA Supplementary series, 81. Journal of Roman Archaeology*, 2011, 127–38; Lisa Pieraccini. "Food and Drink in the Etruscan World" in Jean Turfa, ed. *The Etruscan World.* New York: Routledge, 2013.

162. Maggie Struckmeier and David Connolly, eds. "Ancient Grape Seeds Found in Chianti." *Past Horizons* (Archaeology). Dec. 7, 2012.

163. N. Purcell. "Wine and Wealth in Ancient Italy." *Journal of Roman Studies* LXXV (1985) 10–19, esp. 16.

164. Margarita Gleba. "Archaeology in Etruria 2003–09." Council of the British School at Athens. *Archaeological Reports* 55 (2008–2009) 110.

165. Lew Andrews. "Botticelli's Primavera, Angelo Poliziano and Ovid's Fasti." *Artibus et Historiae* 63 (XXXII) 2011, 4 & ff.

166. Patrick Hunt. *Caravaggio*. Life & Times Series. London: Haus Publishing, 2004, 50 & ff.

167. *Pers. comm.*, according to Charlotte Horton, winemaker at Castello di Potestino. Contemporary sources like Bellori suggest Caravaggio fled south to Zagarola or Paliano; see Hunt, 2004, 108.

168. Fiora Bonelli. "Pestarole etrusche nel castello: I segreti del vino al Potestino." *Il Tirreno-Grosseto*. Jan. 14, 2011.

169. Jean-Pierre Brun. "Le Tecniche di Spremitura dell'Uva: origini e Svi-Luppo dell'Uso del Torchio nel Mediterraneo Occidentale." *Archeologia della Vitivinicoltura nel Mediterraneo Occidentale,* 2007, 56.

170. Some of these *palmenti*—also called *pigiatoi* in the publication noted here below—can be seen in winepress contexts on the island of Ischia at Bosco della Falanga, Punta Chiarito (early 6th c. BCE) and Petralia Sottana as well as elsewhere in Etruria. Gloria Olcese and Stefania Giunta. eds. "I. Ischia: e anfore greco italiche di Ischia: archeologia e archeometria." *Immensa Aequora: Ricerche archeologiche, archeometriche e informatiche per la ricostruzione dell'economia e dei commerci nel bacino occidentale del Mediterraneo,* 2012, 21–22. A parallel Roman word may be *calcatorium* as a "wine press" context for crushing grapes generally by foot-stomping, according to 4th c. Palladius Rutilius Taurus, 1.18.1. See C. T. Lewis and C. Short, *A Latin Dictionary*, Oxford: Clarendon Press, 1879 ed. (or Harper's 1907 *Latin Dictionary* based on Lewis and Short, 267).

171. Alessandro Papo, Gianluca Citi, and Letizia Marini. "Vini etruschi e anfore di Calafuria." *Il Relitto Etrusco di Calafuria*. Nibbiaia, Rosignano Marittimo (Livorno): Gruppo Archaeosub Labronico, 2006. "Agli etruschi viene attribuita la selezione, dalla selvatica vitis silvestris, dei progenitori au-toctoni dei vitigni Trebbiano, Sangiovese, Falanghina… Il Sangiovese, secondo l'opinione di molti ampelografi, è nato nella Toscana etrusca e, anzi, proprio nel territorio del Chianti."

172. Karen MacNeil. *The Wine Bible*. New York: Workman Publishing, 2001, 63.

173. David Way, *pers. comm.*, who also notes "perhaps only Salustri" for other good Montecucco reds; see (http://winefriend.org/about-2/). Also see Simon Hall, London, "Castello di Potentino,"*Bread and Games: Panem et circensis*, Sept. 14, 2011 (http://breadandgames.co.uk/2011/09/wwoof-wine-best-kept-secret.html/); Patrick (Paddy) Murphy, Dublin, "Castello di Potentino Pop-Up" *The Vine Inspiration*, April 12, 2012 (http://thevineinspiration.org/2012/04/04/castello-di-potentino-pop-up/).

174. Jean MacIntosh Turfa. "International Contacts: Commerce, Trade and Foreign Affairs" in Larissa Bonfante, ed. *Etruscan Life and Afterlife*. Detroit: Wayne State University Press, 1986, 75, 78.

175. Gretchen Meyers, *pers. comm.*, Director of Archaeological Materials, 2004 to present, for the Mugello Valley Archaeological Project, excavator of Poggio Colla.

176. Kerin O'Keefe. *Brunello di Montalcino: Understanding and Appreciating One of Italy's Greatest Wines*. Berkeley: University of California Press, 2012, ch.1.

177. J. A. A. de la Fuente. "Some Thoughts on Etruscan **math-* '(Honeyed) Wine.'" *Historische Sprachforschung* Bd. 120 (2007) 305–10. De la Fuente suggests borrowed Luvian-, Anatolian-influenced loan words.

178. Stephanie A. Layton. "Etruscan Bucchero Pottery from Cetamura del Chianti." *Etruscan Studies* 12.1 (2009) 21–60, esp. 24–7.

179. *ibid.*, 26.

180. Jessica Bordoni. "I Top Hundred 2011 di Paolo Massobrio e Marco Gatti." *Civiltà del Bere*, Sept. 16, 2011.

Notes to Chapter 5

181. D. P. S. Peacock and D. F. Williams. *Amphorae and the Roman Wine Economy.* London: Longman, 1986.

182. Patrick Hunt. "Summus Poeninus in the Grand-St-Bernard Pass." *Journal of Roman Archaeology* XI (1998) 265–74; Patrick Hunt. "A Roman Refuge in the Plan de Barasson: Field Reports for 1998–2000." *Vallesia: Chronique du découvertes archéologiques dans le canton du Valais* LIV (Sion, 1999) 300–08; Patrick Hunt, "Bronze Tabulae Ansatae at Roman Summus Poeninus in the Roman Alps." *Acta: From the Parts to the Whole, vol. 2, Proceedings of XIIIth Int'l. Bronze Congress*, Harvard University Art Museums, *JRA Suppl.* 2002.

183. This Roman trade naturally includes other commodities like olive oil and the fish spice *garum* as well as wine. See Jeremy Paterson. "Salvation from the Sea: Amphorae and Trade in the Roman West." *Journal of Roman Studies* 72 (1982) 146–57.

184. Jennifer Moore. *A Survey of the Italian Dressel 2-4 Wine Amphora.* M.A. Thesis. McMaster University, 1995, esp. iii and 9–103 (chs. 2–5).

185. *ibid.*, 29.

186. Paterson, 149.

187. Alexander Conison. *The Organization of Rome's Wine Trade.* Ph.D. Dissertation, University of Michigan, 2012, 6.

188. *ibid.* 32.

189. Christopher Howgego. "The Supply and Use of Money in the Roman World 200 BC to AD 300." *Journal of Roman Studies* 82 (1992) 1–31, esp. 26.

190. T. M. Hickey. *Wine, Wealth and the State in Late Antique Egypt: The House of Apion at Oxyrhynchus.* Ann Arbor: University of Michigan Press, 2012, ch. 4, esp. 90–93& ff.

191. Conison, 4.

192. Pliny, *Nat. Hist.* 14.4.21–22.

193. *ibid.* 14.4.35.

194. As in Virgil's *Georgic* 2.60.

195. Columella, *de Re Rustica* 5.4.1 & 5.5.16.

196. Pliny, *Nat. Hist.* 14. 3; 14.62.

197. Pliny, op. cit. 14.6.57.

198. W. Arrowsmith. *Petronius' Satyricon.* University of Michigan, 1959, 192, where Arrowsmith suggests Trimalchio's attempts to impress his guests display more ignorance than gourmandaise because the wine would not have survived well. Taste may not have been the most important criterion if connoisseurship was as important then as now: Christie's Wine Auction in London (around 1997) had one bottle of 1945 La Tache DRC with an opening bid of £1100.00 sterling or around $1,780.00.

199. Varro, *de Rerum Rusticarum*, Libri III. I.

200. Pliny, *op. cit.* 14.8.70

201. Strabo, *Geography* V.3.6.

202. Athenaeus, *Deipnosphistae* I.26.

203. 2*ibid.*, I.26–27. Athenaeus mentions at least 20 wines from Italy alone.

204. Pliny, 14.8.70.

205. Marcus Gavius Apicius. *De Re Coquinaria* I. (Epimeles) II.1–8.

206. Dayagi-Mendels, 73, 76–7.

207. Horace, *Carmina* III.21.

208. Karl Lehmann. "Ignorance and Search in the Villa of the Mysteries." *Journal of Roman Studies* 52 (1962) 62–68; Karen Pollinger Foster. "Dionysos and Vesuvius in the Villa of the Mysteries." *Antike Kunst* 44 (2001) 37–54.

209. Suetonius, *Life of Domitian* 17, 23.

210. e.g., Brian W. Jones. *The Emperor Domitian*. London: Routledge, 1993 repr., vii.

211. Jeremy J. Paterson, "Classical Rome" in Jancis Robinson, ed., *Oxford Companion to Wine*, Oxford, 1994, 819–20.

212. H. Rushton Fairclough, tr. *Virgil I. Eclogues, Georgics Aeneid 1–6*. Cambridge, MA: Harvard University Press/Loeb Classics Library 63, 1999 rev. ed., 165.

213. N. Purcell. "Wine and Wealth in Ancient Italy." *Journal of Roman Studies* 75 (1985) 1–19, esp. 5.

214. (www.napanow.com/wine.statistics.html) *2010*.

215. M. Stephen Spurr, "Agricultural Writers" in Simon Hornblower and Antony Spawforth, eds. *Oxford Companion to Classical Civilization*. Oxford University Press, 1998, 18.

216. Conison, 50–1.

217. Quoted as an adage footnote to Virgil's *Georgics* 2.412 where it is paraphrased as "Give praise to large estates, farm a small one." (Fairclough translation, 1999 ed., 165.)

218. Notes to Chapter 6

219. Leslie Adkins and Roy A. Adkins. "Vinalia" in *Dictionary of Roman Religion*. New York: Facts on File, 1995, 232–4, 240.

220. Daniel Thomases. "Campania" in Jancis Robinson, ed. *The Oxford Companion to Wine*. Oxford: Oxford University Press, 1994, 183–4.

221. Jeremy J. Paterson "Wine" in Hornblower and Spawforth, 775.

222. Macneil, 70.

223. In Chapter 24 of *Candide*: "'You will at least allow,' said Candide to Martin, 'that these two are happy. Hitherto I have met with none but unfortunate people in the whole habitable globe, except in El Dorado; but as to this couple, I would venture to lay a wager they are happy.' 'Done!' said Martin, 'they are not what you imagine.' 'Well, we have only to ask them to dine with us,' said Candide, 'and you will see whether I am mistaken or not.' Thereupon he accosted them, and with great politeness invited them to his inn to eat some macaroni, with Lombard partridges and caviar, and to drink a bottle of Montepulciano, Lacryma Christi, Cyprus, and Samos wine."

224. *The Count of Monte Cristo*. Signet Classics, 2005. Chapter XXVI, 158, where Vicomte Albert de Morcerf is in the hands of bandits but drinks a glass of *Lachryma christi*.

225. Early in the short story before Giovanni even meets Beatrice, the doomed innocent and beautiful daughter of poison botanist Dr. Rappacini, he is exhorted to drink up a glass of Lachryma.

226. *Tamburlaine the Great*, Part Two, climax of Act I, Scene III.

227. Ian Jenkins and Kim Sloan. *Vases and Volcanoes*. British Museum Press, 1996, e.g., (fig. 7) 26–7, (fig 29) 66, (fig. 33) 71, (fig. 47) 173.

228. Susan Sontag was in residence at Stanford in 1996 and we met for a few hours taking about William Hamilton just before the British Museum William Hamilton Colloquium, where I spoke on his Roman archaeological collection, the bulk of it in the British Museum. See Susan Sontag. *The Volcano Lover*. Farrar, Straus and Giroux, 1992.

229. Maxwell L. Anderson. "Pompeiian Frescoes in The Metropolitan Museum of Art." *The Metropolitan Museum of Art Bulletin*, 45.3 (Winter, 1987–88), esp. 17–36.

230. Milia, A., M. M. Torrente, and A. Zuppetta. "Offshore Debris Avalanches at Somma-Vesuvius Volcano (Italy): Implications for Hazard Evaluation." *Journal of the Geological Society* 160.2 (2003) 309–17.

Notes to Chapter 7

231. Giuseppe Tomasi di Lampedusa. *The Siren and Selected Writings (Il Professore e la Sirena)*. David Gilmour, tr. London Harvill Press, 1995 ed., 80–1.

232. Homer., *Odyssey* IX.119, 142–3 (Robert Fitzgerald translation).

233. Pliny. *Natural History* XIV.6.8, XIV.4.10.

234. J. J. Paterson, "Sicily: Ancient History" in Jancis Robinson, ed. *Oxford Companion to Wine*, Oxford University Press, 1994, 876.

235. Strabo, *Geography* VI.3.102.

236. *Epigrams* XIII.117; the name is unimportant, it is equal to wine anywhere.

237. Andrew Dalby. *Food in the Ancient World: From A-Z*. London: Routledge, 2003, 207.

238. Stephen Hinds. *The Metamorphosis of Persephone: Ovid and the Self-Conscious Muse*. Cambridge: Cambridge University Press, 1987, "The Landscape of Enna" 25–48.

239. Stephen M. Wheeler. "The Underworld Opening of Claudian's *De Raptu Proserpinae*." *Transactions of the American Philological Association* 125 (1995) 113–34, esp. 122.

240. *Claudian, vol. II. De Raptu Proserpinae*. Maurice Platnauer, tr. Cambridge, MA: Harvard University Press/Loeb Classical Library 136, 1998 repr., 292–377, esp, 323–7.

241. Tom Stevenson. *The New Sotheby's Wine Encyclopedia*, 3rd ed., 2001, 341.

242. MacNeil, 407.

243. D. Thomases "Sicily: Modern Wines …" in Jancis Robinson, ed. *Oxford Companion to Wine*, Oxford University Press, 1994, 877; also see the same sub-author's entry on "Apulia," 42.

244. Patrick Hunt. "The Exotic History of Citrus." *Electrum Magazine*, October 2012.

245. Mary Taylor Simeti. *On Persephone's Island: A Sicilian Journal*. New York: Random House, 1986.

246. Hubert Houben. *Roger II of Sicily: A Ruler Between East and West*. Cambridge University Press, 2002, 165.

247. MacNeil, 407.

Notes to Chapter 8

248. Pliny, *Nat. Hist.* XIV.3.16.

249. MacNeil, 357.

250. M. Stephen Spurr. "Roman Agricultural Implements" in Hornbower and Spawforth, 18 (including image).

251. Vini Alto Adige/Südtirol Wein, Consortium Alto Adige Wines, Via Crispi 15 I-39100 Bolzano/Bozen; EOS—Export Organization Alto Adige of the Chamber of Commerce of Bolzano/Bozen, 2011, 5.

252. "Virtually the entire production" (4,940 hectares out of 5,000) according to Daniel Thomases, "Alto Adige" in Jancis Robinson, ed., *Oxford Companion to Wine*, Oxford, 1994, 26.

253. David Molyneux-Berry. *Sotheby's Guide to Classic Wines*, New York: Ballantine Books, 1990, 226.

254. D. Thomases, up to 15% Lagrein in 1994, 849.

255. Molyneux-Berry, 226.

256. Tom Stevenson. *The New Sotheby's Wine Encyclopedia*, 3rd. ed. Dorling Kindersley, 2001, 321.

257. MacNeil, 355.

258. Arthur Hutchings. *Mozart: The Man, the Musician*. New York: Schirmer Books, 1976, fig. 65, 99.

259. As Da Ponte's memoirs tell, p. 155, see first chapter on Anatolia with the Munchausen sultan's tokay and following endnote.

260. This is from the Mozart *Don Giovanni* La Scala 2011–12 score, p. 32 out of 36, Edizione Bärenreiter—Verlag, Kassel; my translation: *Don Giovanni*: "Ah che piatto saporito!"; *Leporello*: ("Ah, che barbaro appetito! Che bocconi da gigante! Mi par proprio di svenir."); *Don Giovanni*: "Piatto."; *Leporello*:"Servo." Evvivano i «Litiganti»!; *Don Giovanni*: "Versa il vino!" (Leporello versa il vino nel bicchiere.) "Eccellente Marzimino!"

261. Heinrich Heine. *Travel Pictures* III, Chapter XIII (1830).

Notes to Chapter 9

262. David Molyneux-Berry. *Sotheby's Guide to Classic Wines*. New York: Ballantine Books, 1990, 144; Conseil Interprofessionnel des Vins d'Alsace, Colmar, 2011 (www.vinsalsace.com).

263. Hanneke M. Wirtjes, "Charlemagne" in Jancis Robinson, ed. *Oxford Companion to Wine*, Oxford, 1994, 219; Einhard, *Life of Charlemagne*, 28.

264. Einhard, 24.

265. Norman Cantor, ed. *Encyclopedia of the Middle Ages*. New York: Penguin/Viking, 1999, 99–101, 110–11.

266. Wirtjes, 219.

267. *ibid.*

268. Hieronymus Bock. *De stirpium commentariorum libri tres*, Strassburg (Strasbourg), 1552. Note also his *Neu Kreütter Buch von underscheydt, würckung und namen*. Strassburg (Strasbourg), 1539; Brian W. Ogilvie. "The Many Books of Nature: Renaissance Naturalists and Information Overload." *Journal of the History of Ideas* 64.1 (2003) 31–33.

269. Conseil Interprofessionnel des Vins d'Alsace, Colmar, 2011 (http://www.vinalsace.com).

270. *Ausonius*. Hugh G. Evelyn-White, tr. Loeb Classical Library. London: Heinemann, vol. I, 1919, 226–7.

271. Tom Stevenson (Sotheby's *Wine Encyclopedia*) is either unclear or ambiguous about if Eiswein can be botrytized; note Stevenson, 31 & 573, but he is the general exception. Most others say quality or hallmark Eiswein should not be botrytized.

272. MacNeil, 534.

273. Ian Jamieson in Jancis Robinson, ed. *Oxford Companion to Wine*, Oxford, 1994, 791–3.

274. *Deutscher Wein Statistik*, German Wine Institute, 2008, Tables 3–4, pp. 7–8.

275. e.g., in New York, these Leitz wines can be obtained from Michael Skurnik Wines, 575 Underhill Blvd., Suite 216, Syosset, NY 11791 (Phone: 516-677-9300 ext. 508, Fax: 516-677-9301, Email: [Kevin Pike] kbpike@skurnikwines.com, Website: <www.skurnikwines.com>.)

276. Elmar Schwinger. *The Jewish Community in Kitzingen*, 1865–1942, Kitzingen archives.

277. Raspe, *Munchausen*, 2010, 61.

278. Victor Hugo. *Les Misérables*. I. F. Hapgood, tr. New York: Thomas Crowell, 1887, vol. 4 ("Saint Denis"), 207.

279. Washington Irving. "The Legend of Sleepy Hollow" and "The Specter Bridegroom," from *The Sketchbook*. Philadelphia: J. B. Lippincott, 1875, 64.

280. Jules Verne. *Five Weeks in a Balloon*. London: George Routledge and Sons, 1876, 54.

281. Don and Petie Kladstrup. *Wine and War: The French, the Nazis, and France's Greatest Treasure*. Broadway/Coronet, 2001. I also recommended this delightful book for my course HIST 177 "History of Wine" at Stanford, 2012.

282. Michael Broadbent. *The New Great Vintage Wine Book*. New York: Knopf/Christie's, 1991, 280–9.

283. Stevenson, 186.

Notes to Chapter 10

284. Jancis Robinson, ed. *The Oxford Companion to Wine*. Oxford, 1994, 935.

285. François Wiblé. *Martigny-la-Romaine*. Martigny: Pro Octodure/Fondation Pierre Gianadda, 2008.

286. Macneil, 584.

287. Robinson, 1994, 333.

288. *Vinum: Le Magazine Européen du Vin*. December 2012, 52–55.

289. *ibid.*

290. Stevenson, 396. Also see *Gesellschaft für Geschichte des Weines*, 2011, "Hermann Müller-Thurgau."

291. Macneil, 584.

292. Robinson, 1994, 117.

293. *Vinum: Le Magazine Européen du Vin*. December 2012, 52–55.

294. A quote from 1932 when visiting his Feldkirch friend Eugene Jolas, while moving from Trieste to Zurich in 1915 during WWI, the Vorarlberg train was inspected by police and officials but Joyce avoided possible arrest and/or likely censorship of his manuscript.

295. Patrick Hunt. "Bruegel's Hunters in the Snow, 1565." *Electrum Magazine*, 2012.

296. See link: (http://www.saxerwy.ch/kontakt.html).

Notes to Chapter 11

297. Homer's *Odyssey* XIV.463–6, S. Butler tr.

298. *Samuel Johnson's Dictionary*. Jack Lynch, ed. Delray Beach: Levenger Press, 2004 ed., 228.

299. John Bourchier, Lord Berners. *The Book of Huon of Bordeaux*. Third Edition, 1601 by Thomas Purfoot. Early English Text Society (S. L. Lee Critical Edition 1882–7) ch. 21, 4.

300. M. K. James. *Studies in the Medieval Wine Trade*. Oxford: Clarendon Press, 1971; P. Timothy H. Unwin. *Wine and the Vine: An Historical Geography of Viticulture and the Wine Trade*. London: Routledge, 1996, 199. Unwin lists thousands of Bordeaux exports from 1305 onward out of Gascon ports, almost 97,848 *tuns* recorded in 1305 alone, but this is by no means the beginning. Unwin's source is also M. K. James, 32–3.

301. Or his father and grandfather were vintners; H. G. Baker in Jancis Robinson, Oxford, 1994, 363.

302. François Rabelais. *Gargantuan and Pantagruel*. Jacques LeClercq, tr. New York: Heritage Press, 1942, Book I, Ch. 5, 19.

303. *ibid.*, Book 4, Ch. 64, 169.

304. *ibid.*, Book 2, Ch. 33, 111.

305. Jane Anson. "Cambridge University to Celebrate Pepys' First Mention of Haut Brion." *Decanter Magazine*, January 18, 2013.

306. *Diary of Samuel Pepys*, vol. II. Richard, Lord Braybrooke, ed. London: Swan Sonnenschein & Co. 1906, 380.

307. *Compact Edition of the Oxford English Dictionary*. Oxford: Oxford University Press, 1971, 2186 (908).

308. Voltaire. *Candide*. Bantam Books/Random House, 2003 reissue. Beginning of Chapter 22, 76-7. The winner, a sage from the north "who demonstrated by A plus B, minus C, divided by Z, that the sheep must necessarily be red, and die of the mange."

309. Voltaire. *Philosophical Dictionary*, vol. 4, Part II, on "Climate": "Certain libations of wine will be naturally enjoined in a country abounding in vineyards; and it would never occur to the mind of any legislator to institute sacred mysteries, which could not be celebrated without wine, in such a country as Norway."

310. Kladstrup, *Wine and War*, 2001, 231-2, 240.

311. Kermit Lynch. *Wine Adventures: A Wine Buyer's Tour of France*. New York: North Point Press/ Farrar, Straus and Giroux, 1988, 262. "I am afraid the day is near when Mouton-Rothschild's beautiful artist's label and all the rest will be marred by misguided, nonsensical health warnings."

312. Robert C. Ulin. *Vintages and Traditions: An Ethnohistory of Southwest France Wine Cooperatives*. Washington DC: Smithsonian Institution. 1996.

313. Sophia Menache. *Clement V*. Studies in Medieval Life and Thought. Cambridge: Cambridge University Press, 1998, 28. This testimony is from his contemporary Geffroy de Nés.

314. Jonathan I. Israel. *Dutch Primacy in World Trade 1585–1740*. Oxford, 1989. The author catalogues Dutch wine shipments from Bordeaux and freight charges from Bordeaux to Amsterdam, 90, 135, 365.

315. Jancis Robinson, 1994, 240.

316. Jame Molesworth. "Bordeaux Roars Back." *Wine Spectator*, March 2012, 43–51, 128–33.

317. Christopher Foulkes. *Larousse Encyclopedia of Wine*. Paris: Larousse, 2001. 141, 171.

318. Hanneka M. Wirtjes in Jancis Robinson, Oxford, 1994, 123.

319. Stevenson, 103.

320. Chris Mercer. "St Emilion Owner 'Seeking Damages' over Classification." *Decanter Magazine*. Jan 17, 2013.

321. *Wine Spectator*, March 2012, 124.

322. *Berry Bros. & Rudd Price List*, October 1998, 35.

323. *Corney & Barrow Wine List* 1998/1999, 32.

324. Raphaëlle Bacqué. "Elysee Aromatic—Journey onto the Wine Cellar of France's Presidential Palace." *Le Monde*, Dec 27, 2012.

325. Clive Coates. *An Encyclopedia of the Wines and Domaines of France*. Berkeley: University of California 2001, 57.

326. Note France's Institut National Recherches Archéologiques Préventives INRAP site for the History of Wine in Southern France: (http://archeologie-vin.inrap.fr/Archeologie-du-vin/Histoire-du-vin/Paleolithique/p-13146-Les-premiers-raisins-sauvages-consommes.htm).

327. G. Barruol, ed. "Lattes-Latara" in *Princeton Encyclopedia of Classical Sites*. Princeton: Princeton University Press, 1976 (but needing revising to reflect INRAP viticultural finds).

328. Barry Cunliffe. *The Ancient Celts*. Oxford: Oxford University Press, 1997, 53, 312, Fig. 28, including Massiliote wine.

329. J. Boardman. *Greek Art*. Thames and Hudson, 1985 ed., 14, figure 103 on 104.

330. Luke, 1994, 24–6.

331. Pliny, *Nat. Hist.* 22.2.5; K. Kristiansen. *Europe Before History*. Cambridge, 1998, 328; S. J. Fleming. *Vinum: The Story of Roman Wine*. Glen Mills, PA: Art Flair, 2001, 3, 5, 22, 96, 101.

332. Jean-Pierre Brun. *Archéologie du Vin et de l'Huile de la Préhistoire à l'Époque Hellénistique*. Paris: Editions Errance, 2004.

333. Cunliffe, 1997, 106.

334. Pliny, *Nat. Hist.* XIV.4.43.

335. James Turnbull. *Rhone Valley: The 90 Greatest Wines*. Paris: Hachette, 1999, 122.

336. *ibid.*, 96–135.

337. Macneil, 254.

338. Turnbull, 1999, 164.

339. Jasper Morris in Jancis Robinson, ed. *Oxford Companion to Wine*, 1994, 1053.

340. To name just a few recent historians: William Younger. *Gods, Men and Wine*. Wine and Food Society (in association with World Publishing, Cleveland, 1966; Desmond Seward. *Monks and Wine*. New York: Crown Publishers, 1979; James Wilson. *Terroir*. Berkeley: University of California Press, 1999, esp. 52 ff.).

341. There are possibly more than a few well-known women with this name in France, but this one in Aloce-Corton is not the doll, the artist musician, nor the northern Rhone Véronique Perrin-Rolin.

342. Bruce Sanderson. "Heaven on Earth." *Wine Spectator*, May, 2010, 49. In New York, 2007, Sotheby's auctioned a case of Romanée-Conti 1990 for $262,900, each bottle at $22,000.

343. *Confrérie des Chevaliers du Tastevin*, 1959 booklet.

Notes to Chapter 12

344. Voltaire, *Philosophical Dictionary*, vol. 4, part 2, section III on "Country."

345. Stephanie Holmes. "'World's Oldest Champagne' Found on Baltic Seabed" *BBC News*, July 17, 2010; (http://www.bbc.co.uk/news/world-europe-10673322); Richard Vines. "World's Oldest Champagne Tastes Sweet After 200-Year Shipwreck." *Bloomberg News*, Nov. 17, 2010 (http://www.bloomberg.com/news/2010-11-17/world-s-oldest-champagne-survives-icy-shipwreck-surfaces-for-wine-tasting.html).

346. Rose Hoare. "An Unforgettable Dinner in Paris." *Wine Searcher*, November 1, 2012.

347. Janet Hulstrand. "Snapshot: The Champagne Country." *Smithsonian Magazine*, July 2008.

348. Nicholas Faith, "Champagne" in Jancis Robinson, ed. *The Oxford Companion to Wine*, Oxford University Press, 1994, 210.

349. *Spumatio –onis*, fem.: a "foaming"; *spumo, spumare*, "to foam" in C. T. Lewis and C. Short. *A New Latin Dictionary*, 1907, 1747.

350. Robinson, 912.

351. The Roman or Gallo-Roman chalk crayères can also be accessed by Veuve Clicquot, Heidsieck, Taittinger, and Ruinart champagne maisons.

352. Robert Blumberg and Hurst Hannum. *The Fine Wines of California*. Third Edition. New York: Doubleday, 1984, 350–1; Frank Prial. "Wine Talk" *New York Times* Dec. 6, 1995, "… the first in modern times to truly match the style and quality of the best French Champagnes is from Jack and Jamie Davies's Schramsberg Vineyards in the Napa Valley …" Hugh Davies is the son of Jack and Jamie Davies who revived the "ghost winery" after it was unused for a generation, not part of the original Schram family.

353. MacNeil, 653–5.

354. Report of the Comité Interprofessionnel des Vins de Champagne (CIVC), 2009; Liger-Belair reports 262 million bottles at $3 billion in 2001.

355. Liger-Belair, 2004, 8 & ff.

356. Other bubble estimates in champagne are far less conservative, with fivefold-higher estimates of up to 250 million bubbles in a single bottle.

Credits

CPSIA information can be obtained at www.ICGtesting.com
Printed in the USA
LVOW02s1918240315

431859LV00001B/1/P